Using Japanese Slang

Using JAPANESE SLANG

Anne Kasschau
and
Susumu Eguchi

YENBOOKS

YENBOOKS
2-6, Suido 1-chome, Bunkyo-ku, Tokyo 112, Japan

© 1995 by YENBOOKS

LCC Card No. 94-60682
ISBN 4-900737-36-4

First edition, 1995

Printed in Japan

Contents

Foreword

This is a book born of frustration. As a long-time student of the Japanese language and a long-time resident of Japan, I have been constantly frustrated by the reticence of my Japanese friends and teachers to answer my questions about slang and underground Japanese, especially as they pertain to matters sexual. This is in pointed contrast to the burgeoning number of books on sale in Japan about colloquial and even vulgar English.

Probably most of you reading this book have had the same experience. Questions such as "How do you say fuck in Japanese?" "What's the word for penis?" or "How do you tell someone he's an asshole?" are invariably met with an embarrassed smile and the immediate response that the Japanese don't have words for these sorts of things. This reflects the *honne* and *tatemae* nature of Japanese society, in which reality *(honne)* is almost always subordinated to appearances *(tatemae)*. And, as the more than 200 pages that follow will amply attest, this assertion simply isn't accurate.

The number of foreigners living in Japan continues to grow, and interest in the Japanese language is strong all over the world. But even those who have lived in Japan for decades have no idea how to make love in Japanese, how to express their displeasure when cut off in traffic by an overeager taxi driver, of derogatory Japanese language, or of the slang and jargon used by the younger generation.

In Susumu Eguchi, my co-author, I finally found a Japanese person willing to be open about such terms. Thus, the 200 columns entitled "Unspeakable Japanese" came to be. Susumu, a journalist and scholar having written several books on the Japanese language under the pen name of Oh Yamanaka, did the formidable job of researching the words and their history and etymology. I am also a journalist who has studied Japanese for more years than I would like to admit. To me fell the task of rendering the work into English and editing each column, as well as re-editing them into book form.

These columns ran from April 1979 to December 1982 on the Friday Page in the *Mainichi Daily News*. Several reader surveys conducted during this period proved them to be the most popular feature of the paper. Not surprisingly, they were also the most controversial.

To this book we have added some of the more scandalous expressions that we were not able to publish in the newspaper. We have also emphasized the spoken language rather than written words, concentrating on expressions, many of which are not yet covered in prestigious Japanese dictionaries.

The basis for our choice of expressions is that they were in use as of the spring of 1994 and can be expected to be around for a while. We have decided to include older and less fashionable expressions only when they are necessary in order to understand the general trends.

There has been little organized slang and jargon research by scholars, in spite of the fact that Japan has experienced a boom over the last ten years in Japanese-language studies and general interest books. With increased interest in Japan overseas as well, several books on colloquial and slang Japanese have been published.

We are often surprised, however, to find that most of them don't go into the origins of the words or how their meaning has developed and changed over the years.

Words are a clue to human psychology; they also provide a window on the culture from which they have originated. In our research for this book, we have examined as much literature as possible and have limited the expressions to ones on which most opinions agree. We offer here what we believe is the most comprehensive and most scholarly research to date on Japanese slang, swear words, underground and sexual terms, scatology, and colloquialisms. We hope you find this book helpful in deepening your understanding of Japanese language and culture.

BAD-MOUTHING
and
DIRTY WORDS

warukuchi, kitanai kotoba

1

Stupidity and Drunkenness

(baka, yopparai)

Baka-Related

Baka (stupid) is a good word with which to start our book. It is literally a four-letter word, and is probably the first—and perhaps only—Japanese swear word that most foreigners learn. *Kenkyusha's Japanese-English Dictionary* fills several columns with translations and explanations of this word, one of which is the quaintly Victorian-sounding old socks. In reality, however, when spoken in tones of disgust or anger, it has the impact of goddamn you bastard, or you son of a bitch.

In 1993, a TV program aired by the Asahi Broadcasting Company in Osaka examined the nationwide usage of *baka* and its synonym *ahō,* and was quite a hit. A book based on the reporter's investigation was subsequently published, receiving even more attention. According to this voluminous work by Osamu Matsumoto, *Zenkoku Ahō Baka Bunpu-kō* (The Nationwide Distribution of *Ahō* and *Baka),* words related to stupidity and idiocy are roughly classified into the *baka* group in eastern Japan (including Tokyo), Kyushu, and far Western Japan; and the *ahō* group in Nagoya and the Kansai region (including Osaka and Kyoto). There are also many colloquial synonyms in dialect, such as *honji-nashi* in the Tohoku and *dara* in the Hokuriku and San-in regions. These are still in use in local conversation. Among them, though, *baka* and *aho* or *ahō* are the two major swear words in Japan, with *baka* being the older of the two.

According to Matsumoto, both *baka* and *aho* derive from ancient Chinese, and even standard Japanese dictionaries offer mistaken etymologies. This is the extent to which even famous linguistic scholars disagree about the origins of words.

Baka, manuke (stupid ass) *omae no kāchan* (your mother) *debeso* (literally, protruding navel), is a typical taunt of children in the Tokyo region. Let's examine the usage of *baka* first.

Bakka, baka ne, or *baka da ne,* when spoken in tones of sympathy, convey that exact sentiment—what a mess you've got yourself into, you poor thing. *O-baka-san,* used to refer to a person, has similar connotations. *O-* in this case is a prefix showing affection and *-san* is a suffix for respect. The inverted form of *baka* (*kaba*) is also used affectionately.

On a somewhat stronger level is *baka yarō,* rarely used by women, which might best be translated as up your ass. *Yarō* means fellow or guy. (Roll the "r" shamelessly for added effect). The impact of this word on the Japanese can be illustrated by the fact that, in 1953, the Diet was forced to dissolve because then-Prime Minister Shigeru Yoshida used it during a main session of the House of Representatives. *Baka tare* has the same meaning and impact, and is used mainly in Kansai.

Kusobaka is very strong and is only used by men. The *kuso* in this expression means shit, and the word should only be used under the most extreme circumstances. *Kuso* can also be added to *babā* and *jijii,* which are derogatory terms for old woman and old man respectively, to create *kusobabā* and *kusojijii.* These words are used to refer to a really disgusting old person.

Women as well as men, however, are allowed to use *bakarashii* or *bakakusai* when they feel that something is absurd or silly. *Sonna bakarashii* (or *bakakusai*) *koto wa dekimasen* means I can't do something that silly. *Rashii* is a suffix meaning look like, seem, or appear, as in *onnarashii* (womanly) or *kawairashii* (lovely, charming). *Kusai* means to smell bad. So *bakakusai* has the connotation of something just reeking of stupidity. *Bakamitai (mitai* also means to look like or appear like) is very similar. These two terms are frequently used in ordinary conversation.

Baka-bakashii, an emphatic form of *bakarashii*, is a popular opening phrase in *rakugo*, Japanese traditional comic storytelling. A typical opening line is *maido baka-bakashii hanashi deshite,* meaning this is a stupid story, as always.

When one adds *ni suru* to *baka*, the meaning becomes to make a fool of. If, for example, you feel someone is making a fool of you, you might say *baka ni suru na* (don't make a fool of me). *Kobaka ni suru*, on the other hand, means to look with disdain upon someone. *Ko-* is a prefix meaning small or little.

Similar irony is present in the expression *usu-baka*. *Usui* actually means thin or weak (as in weak tea or a weak drink), which can then be further interpreted as somewhat or slightly. When used with *baka*, however, the meaning becomes quite the opposite—a great fool, a real ninny. *Usura-baka* is a much stronger word, as is *ō-baka*, *ō-* being written with the Japanese character for big.

Usui- and *ko-*, incidentally, may be used as prefixes with other words to obtain similar effects. *Usugitanai* or *kogitanai*, for example, *(kitanai* means dirty, shabby, or squalid) have connotations of extremely dirty, shabby, or squalid.

Baka used as a prefix, as in *bakashōjiki, bakateinei,* or *bakawarai,* adds the meaning of excessively. So these words, respectively, mean honest to a fault, excessively polite, and horse laugh. Nowadays when prices are high, the word *bakayasu* (*yasu* meaning inexpensive, from the word *yasui*) is also popular for something that seems absurdly cheap.

Adding *ni* to *baka* turns it into an adverb meaning awfully or terribly. Thus, *kyō wa baka ni samui ne* means it's awfully cold today, isn't it? The Japanese also use the expression *bakayōki* (*yōki* is weather) for odd weather. *Baka ni tsukeru kusuri wa nai* (*tsukeru* is to put on or apply, and *kusuri* is medicine) means there's no cure for a fool.

Bakauke and its verb form *bakauke suru* (*ukeru* being to appeal to the public) means an unexpectedly big hit. *Baka no hitotsu oboe* is a common Japanese saying that can be translated as a fool always uses the one thing he knows. In other words, *baka shika shiranai to baka ni sareru* (if stupid is the only word you know, people will think you're the stupid one).

Here are some other synonyms for *baka* that you should know so people won't think you're stupid.

Ahō, or more commonly *aho* (fool, ass, or simpleton), is used all over Japan, but it's particularly popular in Kansai, where its softer sound is more acceptable to the local ear than the explosive-sounding *baka*. One can say *sonna aho na* instead of *sonna baka na* to mean that's ridiculous. *Ahokusai* or *ahokusa* can be used in place of *bakakusai* to mean very smelly. You cannot, however, use the prefixes *ko-* or *usu-* in front of *aho*.

Ahojikara replaces *bakajikara* (*chikara* is physical strength or power; euphonically changed to *jikara*) to mean excessively strong. This expression is used in the common phrase *kajiba no bakajikara* (unusual strength shown in an emergency such as a fire). You can replace *bakajikara* with *kuso jikara*.

Aho has two variations, namely *ahodara* and *ahondara*. They are both compound words made from *aho* and *tara*, and are more emphatic than *aho*.

Antonyms for *baka* and *aho* also show regional variations. Tokyoites say *rikō mono* (clever person), while Osaka people use *kashikoi* and *kashikoi hito*. When praising a child, Tokyoites will say *o-rikō-san* or *ii ko ne,* while people from Osaka say *kashikoi ne* or *ēkoya.*

There are a number of other near synonyms for *baka* that can be used when referring to perceived mental defects or personality shortcomings. Their usage is not as broad as *baka* or *ahō,* as they are usually descriptive of a particular, rather than a general, condition.

Saitei, for example, means the lowest, meanest, stupidest. *Saitei-na yatsu* (or *yarō*) can be translated as he's an asshole. The term can also be applied to inanimate objects, so that *saitei-na koto* becomes what shit or what crap.

Teinō, on the other hand, means a half-wit or bonehead, and can only be used when referring to a person, as in *kare wa teinō da* or *mattaku teinō-na yatsu da* (he's a total dimwit).

Nōtarin is a simpleton or jerk *(nō* is brain, and *tarin* is short for *tarinai,* which means lacking or insufficient). This is never used as an adjective, and only in connection with a person, as in *aitsu wa nōtarin da* (he's a jerk). *Hakuchi* (idiot) is used likewise, but is regarded as discriminatory. Use with care.

Manuke is another synonym for *baka.* The *kanji* for *ma* can also be pronounced *aida,* and here means a pause between rhythms or actions in Japanese music or dance. *Nuke* comes from the verb *nukeru* (to miss or lack). *Manuke* (without modulation), then, signifies a person who somehow lacks a normal sense of what he's doing, a half-wit or dunce. This word can be used both as a noun and an adjective. Thus, *kare wa manuke* or *manuke-na yatsu* or, in a slight variation, *kare wa nukete iru,* are all common expressions to mean he's out of it.

Hema and *doji* are close synonyms of *manuke.* Both can be translated as blunder, bungle, or mess. *Doji* is an abbreviated form of *doshikujiri,* from the verb *shikujiru* (to make a mistake or fail), with the emphatic prefix *do-.*

Hema is thought to derive from *heta* (incompetent) and *manuke; hecho* is its slang variation. Thus, when a person makes a careless blunder, like walking through a puddle instead of around it, you might say *hema, manuke* or *baka, doji*. Used as verbs *(hema o shita* or *doji o funda),* they can be translated as he goofed.

In English, people are sometimes called stupid jerks. They are in Japanese as well, using the expression *tonma*. The *ma* in *tonma,* which is both a noun and adjective meaning nincompoop, ass, or dimwit, is written with the Chinese character for ass or horse. *Tonma da kara muri wa nai,* then, means he's such a dunce, I'm not surprised he did something so stupid.

Ton-chiki and *ton-chin-kan* are two humorous synonyms for *tonma*. *Ton-chiki* (dope) can be used only when referring to a person, while *ton-chin-kan* (absurd, incoherent, or irrelevant) can be applied to people or things. The *ton* in the latter word comes from *ton-ten-kan,* the sound made by blacksmiths when they hammer in concert with each other. The *chin* sound signifies being out of sync with others; thus, *ton-chin-kan* acquired its sense of discordance. Both of these terms can be used by women as well as men.

Noroma comes from *noroi,* meaning slow or tardy, and it is used to describe someone who is dull or muddleheaded. Again, it can be used as a noun or adjective as in *noroma-na hito* or *aitsu wa baka de noroma* (he's a stupid blockhead). *Noro-noro suru na (or noro-noro shinai de* when used by women) means don't be slow.

Guzu-guzu is an onomatopoetic expression that is a close synonym. It has the added implication not only of slow, but irresolute. Thus *guzu-guzu suru na* (or *shinai de*) means stop your dilly-dallying. The *guzu* from *guzu-guzu* can also be used in place of *noroma*. *Kare wa guzu da* means he's a laggard. For emphasis one can say *guzu de noroma*. Or to be more slangy, use *guzura* instead of *guzu*.

Otanchin and *anpontan* are near synonyms for *baka, manuke,* and *tonma,* but their sounds give them a more humorous and colloquial slant. Both of them can be used simply by themselves or in a phrase such as *ano otanchin* (that boob). For greater effect and emphasis, pronounce it *ottanchin.*

Otanko-nasu and *boke-nasu* are similar to *otanchin,* but have stronger meanings. *Nasu* means eggplant. *Boke* here comes from *hōkeru* or *bokeru,* which mean to become senile or absent-minded. Literal translations aside, the image should be clear. Grammatically these two words are used in the same way as *otanchin* and, when used by a woman, should be followed by *ne* or *yo.*

Another word that makes use of the explosive "b" sound (as in *baka*) is *bon-kura* (blockhead). It comes from *yakuza* (gangster) language. *Bon* is the tray on which the mobsters gamble with dice, and *kura* comes from *kurai,* meaning dark or without knowledge. The implication therefore is a gambler who knows little about gambling— despite its being his own occupation. In this way, the expression came to mean a useless person.

Dekunobo is a similar word, a very expressive one, meaning blockhead, dummy or dolt, a person who just doesn't react. *Deku* is a wooden doll or puppet, and *bo* is an affectionate term for a man. *Ano hito wa dekunobo,* then, refers to a man who's a dummy or useless.

Pā is really the ultimate put-down. Used in conjunction with a simultaneous upward thrusting, opening gesture of the palm of the hand by the side of the speaker's head, it means a complete dud, a zero, a nothing.

Dame, meaning no good, is probably a word many students of Japanese are already familiar with. But let's look at some of its colloquial applications. A long-running Japanese comic strip was entitled *Dame Oyaji* (*oyaji* means father), and the protagonist (if we can call him that) was a helpless, hapless father. Perhaps because of this connection, it's more fashionable and sophisticated to say *dame oyaji* than the conventional and grammatical *dame-na oyaji*. The same can be said for *dame otoko* (man) or *dame onna* (woman).

Dame has its origins in the Japanese board game of *go*, in which players compete to secure spaces which then count as their territory. In most cases, useless spaces (*muda-na me*) will remain in the border areas when the game is over. These spaces are called *dame*. Aside from this rather specialized use of the word, *dame* nowadays is applied to anything that is useless, no good, or impossible. *Dame-na musuko* is an oft-heard lament when parents describe a no-good (or perceived as no-good) son. *Deki ga warui ko* is similar, meaning an unaccomplished child, while *deki sokonai* is even worse, literally a failure.

Kono tokei (this watch) *wa dame desu* means this watch doesn't run or, depending on the context, this watch won't do. *Naitemo* (even if you cry) *dame da* means it's useless to cry. When a Japanese mother says simply *dame* to her child, it means don't do that or, more emphatically, stop it. If you reply *dame (desu)* when you're asked to do something, it means that you are unable to help out, or simply, no. This can sound a bit abrupt in Japanese, however. A more common and more polite response would be *muzukashii (desu)*, *muzukashii* being an ordinary word for difficult.

Gūtara is similar to *dame* in meaning good-for-nothing. *Gūtara oyaji* can be used almost interchangeably with *dame oyaji*, and conjures up the image of Dagwood from the comic strip *Blondie*, relentlessly sleeping on the sofa while the lawnmower languishes in the garage.

Ikare ponchi, now archaic, is similar to *dame otoko/onna*. The verb *ikareru* means to become useless or touched in the head. It can be used similarly to *dame* as in *kono tokei wa ikarete iru* (this watch doesn't work). *Ponchi* comes from *bonchi* (a young boy in Kansai dialect), and *ikare* is a shortened form of *ikareta*, the past tense of *ikareru*. The word became popular after World War II, when traditional Japanese ways of thinking were changing drastically, and many young people became *ikare ponchi* in their confusion as to how to adjust to the new (dis)order.

Ikareta is still used and by itself means *dame* in the sense of someone having a hole in his head or being really off his rocker. It can also be used to mean enchanted with as in *kare wa kanojo ni ikareteru* (he's crazy about her), acting like a hoodlum as in *aitsu wa ikareteru* (he's acting like a thug), and to be an idiot as in *kare wa ikareteru* (he's a moron).

Now, we'd like to introduce some terms that sound like the male names *Yotarō, Santarō, Fūtaro,* and *Tōshiro,* but actually connote further meanings. The use of names to imply something else is common in many languages. A john, in English, for example, is used to mean the toilet as well as a prostitute's customer. A cuppa joe is a cup of coffee. And a lulu is an astounding person or thing.

One term derived from a name comes from Japan's sports world. *Dozaemon* is a synonym for the victim of a drowning. It seems that in the Edo era there was an enormously fat sumo wrestler by the name of Dozaemon Naruse, whose swollen body and vast white expanse of stomach reminded people of a drowned person. Although most Japanese today don't know the origin of this term, they use it more frequently than the legal term *dekishisha (deki* is drowned, *shi* is death, and *sha* is person). There are, incidentally, four ways of talking about drowning in Japanese: *dozaemon ni naru, oboreru, dekishi suru,* and *suishi suru.*

Yotarō sounds like an ordinary man's name, but it has taken on another meaning over time. *Yotarō* is a favorite character in *rakugo,* traditional comic storytelling. In classic *rakugo, Yotarō* always appears as an innocently simple fool, his sole purpose being to cause great amusement among the audience. Thus the word *yotarō* has come to be a near synonym for a young *baka manuke* (blockhead or dunce). The shortened form *yota* is used to mean stupidity, or a useless person or thing.

Yota banashi (hanashi is story, changed euphonically to *banashi)* and *yota-mono* are derivatives of *yotarō.* The former can be translated as nonsense or unreliable talk, and the latter as hoodlum or gangster. Thus *yota banashi shinai de* means don't talk nonsense, *yota o tobasu (tobasu* means let fly) means to talk nonsense, and *kare wa yotamon(o) da* means he's a hoodlum. *Yotamon* and *yotakō* are variations of *yota-mono,* the latter being a derogatory word for *yakuza* and other rough characters.

Yotaru and *yotatte iru* are derivative verbs meaning to act like a hoodlum. *Yakuza* and *gurentai,* however, are more up-to-date words for gangsters than *yota-mono.* This will be discussed in more detail later.

Santarō also sounds like an ordinary name. *San* is three, and, literally translated, *santarō* means third son. But it's understood in a broader sense as a half-wit. This is because it's said in Japan that the first and third sons tend to be rather foolish, while the second son, more often than not, is the clever one. Thus *ō-baka santarō* means a dunderhead or a real horse's ass.

Fūtarō (fū being an alternative pronunciation of the character for *kaze,* or wind) means an insignificant person, someone who just blows in the wind and disappears as effortlessly as a spring breeze. Contemporary variations of this word, such as *pūtarō,* will be explained in the chapter on young people's language.

Tōshirō used to be a very common man's name in Japan. It is used now, however, with the sense of amateur or non-professional. *Tōshirō* derives from the word *shirōto* (amateur), which is used particularly in connection with the arts and professions. The two *kanji* with which *shirōto* is written are those for simple and person.

When written with a different character, *shiro* means white and carries implications of pure and innocent. *Shiro*'s opposite *kuro,* on the other hand, also can be written with several different *kanji.* These bear connotations of black, accomplishment, or mystery, depending on the character used.

Several word plays take advantage of these homonyms. Diametrically opposite to *shiroto* is *kuroto (kuro* is black), which means a person who is accomplished, particularly in the arts and crafts, a professional, prostitute, or bar hostess. When a defendant is found not guilty, for example, he or she is called *shiro,* while *kuro* is used for someone found guilty. *Aitsu wa shiro da to omou,* then, means I think that guy is innocent.

The reason that *shiroto* became *tōshiro* is really quite simple. The Japanese, particularly gangsters and entertainers, have a habit of inverting words to create a secret language. Gangsters, for example, refer to women *(onna)* as *naon.* And *hiikō* is often used instead of *kōhii* (coffee). You can use *toshirō* or *tōshirō* as in *aitsu wa honto ni tōshirō da* (he really doesn't know what he's doing). And when you add the emphatic prefix *do-,* it becomes the even more contemptuous *doshirōto, ne* (you're a real amateur).

Yopparai-Related

Nonbei is another word that sounds like a name, but it means a habitual drinker or drunkard. It comes from the verb *nomu* (to drink) and the suffix *-bei,* which in the past was commonly attached to men's names. *Nonbei* can be used when speaking of either men or women, however. *Nomisuke* is a synonym *(-suke* is also a suffix sometimes attached to Japanese men's names). *Ō-zakenomi (sake* is Japanese rice wine and *ō-* means big) is a boozer, and *uwabami* (python) is a heavy drinker. *Nondakure* is a constant drunk, sometimes a bum, while *sakebitari* is to indulge in drinking. The *bitari* here comes from the verb *hitaru* with a euphonic change, meaning to be soaked or immersed in.

In the fall of 1993, some shocking news (shocking for Japan, that is) was reported by Kurihama National Hospital. Japanese under 20 are legally prohibited from drinking; nevertheless, it was found that 14% of high school students (age 15 to 18) consume alcohol one or more times a week.

There are various reasons for this. Unlike in Europe and North America, there are vending machines nationwide in Japan where alcohol can be easily purchased by those underage without any ID check, though the machines are expected to be closed down at 11 P.M.

As of 1990, the number of alcohol vending machines reached 200,000 (one per 600 persons), 70% of them selling beer. The Ministry of Health and Welfare has asked retailers to exercise restraint in this matter, but the Ministry of Finance is not too enthusiastic about it since the machines are a lucrative source of tax revenue. Recently there has been serious criticism of this state of affairs, and plans to remove alcohol and cigarette vending machines have been carried out at the local level.

Sake is sometimes called *kichigai mizu* (literally, crazy water), and is thought to paralyze a part of the brain and create a condition of stupidity. *Shirafu* (literally, white face) means sober. This is because the Japanese characteristically become very red in the face when they drink.

Horo-yoi means tipsy. Here *horo* means a little, and *yoi* means to become drunk. *Ippai kigen* can also be translated as tipsy, with *ippai* meaning one glass and *kigen* meaning humor or mood.

Yopparai is used when tipsiness passes into drunkenness. It is similar to *nonbei,* but more colloquial. Also, while *nonbei* describes a habitual drinker, *yopparai* can describe someone who occasionally gets drunk. It comes from the verb *yopparau,* meaning to get very drunk or sloshed, which, in turn, is derived from the verb *you*. *You* has three interpretations: to get drunk, to get seasick, and to be fascinated by music, etc. If you call someone *yopparai* in an angry tone, it's equivalent to saying you goddam drunk, get out of here.

Jōgo is a tippler. It can be used in compounds, such as *warai-jōgo* (a happy drunk), *naki-jōgo* (a maudlin drinker), and *okori-jōgo* (a mean drunk).

Geko is a bad or weak drinker. It can also mean a teetotaler. It is always used by itself, never in compounds.

Strong drinkers are generally called *hidari-tō* (literally, left-handed party). *Hidari* comes from the word for left, as in left-handed, and implies people who want to continue drinking so badly that they will drink with their left hand, while using their right to eat simultaneously.

Geko are thought of so contempuously that they are called *ama-tō* (lovers of sweets). *Ama* comes from *amai mono* (sweets), and *tō* means party or faction. *Ama-tō* are often regarded as *buchōhō* (impolite, awkward, or unccomplished). An antonym for *ama-tō* is *kara-tō* (literally, hot and dry), which is also used to refer to a drinker.

Japanese people often inquire as to whether their guests can drink or not by asking *ikeru kuchi desu ka?* (*ikeru* means literally to be able to go, but can also mean to be nice or good). When one says *kono sake wa ikeru,* it means the *sake* is not bad, with the connotation that it's actually good. *Ikenai-kuchi* is similar to *geko* and *buchōhō*.

One reason why most of the so-called *geko* don't drink is that Japanese people tend to get red *(akaku naru)* in the face when they drink. Thus, *akaku naru kara nomanai* is a favorite excuse for declining a drink, used especially by young women.

The onomatopoeic expressions *hebereke* and *berobero* both mean to be in a state of dead drunkenness. *Kare wa hebereke da* or *hebereke ni yotte iru,* then, mean he's dead drunk. The expression *watashi wa anata ni yotte iru* literally means I'm drunk over you, or I'm in love with you.

Ō-tora (big tiger) is a violent or roaring drunk. *Ōtora* are often found sleeping it off in the *torabako* (tiger box) at local police stations all over Japan.

Yoitsubureru (tsubureru is to be crushed or destroyed) is almost identical to its English equivalent, smashed. *Waru-yoi* (bad drunk) is used when someone gets sick from drinking. This often happens in Japan, especially around the end of the year. It's a regrettable fact that, in the evening, it's usually wise to watch where you're stepping in certain areas of the city or on train platforms. *Futsukayoi* (literally, to be drunk for two days) is the Japanese word for a hangover. *Aru-chū,* which is a derogatory abbreviation for *arukōru chūdoku* (literally, alcohol poisoning) is used to refer to an alcoholic.

Hashigo (ladder) or *hashigo-zake* is a good way to become an *aru-chū. (Zake* here is a euphonic change of *sake,* which in addition to meaning Japanese rice wine is also a generic term for any alcoholic beverage). These terms refer to pub-crawling or bar-hopping. And when one has been bar-hopping long enough, one's gait becomes *chidori-ashi. Chidori* is a plover, which is a long-legged water bird, and *ashi* is a foot or leg. Plovers walk rather clumsily, zigzagging along like a drunk, and this, obviously, is the origin of this term.

Nomi-ya is a general term for a drinking house. Traditionally, drinking in Japan involves eating as well. Typical locations for drinking in Japan are *yakitori-ya* (restaurants serving skewered grilled chicken), *oden-ya* (restaurants serving *oden* or Japanese stew), and *sushi-ya* (sushi restaurants). The least expensive and most popular, though, are the *biya hōru* (beer halls), and *ippai-nomi-ya* or *izaka-ya* (drinking houses or pubs). In beer halls a large variety of items is served, from little plates of hors d'oeuvres to full meals. In *izaka-ya,* customers can get a large variety of *o-kazu* (side dishes) to accompany beer, *sake,* whiskey, *shōchū* (a cheap liquor made from potatoes, rice, or wheat), and other alcoholic beverages. Restaurant/bars called *robata-yaki* (literally, fireside grill) are also very popular. These establishments serve food that is grilled right in front of the customers.

Cheap drinking houses often hang red lanterns at the entrance; thus, they are collectively called *aka chōchin* (red lanterns). After having a few drinks and some snacks at such an establishment, a *nomisuke* might *hashigo* on his *chidori-ashi* to a *bā, sunakku,* or *karaoke-bā* (bar, small night club, and karaoke bar, respectively).

Speaking of food and drink, although *sakana* is now used to mean fish, the word actually originates from *sake no na, na* being literally edible grass or vegetables. Later it came to be a general term for food to enjoy while drinking *sake*. The redundant *sake no sakana* has now come to mean the butt of a joke made while drinking. The word *sakana* by itself can also be used in this context, as in *oi, ore o sakana ni shitarō?* (you enjoyed making fun of me, didn't you?).

2

Parts of the Body

(shintai kanren)

In Japanese there are many derogatory words related to parts of the body. We'll start with the face.

Busu and *buotoko* mean, respectively, ugly woman and ugly man. *Busu* is most derogatory when it is applied to a young woman, and can be regarded as a discriminatory term. One of the largest bookstores in Japan, Kinokuniya, was found guilty of discrimination in a trial held some time ago. The management had apparently set standards of appearance in employing young women. Those considered *busu* (ugly), those wearing *megane* (glasses), and those labeled *chibi* (a derogatory term for a very small person) were not hired.

Busutto shita or *busutto shite iru* mean to look sullen or sulky, and this may be the etymology of *busu*.

Okame and *hyottoko* are a pair of synonyms for *busu* and *buotoko,* but they are now rather archaic. You can understand the looks they signify if you've ever had the chance to see the masks used in *okagura,* sacred Shinto dancing. The female variety has a tiny nose, small narrow slits for eyes, a high forehead, and large round cheeks. Her male counterpart has big, round, stupid-looking eyes and a very protruding mouth. These masks are believed to symbolize the genital organs of the respective sexes, the mouth being the vagina, the nose the clitoris, and the cheeks the testicles. If this seems curious, remember that the Shinto religion celebrates all aspects of life, and many of its ceremonies—the renowned phallic festival, for example—are blatantly sexual.

Okame originally comes from the term *otafuku* (ugly woman). The *kanji* for this word mean full of happiness, presumably because a man who marries an ugly woman need have little fear of her infidelity.

During the New Year season, the Japanese play a variety of traditional games. Among them is *fuku-warai,* which is somewhat like pin-the-tail-on-the-donkey. In *fuku-warai,* the player is supposed to arrange the parts of the *okame* face with his or her eyes closed. If the player does well, this assures good fortune in the coming year. *Okachimenko,* a derivative of *okame,* is frequently used today as a synonym for *busu.*

Bukiryō, or *busaiku,* and *fubijin* are other rather formal terms for ugly persons. The former can be applied to both sexes; the latter literally means not beautiful person and is applied only to women. *Bu-* and *fu-* in this case are prefixes meaning un- as in unattractive. *Kiryō* means face or personal beauty, and *saiku* is fine work or ware. Close synonyms are *minikui hito* (ugly-looking person), *hen-na kao* (odd or grotesque face), and the slangy *mazui tsura* (plain or bad-looking face). *Tsura* is a vulgar synonym for *kao* (face).

The worst expression for an ugly woman, though, is *obake* (monster). This term and the stronger *bakemono* (goblin or monster) are often used in a derogatory and critical sense for women who put on too much make-up *(atsu-geshō)* or who have had cosmetic surgery *(seikei shujutsu)* with bad results.

Oiwa-*san* is the name of a famous *obake* character in *kabuki* theater who is ultimately poisoned by her own husband. She appears on stage as a hideous monster; thus the term *oiwa-san* can be extremely insulting to a woman.

Daburu hatto is a rather odd slang expression often used by students. It refers to a woman who looks great from behind, but, when an admirer catches up sufficiently to see her face, finds she's really quite ugly. *Hatto* is a mimetic word meaning a surprise, and *daburu hatto* means doubly surprised. A synonym for this is *bakku shan*. *Bakku* comes from the English back and *shan* from the German *schon,* meaning a beauty or a belle.

Nafutarin comes from napthalene, the chemical in mothballs that repels moths and other insects. The abbreviated *nafu* means a really ugly girl.

While we're on the subject of insects, we might mention that the idiomatic expression *mushi ga tsuku* (an insect catches on a flower or tree) means for a woman to have a lover. Its negative form *mushi mo tsukanai* (even an insect wouldn't alight), means hopelessly unattractive.

A particularly graphic term that can be applied to a very ugly person, either male or female, is *chinkusha.* The *chin* here refers to a Pekingese dog, with its funny face—the eyes, nose, and mouth all seeming to come together in the middle. *Kusha* is short for *kushami* (sneeze). Just imagine what a Pekingese dog looks like sneezing and you'll get the idea of the type of person to which *chinkusha* refers.

Abata-zura and *kabocha-zura* are used to mean a pockmarked or pitted face. *Abata* is literally a pockmark or pit, while *kabocha* is a pumpkin. *Zura* is a euphonic change of *tsura,* or face. *Nikibi-zura* is used to describe a face covered with pimples, *nikibi* being pimples. *Sobakasu* are freckles in Japanese, and, when a person is heavily freckled, he can be described as *sobakasu-yaro* or *sobakasu-darake.* *-Darake* is a derogatory suffix meaning full of or covered with. In the West, a moderate amount of freckles is often regarded as cute, or at least aesthetically acceptable, but the Japanese seem to have an aversion to them.

Shiwa-darake or *shiwakucha* are used to refer to a very wrinkled individual. *Shiwa* is a wrinkle, line, or furrow, and *kucha* is an onomatopoetic device for the sound that accompanies crumpling or wrinkling. Thus, *shiwakucha babā* is a commonly heard derogatory term for a heavily wrinkled old lady. Small wrinkles are called *kojiwa, ko-* being a prefix meaning small, and *jiwa* a euphonic change of *shiwa*. *Kojiwa* are also called, more elegantly, *karasu no ashiato* (crows' tracks), equivalent to crows' feet in English. Whether they are called *kojiwa* or *karasu no ashiato,* they are particularly dreaded by middle-aged women the world over.

Hige-zura (bearded face), *hige-darake* (covered with a beard), and *higeyarō* (bearded fellow) are all derogatory terms for a bearded person. Until recently most Japanese didn't grow beards, and people who did so were thought of as odd and somehow dirty. Thus, there are a number of derogatory terms for such individuals.

Hige is a general term for the beard, or the hairs that grow around the mouth *(kuchi),* cheeks *(hoho),* and jaw *(ago). Kuchihige,* then, is a mustache, *hohohige* is whiskers, and *agohige* is a beard. Sideburns are called *momiage* from the verb *momiageru* (to massage up), the action required when attempting to shave them off.

Nowadays, though, beards are becoming more popular among young Japanese. Such young men are called members of the *hige-zoku* (beard tribe or beard gang). This tendency reveals a change in social customs and the influence of foreign fashions.

Schick, an American manufacturer of razor blades, now sponsors a yearly beard contest in Japan and reports that the number of applicants has been growing steadily through the 80s and into the 90s. Japanese companies, too, may be taking a slightly more tolerant attitude towards employees who grow beards.

Uma-zura (horse-faced), *geta* (Japanese square wooden clogs), and *rakkyō* (shallot) are used to describe a face that tapers toward the chin.

As for the head as a whole, *atama dekkachi* (from *atama* meaning head and *dekai* meaning huge) refers to a person whose head is too large for his body. It also implies a person who has lots of book learning but no common sense. When someone says *atama dekkachi shiri subori* (or *subomari),* it means something that starts with a bang but ends with a whimper.

Tongari atama (tongari means sharply pointed) or *biriken atama (biriken* comes from Billiken—an American "happy god" with a sharply-pointed head created by a female artist in the early 20th century), both mean pointed head. *Zeppeki (atama)* refers to a person whose head is flat in the back, usually as a result of the traditional Japanese custom of laying infants on their backs. The Japanese traditionally fear laying babies on their stomachs. Fortunately, this fear is gradually coming to be understood as unfounded, and we see fewer and fewer cases of *zeppeki atama* these days. *Zeppeki* here means cliff.

Hage or *hage atama* are derogatory terms for bald men, *hage* being the word for bald. *Hage* has a number of variations, such as *hage chabin* (totally bald like a teapot), *tsuruppage* (entirely bald), *zenippage* (literally, coin bald; figuratively, bald in spots), *jarippage* (literally, gravel bald; likewise, bald in spots), and *hage choro* or *usuppage* (both meaning baldish). *Choro* actually means the state of sneaking or flitting about, as in *shimi choro* (a slip which occasionally shows). *Teka-teka* (bright), *pika-pika* (shining), and *tsuru-tsuru* (slippery) are additional terms used to describe bald people. *Bōzu* is a derogatory term both for bald people and for Buddhist monks, who usually shave their heads. *O-bō-san,* which uses the two honorifics *o-* and *-san,* is the accepted term for a monk. *Taiwan bōzu* (Taiwan monk) is a derogatory expression for someone with *enkei datsumō-shō* (a round patch of baldness). *Hage* and *bōzu* can refer to a sexually vigorous male as well, though.

Today, due to the variety of available wigs, *hage* people don't suffer as much as in the past. One of the biggest makers of wigs in Japan is a company called

Aderansu, so the word has been adopted as a synonym for wig.

Even people lucky enough to have hair growing on their heads can become the target of ridicule with terms such as *shiraga* (gray hair), *wakajiraga* (prematurely gray), and *gomashio atama* (sesame-salt head), which is equivalent to the English salt-and-pepper.

Akage means red-head or carrot top. It has become less effective as an insult due to the popularity of an animated TV series entitled *Akage no Ann,* based on the book *Anne of Green Gables.* In fact, many Japanese young people nowadays dye their hair a great variety of shades of red.

Moving to the eyes, *demekin,* a somewhat exotic species of goldfish with round, protruding eyes, as well as *deme,* a derivative of this word, can be used for a pop-eyed or goggle-eyed person. *Ano hito wa demekin* means that guy's got bug eyes. When you want to convey the same meaning more politely and indirectly, you can say instead *kare wa me ga chotto dete iru* (his eyes protrude a little).

Chikame (chika is near, and *me* is eye or eyeball), or *kingan,* which is an alternate way of pronouncing the same characters, refer to near-sighted or short-sighted persons. *Do-kingan* is more derogatory. *Kingan* comes from *kinshi* (myopia or short-sightedness) and *gan* (eye). The expression *kinshigan-teki* is used as an adjective to describe a short-sighted viewpoint on something.

Yabunirami, shashi, and *yorime* all refer to cross-eyed persons. *Yabunirami* and *shashi* refer to a person with one eye in the correct position and the other either looking excessively outward or inward. *Yorime* is the condition of both eyes looking inward, toward the nose. As for *shashi, sha* is slant and *shi* is the direction of the eyes. The origin of *yabunirami* is more obscure. *Yabu* means growing willy-nilly in all directions, and *nirami* means staring or glaring. *Yabunirami* can also be used to refer to a twisted viewpoint on something.

Ronpari is an amusing variation. It comes from the *ron* in London (as it is rendered in Japanese) and the *pari* in Paris, and implies one eye on London, the other on Paris; in other words, both eyes positioned outward.

Donguri-manako means goggle-eyed, *donguri* being acorn and *manako* being eyeball. *Gyoro-me* is a synonym; *gyoro* is a mimetic expression for glaring. *Kitsune-me* describes a person with narrow, slanting eyes; *kitsune* means fox in Japanese.

As for the ears, *tsubureta mimi* (literally, destroyed ear) is rendered into English as cauliflower ear. *Mimidare* is a runny ear. The *-dare* here comes from the verb *tareru,* which means to run down, ooze, or fall in drops. *Fukumimi* (literally, happy ears) is used to describe someone who has big ears, especially when the lobes are thick. People with big, thick earlobes, it is said, will be blessed with good luck and wealth.

Dangoppana and *shishippana* refer to a snub or pug nose. *Dango* is a kind of dumpling and *shishi* is lion. *-Ppana* is a euphonic change of *hana,* or nose. *Butappana* is a pig nose. In Japan, there are quite a number of *hanapecha* (flat-nosed people) who keep the pockets of the nation's plastic surgeons full of crisp, new yen notes. *Pecha* comes from *pechanko,* a mimetic expression which means the state of being crushed or smashed.

Hana ga hikui is a low or flat nose, in contrast to *hana ga takai,* which means either a long nose or to be proud of something. Japanese people often speak admiringly of Western noses, describing them as *hana ga takai.*

Washippana or *kagippana* (Roman or hooked nose) are rarely seen among the Japanese. In these expressions *washi* means eagle and *kagi* is hook.

Hana no shita literally means under the nose. When *hana no shita ga nagai* (long under the nose) is said of a man, it means he is somewhat foolishly amorous or lecherous. *Bikachō* has exactly the same *kanji* characters and meaning, but uses the pronunciations *bi* instead of *hana,* *ka* instead of *shita,* and *chō* instead of *nagai.*

Dekai kuchi, ōki-na kuchi, and *ō-guchi* are all derogatory expressions used to describe a person with a large mouth. *Dekai* is a colloquial term for big. Traditionally, a small mouth was considered more acceptable in Japan than a large one; thus these derogatory expressions for big mouths. When you say *dekai kuchi o tataku* or *kiku,* it means to talk big.

Mitsukuchi (three mouths) refers to a harelipped person. *Ukeguchi* (receiving mouth) describes a person with a protruding lower lip. Kaō, one of the largest manufacturers of soap in Japan, has as its trademark a crescent-shaped face with an *ukeguchi.* Thus people use the expression *kaō sekken (sekken* is soap) as a synonym for *ukeguchi. Deppa* (protruding teeth) means bucktoothed.

Still in the mouth, *shitatarazu* is used to mean a person who easily becomes tongue-tied or a person who lisps. *Shitatarazu* also means lacking sufficient explanation.

Moving down to the shoulders *(kata),* there are two types of expressions: *ikari-gata* and *nade-gata.* The former literally means angry shoulders, but is used colloquially to signify someone who is, in fact, square-shouldered.

The term *nade-gata,* from the verb *naderu* (to stroke), means drooping or sloping shoulders and is used in reference to an attractive, elegant woman.

Moving to the back, *nekoze* means round-shouldered or a stooped or bent back. This comes from an association with the round back of a cat *(neko). Nekoze de megane* (glasses) is a caricatured description of a typical hunched, bespectacled Japanese. When the stoop is very pronounced, the word *semushi* (humpback or hunchback) is used, though this term is now regarded as discriminatory.

As mentioned earlier, *debeso* is a protruding belly button. This term comes from the expression *heso* (navel) *ga dete iru* (is protruding). *Hesomagari* or *ohesomagari* (crooked or twisted belly button) means perverse or obstinate, or people with these traits.

After the face, it is the hands *(te)* that are usually the most visible part of one's anatomy. Not surprisingly, then, there are a good number of Japanese terms used to describe and make fun of the hands. *Tenagazaru* originally meant a gibbon or long-armed ape, and is now used derogatorily to refer to a long-armed person. *Te* in Japanese, incidentally, includes both hands and arms, as *ashi* is both feet and legs.

Futoi ude and its slang variations *buttoi ude* and *marutanbo* (log) refer to big, brawny arms. Physically slender arms are *hosoi ude,* but the slightly altered *hoso-ude* (literally, thin arms) refers to a woman's management of a shop or company. Corresponding terms for big hands are *gotsui te, kumade,* and *gurōbu. Gotsui* is rough and thick, *kumade* is literally bear hand, and *gurōbu* is baseball glove.

In a world dominated by right-handedness *(migi-kiki),* the left-handed minority *(hidari-kiki)* is sometimes the object of scorn and contempt. *Gitcho* (lefty) is a slang expression for a left-hander. Interestingly, *gitcho* is an abbreviated form of *hidari-gitcho,* the original form of which is *hidari-giyō. Kiyō* and its euphonic change *giyō* mean skillful hand.

In Japan, being left-handed has traditionally had at least one advantage. Lefties have generally been thought of as skillful at handicrafts. A sculptor who lived in the early Edo era and left many masterpieces, including the "Sleeping Cat" relief in Nikko, was given the name Jingorō Hidari.

For most of history, though, *hidari* has usually been thought of as symbolizing something bad or unfortunate, and *migi* just the opposite. The same is true of *sinister* and *dexter* in Latin. From the former, meaning left, derives the English word sinister with its connotations of misfortune and evil. Dexterity, which comes from the Latin for right, means handiness, skillfulness, and cleverness.

Though not directly related to a part of the body, *hidari-mae* (literally, left in front) means adversity, decline, or a business that has gone the wrong way. *Ano ie wa hidari-mae ni natta* means that family is going out of business.

This expression comes from the custom of wearing a kimono for one's last journey, (i.e., to the grave), *hidari-mae* (left side over right side). This is a little confusing because, when the *kimono* is put on in *hidari-mae* fashion, it is done from the point of view of the living who put the kimono on the dead. *Migi-mae,* with the right side in front (left to the onlooker), is the one and only way for the living to wear their kimono. Dress with care.

Hidari-maki (counter-clockwise) colloquially means a screwball. A person with a counter-clockwise cowlick on his head is considered nutty or eccentric.

A derogatory expression often used to describe the skin *(hada)* is *samehada* (shark skin). Like other cultures, the Japanese value smooth and compact skin very highly. *Torihada* (literally, chicken skin) means gooseflesh. A common synonym is *zara-zara* or *butsu-butsu shita hada,* as in *kanojo wa bijin da kedo hada ga zara-zara da* (she may be a beauty, but she has rough skin). You may also simply say *hada ga kitanai* (dirty) or *hada ga arete iru* (chapped). Chapped skin is also known as *hada-are* or *arehada.*

Although it is not as highly prized in Japan as it used to be, a traditional beauty always has white, translucent skin. Thus, the proverb *iro no shiroi wa shichi nan kakusu* means, literally, that white skin can hide many faults, or a fair complexion compensates for other poor features. Correspondingly, *asaguroi hada (guroi* is black) is something most darker Japanese wish they didn't have. This prejudice comes from the old days when only farmers and other menial workers spent long hours in the sun. The mark of the leisure class, who could spend its days indoors in intellectual, artistic, and amorous pursuits, was very pale skin.

Here we move on to *ashi* (feet or legs). Long, slim, shapely legs are much admired in Japan, despite, or, possibly on account of, their rarity. *Ashi ga mijikai* (he has short legs) or *mijikai ashi* (short legs) are ordinary expressions. But *tansoku,* an alternative reading for *mijikai ashi,* is much more a term of ridicule for someone with stumpy legs.

Dōnaga-tansoku literally means long-waisted, short-legged, and is a typical insult for fat, middle-aged men in Japan. A more amusing synonym is *dakkusufunto* (dachshund).

Daikon-ashi (radish legs) can be aptly translated as piano legs, and is commonly applied to women with thick, definitionless legs. *Futoi ashi* is a common way of describing fat legs. *Ganimata* means bowlegged. *Ganimata* comes from *kani mata, kani* being crab, and *mata* being crotch or thigh.

It's interesting to note that the Japanese language originally did not have voiced sounds at the beginning of its words. Later people began to add voiced sounds to word beginnings in order to emphasize derogatory or indelicate meanings. This explains a change such as *kani* to *gani. Ganimata* sounds really awful to the Japanese ear; therefore, it's appropriate only when someone wants to be really disparaging.

Ganimata, or bowleggedness, is said to be the result of mothers putting excessively thick diapers on their babies. *Uchimata,* on the other hand, means pigeon-toed or knock-kneed. One sees quite a few pigeon-toed women in Japan, perhaps because of the country's long custom of wearing kimono, in which one must walk with short, mincing steps.

Another expression, *wani-ashi,* can be used to describe a person who is either bowlegged *(soto-wani)* or knock-kneed *(uchi-wani). Soto* means outward, and *uchi* is inward. *Wani* is alligator or crocodile.

The phrase *kōdaka banbiro* is used to describe the typically wide, high-instepped foot of the Japanese. *Kōdaka* means high instep or high back, and *banbiro* is wide feet. Such feet are thought to have developed from wearing traditional *geta* (wooden clogs), which do not constrict the feet in any fashion. But this expression is going out of use as *geta* are rarely seen nowadays.

In speaking of one's body shape as a whole, there are any number of amusing Japanese terms. *Noppo* (tall, gangly fellow), *seitaka noppo* (stilts or lampost), and *kirin* (giraffe) are all humorous ways of referring to a very tall person. *Udo no taiboku* is a near synonym. *Udo* is a Japanese plant similar to asparagus, and *taiboku* is a big tree. The stalk part of *udo* is edible when it's young, but after it grows to six feet or so in height, it becomes inedible. This phrase, then, means something like a big boob, someone who's big but useless.

Chibi or the more slangy *chibikō* are used to describe a very small person. When applied to children, these terms mean tot or kid, and the term *chibikko* is now commonly used when referring to children in a collective sense. *Chibita* is only used for male children.

The nouns *chinchikurin* and *chinchikurin yaro* describe a person who is small both physically and mentally (a pipsqueak or squirt). A more slangy adjective for these two nouns is *chinke-na. Chinke-na onna* means a short, unattractive, or awkward girl or woman.

Kobito, which is not to be confused with *koibito* (lover), is a dwarf, as in *Shichinin no Kobito* (The Seven Dwarfs).

Totchanbōya comes from *ototchan* (slang for father or grown male) and *bōya* (boy), and means a short, physically mature—but mentally immature—man.

Even more than people who are short or tall, those who are excessively thin or fat are likely objects of ridicule. Here are some words used to describe such people.

Yase or *yaseppochi,* which come from *yaseta hito* (thin person), is slang for someone who is very skinny. *O-yase-san* is a more ladylike expression. *Gari* or *garitcho* mean skin and bones, with *gari* being an onomatopoetic device for the sound of biting or scratching. *Gari-gari ni yaseta* describes an extremely skinny person. *Honekawa sujiemon,* which sounds like a person's name, also means skin and bones. Its components are *hone* (bone), *kawa* (skin), and *suji* (tendon). The *-emon* is added to make it sound like an old-fashioned male name. Finally, the envy of many of us are *yase no ō-gurai* (slim people who eat all they want).

Gaikotsu refers to a skeleton. Japanese sometimes make a pun on this term and the word *gaikokujin* (foreigner), creating the expression *gaikotsujin* to describe a tall, skinny, funny-looking foreigner. Two other expressions for skinny people are *hyoro* or *hyoro-hyoro* (beanpole) and *moyashi* (bean sprout). *Hyoro* or *hyoro-hyoro* refer to a person who is tall and lanky almost to the point of being unsteady, like certain varieties of water birds. *Moyashi* describes an immature, skinny person. *Rōsoku* (candle) is simply someone who is tall and thin.

Debu (fat person or the state of being fat) is the most common all-embracing slang term used to describe fat people. *Debu-chan,* with the diminutive suffix, implies some degree of affection when applied to roly-poly children or young people.

O-debu (-san) is mainly used for young women, and *debuchin* or *debutcho* for men. Fatty, fatso, or butterball would be English equivalents. *Debu-debu* (a ton of lard) is appropriate when one wants to emphasize merely the fact that a person is fat. *Hyakkan debu* might also be translated as a ton of lard. *Hyakkan* is 100 *kan, kan* being an old Japanese unit of weight equalling approximately 3,750 grams, or a little more than eight pounds. Konishiki, a sumo wrestler from Hawaii who weighs in at over 200 kilograms or 440 pounds, is regarded as *hyakkan debu*. Akebono, also from the U.S. and a sumo grand champion, is not called *debu* because he's relatively tall.

Deppuri is an adjective that can be applied to a stout, yet rather wealthy, gentleman, as in *deppuri shita shinshi* (portly gentleman) or *deppuri futotta hito* (portly person). *Futotta* is an adjective formed from the verb *futoru* (to become fat).

Maru-maru shita (round and full) is an expression commonly used when commenting on a chubby or roly-poly baby. *Marupocha* (cutie) describes a short, plump, but nevertheless charming young girl. *Pocha* comes from the mimetic adjective *potchari* (plump yet attractive). Another expression making use of this term is *pocha-pochatto shita ii onna,* the *ii onna* in this case being a very appealing woman. When this woman gets a little older, however, she might be described with the adjective *kobutori* (dumpy). *Ko-* is a prefix meaning small or little, and *butori* is a euphonic change of *futori* (fat).

Zunguri (shita) or the stronger *zunguri mukkuri (shita),* both mimetic expressions, are commonly applied to people who are short and fat and, at the same time, somewhat unattractive. Pudgy, stumpy, or tubby would be among the many English translations. *Gasshiri shita* (solidly built) would be well-built, stout, or sturdy.

Futome is a rather fashionable word these days. *-Me* is a suffix implying a little bit or rather. *Hosome*, for example, means rather thin, and *katame,* rather hard. *Futome* is a more gracious term than *debu.* If you say *kanojo wa debu,* it sounds as if you are just being nasty, but *chotto futome* is closer to pleasingly plump. *Futome* can also be used to describe animals.

Speaking of animals, *butanko* and *tonko* for women and *bū-chan* for men are other close synonyms of *debu.* *Buta* is pig, and *bū-bū* is the sound a pig makes, similar to oink oink in English. *Bū-bū iu* means to constantly complain. *Ton* is an alternative pronunciation of the same character for pig. *Tonko* is most often used to describe an unattractive young woman, while *bū-chan* is an affectionate expression often used in nicknames for men.

Hara or *onaka* (belly) *ga dete iru* (swelling out) is the most commonly accepted expression for paunchiness. Some slang variations are *biya-daru* (beer barrel) and *zundo* (thick trunk). *Kono goro hara ga detchatta* (I've recently started growing a paunch) is a commonly heard lament among middle-aged men. *Sandan-bara* (literally, triply undulated fat belly), on the other hand, is greatly dreaded by middle-aged women.

A word of caution: when you say *ōki-na onaka* about a woman it means she's pregnant, as in *kanojo wa onaka ga ōkii* or *ōki-na onaka o shite iru.* Slang variations for this are *boteren* and *botebara.* Another tricky expression to watch for is *hara ga futoi* (literally, fat stomach) or *futoppara* in reference to a man. This means he's broadminded.

Dekai o-shiri and the abbreviated *detchiri* (big backside), as well as the more slangy *dekkai ketsu* (big butt), are popular derogatory terms applied to women. In Japanese, *shiri* or *o-shiri* (literally, latter or hind end), and *ketsu* (hole) all mean butt, hips, or ass. *Ketsu* also implies anus.

Koshi means waist and hips. Japanese people favor *yanagi-goshi* (a willow-tree shaped waist or slender figure); this shape is perceived as being most attractive in the bulky, traditional kimono. *Hatomune desshiri* or simply *hatomune* (both meaning pigeon's chest or big breasts) tends to throw the elegant shape of the kimono out of proportion.

Tareta o-shiri (hanging butt or droopy ass) is another bane of middle-aged women. The noun form for this is *tare-jiri.*

There are many idiomatic expressions using *shiri.* They include *shiri-uma* (blind imitation), *shiri-kire* (abrupt ending), *shiri-nuke* (leaving something half-done), and *shiri-nugui* (literally, wiping another's ass; figuratively, paying a debt on another's behalf).

Now that we can insult almost any kind of person's appearance, this might be an appropriate spot to introduce some complementary (and complimentary) words of praise.

Bijo refers to a good-looking woman, and *bidan*, or *bidanshi*, a handsome man. *Bidanshi* is often pronounced *binanshi* or simply *binan*. *Bi* means beauty. *Bijin* (literally, beautiful person) is used only to refer to women. *Beppin* is a synonym for *bijin,* implying elegant beauty. *Kanojo wa sugoi beppin da* can be translated as she's a real knockout. Adjectives such as *utsukushii* and *kirei,* both meaning beautiful or pretty, have traditionally been used only in reference to women. But with the advent of the feminist movement, they are now occasionally used in decribing a man. *Otokomae,* on the other hand, can only be used when speaking of a man, as in *kare wa otokomae* (he's a handsome man).

A very popular expression used to describe a beautiful person is *ii onna* or *ii otoko. Ii* is the colloquial form of the adjective *yoi* (good, beautiful, fine). Nowadays one rarely hears *yoi* in common conversations: it's *ii tenki* rather than *yoi tenki,* for example. *Ii onna* implies many things, but most commonly it describes a mature, attractive, and independent woman. *Kanojo wa boku no ii onna,* however, means she's my lover. *Ii hito* can also mean lover or steady partner, as in *watashi no ii hito* (my boyfriend). When you want to ask someone if he or she has a girl (or boy) friend, a rather nice way of putting it is *(dareka) ii hito iru no?*

An expression used to praise a good-looking woman is *hatto suru hodo ii onna. Hatto suru* is an intransitive verb meaning to be suprised or given a start. *Hodo* indicates degree or comparison. So the expression roughly means a suprisingly gorgeous woman.

Me (eye) *no sameru* (to awake) *yō-na bijin* is a woman of dazzling beauty. In the same vein, *iki* (breath) *o nomu* (to drink or inhale) *yō-na bijin* can be almost directly translated as a breathtaking beauty. Japanese often add the adverb *omowazu* (unconsciously) before *iki o nomu* to indicate that the person's breath has been taken away without his even being aware of it.

Nimai-me is a traditional expression that is still used for a handsome man. *Nimai-me* (literally, the second ranked) originally came from *kabuki.* When a play was being performed, the names of the main actors would be displayed on the marquee outside the theater. The name of the biggest star would always be followed by that of a handsome young actor. This tradition still lingers in the film and theatrical worlds today. *Sanmai-me* (the third ranked), according to this system, is a fun-loving character. So, when one says *nimai-me han (han* means half), it means a man who falls between *nimai-me* and *sanmai-me,* a man who is both handsome and fun-loving.

3

Discriminatory Language

(sabetsu yōgo)

Buraku-Related *(buraku kanren)*

As in the U.S., discriminatory language in Japan is a major social issue. In the past 20 years or so, there has been extensive *kotoba-gari* (word hunting) by the Buraku Kaihō Dōmei (Buraku Liberation League, or BLL). *Buraku* literally means a community in a small village, or a hamlet, but in today's Japan it means a population that has historically suffered social and economic discrimination. The BLL systematically examines newspaper and magazine articles, radio and TV broadcasts, movies, and literary publications for so-called forbidden words, and, if it finds them, issue a *kyūdan* (violent censure or protest by a group) even if the publication, film, or broadcast as a whole is against discrimination.

Just like the political correctness (PC) movement in the United States, the anti-discrimination efforts of the BLL have gone a bit too far in many people's opinions. As a result, it is not gaining the whole-hearted support of the Japanese people. Nevertheless, the mass media in Japan have been overwhelmed by the BLL's strident campaign and now refrain from using many words that have been identified by the organization as being discriminatory.

In September of 1990, *The Enigma of Japanese Power* by well-known journalist Karel van Wolferen was censured; subsequently, van Wolferen appeared in a public debate with the BLL at the Foreign Correspondents' Club of Japan. In his book, van Wolferen wrote that the BLL preferred to threaten the mass media rather than undertake legal procedures, and that this strategy had proven effective.

He was correct. While the media overall had been sympathetic to the plight of the *burakumin* (those suffering discrimination), the BLL still claimed that "nobody except the person whose own foot was stepped on could really feel the pain." In so doing, they wrung out further concessions. More recently, as a result of "self-censorship" on the part of the publisher, a portion related to *buraku* was cut from the Japanese translation of the best-selling book *Rising Sun* written by Michael Crichton.

In less enlightened days, *burakumin* were simply ignored by the rest of Japan. Their plight was very much like the untouchables of India. Their residential areas were confined to the worst parts of the village or town, and only occupations regarded as mean or filthy were allocated to them. Marriage with other villagers outside the *buraku* group was forbidden, and there were many other similar regulations imposed to keep *burakumin* "in their place."

Other derogatory expressions for *burakumin* included *eta* (untouchables), *hinin* (literally, not human beings; this refers to people who were engaged in the cremation and burial of the dead), and *yotsu* (four). *Yotsu* came from the fact that it was *burakumin* who butchered four-footed animals such as cattle and pigs and processed their various components into meat, leather, and so on.

Japanese Buddhism has traditionally regarded the killing of animals as unclean.

In 1969 the "Special Measures on Enterprises Regarding *Dōwa*" was enacted by the Japanese government *(dōwa* is an acceptable term for *buraku).* Since then the term *dōwa mondai (mondai* is problem) instead of *buraku mondai* has been used. A large amount of tax money has been put into aid for the *dōwa,* helping them with affordable housing, financial aid for education, and job opportunities. As a result, institutionalized discrimination against them has just about disappeared, but prejudice still strongly lingers in the minds of many Japanese.

In addition to the BLL, organizations representing the handicapped and lowly-regarded occupations have also participated in *kotoba-gari.* This has resulted in self-censorship by the mass media, through the use of *iikaeshū* (literally, glossary of word-changing; here, a style book that lists forbidden expressions). Thus, most of the words introduced below cannot be used by the media any more and should be used very carefully by individuals.

Mental and Physical Handicaps *(shinshōsha kanren)*

In 1981, the International Year of the Handicapped, the Japanese government replaced the words *mekura* (blind), *tsunbo* (deaf), *oshi* (deaf-mute), *katawa* and *fugu* (deformed), and *bikko* and *chinba* (lame) with expressions that were more acceptable to those affected. The trend to ban discriminatory words comes from the desire of the handicapped, who have long been victims of prejudice, to have a chance at normal lives and equal opportunities.

When this kind of word-hunting goes to excess, however, it can have absurd results. Some years ago, for example, a Japanese record company wanted to release a song titled "Love Is Blind." The only suitable Japanese equivalent they could find for this title was the direct translation *Koi no Mekura*. Because *mekura* had been deemed inappropriate, the firm withheld its release for several years.

Mekura comes from the simple expression *me ga kurai* (the eyes are dark). As it is now considered contemptuous and discriminatory, new expressions have been coined, such as *me no fujiyū-na hito* (a person with impaired vision), *me ga mienai hito* (a person whose eyes cannot see), and *mōjin* and *mōmoku*, which come from blind person and blindness, respectively. *Mekura-ban* (literally, blind approval; figuratively, to rubber stamp) has also become unacceptable.

In the early 70s, the former governor of Tokyo, Ryokichi Minobe, coined the word *o-mekura-san* (literally, my poor dear blind people). Even though Minobe was known for his compassion and welfare policies, the term was taken by the people it describes as patronizing. Thus he was forced to resort to more acceptable expressions, such as *shiryoku shōgaisha* (eyesight-handicapped person). The most acceptable terms and those commonly used today in the mass media are *me no mienai hito* and *me ga fujiyū-na hito*.

A related term is *akimekura* (illiterate), now banned from media usage as well. An earlier substitute, *monmō* (*mon* is literature or text, and *mō* is blindness or ignorance) has been abandoned in favor of the less offensive and very difficult to pronounce *hi-shikijisha* (a person unable to decipher words).

As for deafness, *tsunbo* has been replaced by *rōsha* (deaf person) and *chōryoku shōgaisha* (listening impaired person). But again, the most acceptable expressions are *mimi no kikoenai hito* (a person whose ears cannot hear) and *mimi ga fujiyū-na hito* (a person with impaired hearing).

For speech-impairment, *oshi* was replaced by *asha* (deaf-mute), and then by *kuchi ga kikenai hito* (*kikenai* is the negative form of the verb *kiku*, meaning to work or be effective). *Kuchi no fujiyū-na hito* is also acceptable. *Oshi de tsunbo* (deaf and mute) was replaced by the slightly more acceptable *rō-asha* (deaf and dumb person), and then by *mimi to kuchi ga fujiyū-na hito.*

Domori is stutter or, by extension, a stutterer. Some feel that *domori* is a discriminatory word, and Japanese newspapers often prefer the terms *kitsuonsha* (stammering person) and *shita* (tongue) *no fujiyū-na hito.* Since *domori* is not definitely discriminatory, however, it is often used as is. There is no substitute for the verb *domoru* (to stutter). But some people prefer the expression *shita ga nameraka de nai* (the tongue is not smooth).

Katawa and *fugu,* in the war of words, first became *shintai shōgaisha* (literally, bodily-handicapped person), which can be shortened to *shinshōsha,* and then the more acceptable *karada no fujiyū-na hito.* Also in this group, the words *chinba* (cripple), *bikko* (lame person), and *izari* (someone crippled in both legs) have all become *ashi ga fujiyū-na hito.*

Tenashi and *tenbō* (handless) became *katate* (one-handed), then *te ga fujiyū-na hito* and *te ga nai hito.* The term *katateochi* (partiality or one-sidedness) has also come to mean missing one arm. But this is gradually being replaced by the terms *ippō-teki* (one-sided) and *fukōhei* (unfairness).

Kichigai (insane) has also been deemed unacceptable. This is a frequently used word, as in *kichigai ja nai no?* (are you crazy?) or *mattaku kichigaijimite iru* (it's totally insane). But expressions such as *kuruma kichigai* (car crazy), *otokichi* (abbreviation for *ōtobai kichigai,* or motorcycle maniac), *tenikichi* (abbreviation for *tenisu kichigai,* or tennis nut), *tsurikichi* (abbreviation for *tsuri kichigai,* or fishing freak), and *kyōjin* (lunatic, madman) have all disappeared from mass media usage. *Kichigai* has become *seishin shōgaisha* (mentally handicapped).

Finally, *chie okure* (slow-witted) and *hakuchi* (idiot) have been replaced by *chiteki shōgaisha* and *chinō shōgaisha* (both meaning intellectually or mentally handicapped).

Profession-Related *(shokugyō kanren)*

In Japan, as elsewhere, certain occupations are the objects of ridicule and derision.

Hyakushō, inakappe, and *tagosaku,* for example, all are used to mean farmer, boor, hayseed, hick, or country bumpkin. In English there are many such words, but in Japanese there are only a few. We're not sure of the reason for this discrepancy. It may be, though, that farmers in Japan have long formed a fairly large and powerful bloc and, thus, they're a group that's best not offended. In the Tokugawa era, for example, farmers were nominally given the second highest of the four social ranks, after the samurai. The truth of the matter is that they were the poorest, as they were always prime targets for heavy taxation.

Hyakushō literally means a hundred names. Originally it was used to refer to individuals without any rank and, over time, it came to mean farmer. Now it is used rather disdainfully, as are *tagosaku* or *inakappe,* when speaking of someone who is uneducated, boorish, or rude, regardless of his native place or occupation. *Donbyakushō* is even more disdainful.

When you want to use *hyakushō* to refer respectfully to a farmer, add the honorific prefix *o-* and the suffix *-san.* In ordinary conversation today, however, most Japanese use the terms *nōmin* (farming people) and *nōka* (farming family).

Inakappe, originally *inaka-bei,* consists of *inaka* (countryside or native place), and a euphonic change of the suffix *-bei. Kappe* by itself is much more popular, as in *aitsu wa kappe da ne—wakatcha inai* (he's such a bumpkin—he doesn't know anything).

Bun-ya derives from the word *shinbun-ya* and refers to the press or a journalist. *Shinbun-ya* is also a collo-quial expression for *shinbun hanbai ten* (newspaper sales agency). *Bun-ya* is now used when speaking about a journalist in a derogatory manner. The *yakuza* and their associates hate journalists almost as much as they hate the police, and they're fond of this expression.

It's interesting that once *kisha* (journalist), *yakusha* (actor), and geisha were regarded as *yakuza (-na) kagyō* (shady, suspicious, or good-for-nothing occupations). People in these professions were thought to be scandal-ous parasites living off common, decent folk. It's true that journalists can be fairly unscrupulous individuals, but in general journalism is regarded by young people today as one of the most desirable occupations to pursue.

As with *bun-ya, -ya* is used as a derogatory suffix in politics, too. *Seiji-ya,* then, would refer to a shrewd or manipulative politician. *Seijika,* on the other hand, is a neutral word for politician.

Ongaku-ya (ongaku is music) and *oto-ya (oto* is sound) are words used to describe musicians, and are more colloquial than the standard *ongakuka* (musician). The same can be said of *gakutai* (musical group) as opposed to *ōkesutora* (orchestra). We aren't authorities on what is or isn't art, but nowadays any popular musician or singer, no matter how bad, is called *āchisto* (artist) in Japan.

Peinki-ya (painter, as in house painter) is the most degrading expression for *gaka* (painter or artist). *Ekaki* is a colloquial expression for a painter that is often used with derogatory connotations. This term comes from *e o kaku* (to draw a picture).

Sakka refers to a writer or novelist. *Saku* means to create, make, or write. *Bunshi* (literary man, writer), on the other hand, can be used contemptuously, as in *sanmon-bunshi* (hack writer). *Sanmon* here means three cents, implying worthlessness. *Monokaki* (literally, a person who writes things; also a secretary), as *ekaki* above, has even more derogatory connotations because it implies a lack of creativity. *Takaga monokaki* means I know he or she can write, but so what? *Takaga* here is a belittling term meaning only, merely, or at best.

In profession-related vocabulary, new words have been coined to replace older ones. *Tosatsujō* is a slaughterhouse, but its use is considered unacceptable. *Tojō* is better, though the lengthy official expression *shokuniku shorijō* (meat-processing center) is even more acceptable, if harder to say. The old expression *gomi-ya* (literally, garbage collector) has recently become *seisō sagyō in,* shortened to *seisō in* (literally, person who cleans the city, or sanitary engineer).

Un-chan (car driver) has become *untenshu*. *Takushii no un-chan* is now *takushii untenshu* or *takushii doraibā* (from the English driver).

Bōzu (monk) is now *obō-san*. *Sōshokusha* (priesthood person) has been shortened to *sōryo*. *Yabu-isha* (an incompetent doctor or quack) is now unusable. In this case, *yabu* comes from the word for a shrine maiden, particularly in the remote countryside, who is somewhat of an amateur in her profession. *Yabu* alone can also mean a quack, and *yabo-isha* or *hebo-isha* are both used to mean a doctor who is not very skillful.

Dokata (coolie) is now unusable. The politically correct word is *kensetsu rōdōsha* (construction worker) or *kensetsu sagyō-in* (construction operations team member).

Bataya, which used to mean a rag-picker or bum, is now *haihin kaishū gyōsha* (*haihin* is waste articles, *kaishū* is collection, and *gyōsha* is trader or dealer).

Nowadays, the old familiar expressions for occupations such as barber or greengrocer are rarely seen in newspapers. These traditional words have no derogatory connotations, but people engaged in these trades want to be referred to in a more modern fashion. Thus, *toko-ya* (the old familiar expression for barber) is now *rihatsu ten* (literally, hair adjusting shop). In conversation, though, *toko-ya* is made acceptable by adding the honorific suffix *-san* to create *toko-ya-san*. *Yao-ya* (greengrocer), *niku-ya* (butcher's shop), and *sakana-ya* (fishmonger) are now officially *seikashō*, *shokuniku hanbaigyō*, and *sengyoshō*, though the old terms are also used by adding the suffix *-san*.

The Elderly and Women *(rōjin, josei kanren)*

Ijiwaru bāsan (mean old woman) and *yokubari jiisan* (greedy old man) are derogatory terms for the stereotypical bad characters who appear in Japanese folk tales. As Japanese society ages, there has been an increase in cases of Alzheimer's disease, and *boke* (senility) is becoming a large social problem. A typical derogatory term that has appeared from this is *boke rōjin* (senile old man or woman).

The standard word used to describe the elderly is *toshiyori* or, more politely, *o-toshiyori*. The Japanese concept of getting old has been compared to waves continuously lapping up on the shore. Thus, there is an old saying *yoru toshi-nami ni wa katenai* (literally, you cannot triumph over your increasing years). Similar expressions in English might include time and tide wait for no man, or nothing is sure but death and taxes. In any case, *toshi-nami* in this expression literally means age-wave, and *yoru* is to draw near.

Another expression connected with the elderly is *toshiyori no hiyamizu* (*hiyamizu* is cold water), meaning an old man's indiscretion or, in English, there's no fool like an old fool.

In the traditional sumo world, on the other hand, *toshiyori* is a retired wrestler who still holds great influence both politically and economically. It's said that in order to become an official *toshiyori,* a fee of more than a million dollars is required.

Jijii and *babā* are derogatory words for an old man or woman. We have already mentioned the expressions *kusojijii* and *kusobabā,* which mean a disgusting old man or woman. *Jiji-musai* and its modern equivalent *ojinkusai* both mean old-mannish or slovenly. *Jiji-musai* comes from the *jii* in *ojii-san* (old man or grandfather) and *musakurushi* (sordid or squalid). Take care, though, for there is no such expression as *baba-musai.*

In 1972 the late Sawako Ariyoshi, a well-known female author, wrote a novel entitled *Kōkotsu no Hito (The Twilight Years).* It concerned the problem of the aging *(rōjin mondai)* and was considered a harbinger of Japan's present concern with this issue. The central character of the novel was a senile 84-year-old widower who had forgotten everything about his past, including the names and faces of his closest relatives. With no enjoyment or hope in his life, he just hung on while his family tended to his needs. As a result of this novel, the terms *kōkotsu* and *kōkotsu ningen* have become popular expressions that describe an extremely senile person. The word actually means in a state of ecstasy, trance, or rapture.

Boke, which comes from the verb *bokeru* (to grow senile) is a popular synonym for *kōkotsu* or *kōkotsu ningen. Boke* is often used in ordinary conversation as an interjection like *baka,* or as in *boketeru nē, mō wasureta no?* (you're spaced-out—have you forgotten already?). *Netakiri rōjin* (an old person who has taken to his bed for good) is another expression used in connection with the aging.

There are many more slang terms for the elderly. *Oibore* means dotard or withered up. *Oibore babā* is a withered old woman, a hag, or an old witch. *Mōroko* also refers to dotage. *Kare wa mōroko shita* means he became senile.

Shobokure is a dull old man, but it can also be used when referring to a wretched state, even in relation to a young person. *Dōshita no shobokure-chatte?* means why do you look so miserable?

Yoi-yoi is a derogatory slang expression for paralysis or a paralyzed person. This is often used in reference to elderly people. *Yoi-yoi* includes the concepts of *rore-rore* and *tare-nagashi*. *Rore-rore* means inarticulateness or an inarticulate old person, while *tare-nagashi* means incontinence. *Tare* comes from the verb *tareru* (to drip), and *nagashi* comes from the verb *nagasu* (to let flow or run out).

Tasogare (literally, twilight time) is also used in relation to aging. *Jinsei no tasogare*, for example, refers to people in their 60s who are starting to show real signs of aging. *Tasogare jiisan* is a derogatory term for such men who also have lots of money and like young girls. *Tasogare* is an expression that is more than 1,000 years old, coming from *tarezo, kare?* (who is that man?), a question that might well be asked as dusk sets in and vision becomes more difficult.

The expression *me-ha-ma* (eyes, teeth, and cock) lists the body parts to be checked for symptoms of aging, as well as the order in which they occur. *Me* are the eyes, and farsightedness is thought to begin in the 40s and get worse with age. Next is *ha* (teeth), which over time become vulnerable to cavities and gum disease, even loss. Last is *ma* from *mara* (penis), implying that *bokki* (erection) becomes difficult. Thus the question *me-ha-ma, daijōbu?* (are your *me-ha-ma* OK?) becomes commonplace as men enter their 50s. If the situation worsens, men are visited by the unwelcome trio of *kasumi-me, sō-ireba,* and *yakutatazu no inpo* (bleary eyes, false teeth, and limp dick).

Naturally there are various discriminatory expressions used to describe women in Japanese.

Onna (woman) is the word most commonly used in conjunction with *otoko* (man), but with the tentative spread of feminism, *onna* is starting to become less popular. Expressions such as *ano onna* (that woman), *ii onna* (beautiful woman), *dame-na onna* (bad or useless woman), *wakai onna* (young woman), *hataraku onna* (working woman), and *kekkon shinai onna* (unmarried woman), must, in order to be acceptable, all add *no hito* (becoming *onna no hito,* redundant, but meaning female person). Or, *onna* may be replaced with *josei* (literally, female sex). So far, there's no corresponding restriction on *otoko*.

Feminists strongly criticize some of the older expressions created in Japan's male-dominant society. For instance, the words meaning widow, *goke* (part left behind in the family) and *mibōjin* (not yet dead person), are under heavy attack these days. What is offensive is the implication that a woman is less than a person because her husband is dead. *Memeshii* (very womanly) has a negative connotation of womanish or sissy, while *ōshii* (very manly) is always used in a positive sense.

The expression *oba-san* (auntie) used to be a convenient expression for older women, but is now perceived by middle-aged women as derogatory. It is now becoming necessary to call even women in their 40s *onē-san* (elder sister).

In 1989, the slang word *obatarian* was coined to refer to obnoxious middle-aged women. Despite protests from women's groups, it's in extensive use nationwide. *Obatarian* is the name of a hit comic strip and derives from a combination of *oba-san* and *Batarian,* the name of an immortal cartoon monster. *Obatarian* are the kind of dumpy, indifferently dressed women one sees at department stores fighting for bargains or forcing fellow train passengers to make a place for them to sit down.

Traditional discriminatory expressions for middle-aged women are *toshima* (aged) and *ō-doshima* (very aged). A new word that has replaced *toshima* is *jukujo* (mature woman). The term *jukujo jidai* is a synonym for *onna zakari* (prime of womanhood). Here *juku* means to mature or ripen, and *jo* is the same *kanji* as *onna* or woman. Some new expressions such as *jukunen* (mature or ripened age) and *naisu midoru* (nice middle) were created, but they haven't become too popular.

Spurred by the feminist movement in America, there has been a trend toward nonsexist expressions in Japan as well. Finding new words to replace terms such as *go-shujin* (literally, master; meaning husband) or *oku-san* (literally, lady of the house; meaning wife), however, has been difficult, with ongoing trial and error. *Tsureai* (partner) and *haigūsha* (spouse), for example, don't sound natural in conversation and have not caught on so far.

Otoko masari (stronger than a man) means a spunky woman. Note that there is no such expression as *onna masari*. *Demodori* (a person returning home after a divorce) applies only to women, as do *akusai* (bad wife) and *akujo* (undesirable woman). There are no male equivalents for these two expressions. When criticizing a bad male partner, such expressions as *binbō-kuji* (literally, a poor lot; in this context, unluckiness), *kaishō-nashi* (shiftless), *hajisarashi* (shameless), *ikuji-nashi* (weak-minded), or *waru* (villain) are used.

As women have started to gain financial independence through employment, the number of divorces among those over 50 has increased, and men who haven't bothered with family life till now are beginning to feel threatened. Under such circumstances, while it may not actually come to divorce, there are many *kateinai bekkyo* (separate beds in the house) and *kateinai rikon* (in-house divorces). Thus, the *teishu kanpaku* (bossy husbands) who only had to utter three words in their homes, *meshi, furo, futon* (dinner, hot bath, and bed), are now being treated as *sōdai gomi* (big trash, such as worn-out furniture, refrigerators, and so on). *Sōdai gomi* refers to the husbands who are *goro-goro shite iru*, that is, loafing around the house. There are also terms like *nure ochiba* (wet fallen leaves that stick on the ground and are difficult to remove) for husbands who reach *teinen* (retirement age) and hang around the house, demanding extra meals and other services and becoming increasingly critical of their wives.

Race-Related *(jinshu kanren)*

Because of the prejudice directed by Japanese against Koreans and other Asians after the Meiji era, especially during the period surrounding World War II, derogatory language based on race is a very sensitive and controversial subject. Many Asians still resent the Japanese because their memories of the cruel treatment dealt by the Japanese are so bitter. So the terms introduced here should be used with great care—if at all.

Asakō is a derogatory term for Koreans. The etymology of this word is a little convoluted, but here goes. In Japan, ordinary expressions for Koreans are *chōsen-jin* or *kankoku-jin,* and we'll go into the difference between them a little later. According to the usual way of making a derogatory term, one would take the *chō* of *chōsen* and add the contemptuous suffix *kō* as in *sen-kō,* which is sometimes used by disgruntled students as a derogatory term for their *sensei* (teacher). But *chō-kō* was rejected because it was potentially insulting to the *chōtei* (Imperial Court) especially because the *chō* in *chōtei* and *chōsen* are the same *kanji* (morning or dynasty). As this character can also be pronounced *asa, chō* was changed to *asa* before adding the derogatory suffix *kō. Asa-chan, -chan* being a diminutive suffix, is a contemptuous variation, slightly milder than *asa-kō.*

Senjin, an abbreviated form of *chōsenjin* (Korean

person), is as historically insulting to Koreans as *asa-kō* and *asa-chan*. These days *chon-kō* is frequently used as well, along with derogatory derivatives such as *chon-baggu* (bag) and *chon-gutsu* (shoes) to describe possessions of Korean students in Japan.

After World War II, when Korea was freed from Japanese domination, the South Korean people insisted that they be called *kankokujin*. The matter is further complicated because the North Koreans have demanded that the term *chōsenjin* be used, stating that *kankoku* is not an authorized name for the unified peninsula.

The North Koreans are also opposed to the expression *hoku-sen,* which is a derivative and abbreviation of *kita chōsen* (North Korea). The character for north in Japanese can be pronounced *hoku* as well as *kita*. Thus, one must be careful to choose the proper occasions to use *chōsenjin* or *kankokujin*. Caution also needs to be exercised with *hantōjin* (people of the peninsula), a term implying that Korea isn't even a nation at all, but perhaps rather an annex of Japan.

Bakachon, as in *bakachon kamera* (foolproof camera or idiot's camera), is a popular expression that has been criticized as being discriminatory against Koreans. Critics claim that it came from the expression *baka de mo chon de mo utsuseru* (even a fool or a Korean can take a picture), with *chon* being a derogatory expression equivalent to *chon-kō*. But etymologically, this is not correct.

The word *chon* was actually created in the Edo era to mean an immature or foolish person, and had nothing to do with Koreans. People today, however, without knowing this history, have adopted the discriminatory folk etymology. The *chon* in a phrase like *baka de mo chon to osu dake* (even an idiot can take a picture by just pushing the button) actually came from the sound of the clappers heard at *kabuki*. But after being criticized by pro-Korean groups, the mass media decided some years ago to try to avoid controversy, and so it's rare to see this expression in Japanese newspapers nowadays. Alternatives are *zenjidō kamera* or *ōtomachikku kamera* (fully automatic camera).

Chan-koro, an extremely contemptuous expression referring to the Chinese, was used until the end of World War II. It is thought to have come from an onomatopoeia used in the Edo era. The story goes that a Chinese in the costume of the Ching Dynasty sold sweets in Edo by striking a small gong *chang, chang. Koro* is said to be a suffix to indicate something small, like *inu-koro* (puppy dog) or *ishi-koro* (small stones). Regardless of the etymology, the expression became more and more derogatory as Japanese imperialism rode to victory in the Sino-Japanese War and, in the process, killed many Chinese. Japanese used the expression so disdainfully that *koro* became associated with *korosu* (to kill).

Shinajin (Chinese people, similar to the English use of Chink) was used around the same time as a derogatory synonym for *chan-koro. Shina-pokopen* is even worse, adding the nuance of China being a weak nation. *Pokopen* came from a Chinese word meaning no good.

After World War II, when China became the People's Republic of China, the acceptable expression for Chinese people became *chūgokujin.* Later, even *shina-soba* (Chinese noodles) was changed to *chūka-soba,* and it would be very difficult to find a Chinese noodle shop that uses the expression *shina-soba* any more.

The most up-to-date expression for a Chinese restaurant is not *chūka ryōri ten,* but *chūgoku ryōri (ten).* The reason for this, it is said, is because the owners of such restaurants will be thought of as being pro-Taiwanese (Taiwan is called *chūka minkoku)* if they use the word *chūka.*

Because of the close geographical and historical relations between Japan, Korea, and China, there are many derogatory expressions in Japanese for the people of these two neighboring nations. Because of an historical lack of such relationships, there are not as many terms for other foreigners. Nonetheless, here are a few of them.

Gaijin (literally, outside person) is the most common term used for non-Japanese in Japan. It's short for *gaikokujin,* or outside-country person. Neither term is particularly derogatory in themselves, though non-Japanese quickly tire of hearing them. But when they're spoken in a derogatory tone, they're undoubtedly meant to be just that.

Ketō is a typical disparaging word for a foreigner, particularly one from the West. It comes from the now archaic *tōjin* (literally, Tang dynasty people in China). Both before and during the Tang dynasty, Japan imported various aspects of other cultures, mainly from China. To be foreign in Japan, therefore, was to be Chinese. In this context, *tōjin* was adopted to mean foreigner, even for people from countries other than China. This term was even adopted to apply to the Japanese wife of the first American consul general to Japan, Townsend Harris. Her name was Okichi, but she was popularly known as *tōjin* Okichi.

Ketō or *ketōjin* was made by adding *ke* (hair or hairy) to *tōjin* to mean outlandish hairy foreigner. Western men, with their profuse (compared to the Japanese) facial hair and custom of wearing beards, appeared truly outrageous to the Japanese who first saw them. Artists have immortalized Japanese visions of these men in the woodblock prints of the Tokugawa era. These artists invariably portrayed Western men as having huge noses, red faces, and lots of hair, and the prints they made were called *nanbanjin* prints after the common word of the day for foreigner. *Nanbanjin* literally means barbarian from the south, presumably because the first European ships from Portugal came from the south some 450 years ago.

Ame-kō is a combination of *amerika* (America) and

the contemptuous suffix *-kō*. This term appeared after World War II when the United States occupied Japan, but is no longer used, reflecting the close relationship between the two countries.

Ita-kō is a derogatory expression for Italian people and was created in the same way. We don't know exactly why it was coined, but it may have been because Italy was the first among the Axis powers—Japan's allies in the war—to surrender to the Allies in World War II. Since the Japanese at that time considered surrender to be the supreme disgrace, they must have looked upon the Italians with utter contempt.

The word *rosuke* comes from *roshiya* (Russia) and the contemptuous suffix *-suke,* and was coined after Japan's victory in the Russo-Japanese War of 1904. It can be translated as Russkie.

Dojin (natives or aborigines) is a derogatory word for the inhabitants of developing areas, such as South Pacific islanders *(nanyō no dojin)* or African natives *(afurika no dojin).* These expressions appeared quite often in the Japanese mass media, especially on TV comedies and variety programs, until people in the developing nations became aware of it and protested the insensitive treatment. Since then the mass media have been using a modern alternative, namely *genjū-min* (native people).

Kuronbo or *kuronbō* can be translated as the distasteful word nigger. They derive from *kuro* (black) and the derogatory suffix *-bō,* with an "n" for euphonic purposes. Another derogatory word for blacks is *niguro,* which comes from the English negro.

Ai-no-ko (half-breed) refers to children of mixed marriages. Traditionally the Japanese have rarely married non-Japanese, so children from such unions come in for their share of contempt. *Ai* is from *aida* (in between), and *ko* is child. *Konketsu-ji* (literally, mixed-blood child) is a proper word, but it is often used contemptuously as a synonym for *ai-no-ko.* Both were often used to describe babies fathered, legitimately or otherwise, by Americans in the postwar period.

Hāfu (half) is more up-to-date and is used in such expressions as *ano moderu wa hāfu* (that model is of mixed blood) or *kare wa Amerika to Nihon no hāfu da* (he's half American and half Japanese). We prefer another approach—the one that says that children of mixed marriages are not half anything, but rather both.

4

Scatology

(sukatorojii)

Scatology is defined as obscenity, especially in language or humor, related to excrement. Although many people think of excrement exclusively as feces, the word really refers to waste matter from all parts of the body. As you will see, the Japanese language is rich in scatological terms.

Kuso is a rather basic term, meaning—vulgarly—shit, or, more politely, excrement or feces. *Kuso* usually means human fecal discharge, but, when certain prefixes are added, as in *tori no kuso* (bird shit) or *ushi no kuso* (cow shit or bullshit), it can be applied to animals as well. In this sense, it can be translated as ordure or dung. *Kuso* sounds fairly rough and is rarely used by women. The term is also used to describe secretions from various parts of the body, such as the eyes, nose, or ears, as in *me-kuso, hana-kuso,* and *mimi-kuso,* respectively.

Kuso can be used in four different ways. The first is described above. The second comes close to the English bullshit or horseshit. *Kusomitai-na koto* means nonsense or foolishness in precisely the same manner as bullshit. You can apply this phrase to a person as well, as in *aitsu wa kusomitai* (that guy is nothing but bullshit).

The third usage of *kuso* is for emphasis, as in *kuso dokyō* (reckless courage), *kuso benkyō* (a grind, in the sense of someone who studies all the time), *kuso majime* (absurdly serious), *kuso jikara* (enormously strong) and *kuso atsui* (awfully hot). In these expressions *kuso* is very similar to *baka ni,* as in *baka ni atsui* (ridiculously hot).

Synonymous to *kuso benkyō* are *gariben* and *gachiben,* as in *ano hito wa gariben* (he's nothing but a grind). *Ben* is a shortened form of *benkyō* (study). *Gari* comes from *gari-gari* (greedy) and *gachi* from *gachi-gachi* (stubborn, inflexible).

The fourth application of *kuso* is for cursing, such as damn it, go to hell, oh shit, and so forth. You can simply say *kuso* or *kusottare* (literally, you shit dripper) or *kusokurae* (go eat your own shit).

There aren't very many curse words associated with religion in Japan, unlike countries with Christian backgrounds. But there are plenty of substitutes. *Chikushō* (literally, you beast) and its more emphatic version *kon chikusho* are very popular curse words meaning exactly the same as damn it. *Baka yarō, ahō,* and *roku de nashi* mean you fool or you son of a bitch. *Shinjimae, shinjae, kutabare, kutabatchimae, jigoku e itchimae,* and *bachi atari* can all be translated as drop dead or go to hell. The expression *kutabare* is often used in headlines of weekly magazines meaning down with something or someone.

Kuso o suru is the verb form of *kuso,* and it means to take a shit. As in English, this is a very vulgar term and should not be used in polite conversation.

Daiben (literally, big convenience) is a medical word for excrement and more formal than *kuso. Daiben suru* is a relatively polite way to talk about a bowel movement, but it has a rough, sonant sound, and women generally don't like to use it.

Unko and *unchi* are baby-talk equivalents, similar to poo-poo or poop in English. Japanese mothers can be heard asking their children *unchi shita?* or *un shita?* (did you go poo-poo?). Young girls often use these words. *Okii hō* (the bigger one) is equivalent to number two in English.

Fun is an alternative pronunciation of *kuso,* and can be used in a number of compounds. *Jin-pun,* for example, means human excrement, *ba-fun* is horseshit, and *fun-nyō* is both feces and urine. *Fun o suru* is applied to the bowel movements of animals.

Bentsū (literally, convenient passage) means both bowel movement and urination. *Bentsū* (or *osūji) ga aru* are also acceptable expressions meaning to have a bowel movement. *Osūji* is another term for passage. *Yoku tabe, yoku dasu* is a set phrase referring to the good food and good "convenience" essential for good health. *Kaishoku, kaiben* means the same thing.

Kaiben (pleasant movement) or *otsūji ga ii* (nice movement) can be used when the going is easy. When the going gets rough, *katai* (hard or tough) *ben* and *ben ga katai* are used. When *katai ben* becomes an habitual problem, one is described as *benpi* (constipated). *Funzumari* (stuffed up with feces) is a slang equivalent. On the other hand, when the bowels are very loose, the terms are *nan* (soft) *ben, hara-kudashi* (loose bowels), and *geri* (diarrhea).

People, especially women, avoid using direct expressions such as *kuso shitai* or *unko shitai* when they need to go to the bathroom. Instead, they will say something like *toire ni iku* (I'm going to the toilet) or, more euphemistically, *chotto shitsurei* (excuse me).

Raku ni naru, which simply means to relieve oneself or to make oneself comfortable, is a euphemistic expression for going to the bathroom, as is *onaka o kara ni suru* (to make one's stomach empty). When a man is in an isolated place where there are no public facilities, he does *kiji o utsu,* meaning to shoot a pheasant. We don't know how this expression originated, but we do know that the experience is universal. *Hana o tsumu* (to pluck a flower) is the counterpart used by women.

Chiisai hō (the smaller one) is equivalent to number one in English. The most popular colloquial expressions for urination are *shōben* and *o-shikko,* both of which mean urine. *Shōben* (small convenience) corresponds to *daiben* (big convenience) and is used mainly by men.

Shonben (piss) is its slang variation. *Uma* (horse) *no shōben* is a long piss.

O-shikko, an onomatopoetic expression based on the sound of urination, is used mainly by women and children. *Inu* (dog) *no o-shikko,* corresponding to *uma no shoben* above, is a short piss. *Shi,* the onomatopoetic stem of the word, is an abbreviated version of *shii* or *shii-shii.* Japanese mothers can often be heard saying, *sā, shii-shii shite,* when they encourage their children to go to the bathroom. *Jā-jā* is an onomatopoetic expression for splashing, and is only applied to urinating adults.

Some other expressions for urination are *shōyō* (a euphemistic term meaning small business) and *hai-nyō* (passing or discharging urine), but these are rather square words.

As for verbs, *shōben suru* and *o-shikko suru* both mean to urinate or to go pee-pee. *Shōyō o tasu* is to make or pass water, and the more vulgar *jā-jā yaru* means to splash or piss noisily. *Yō o tasu* is a polite and euphemistic verb meaning to do one's business or go to the bathroom, regardless of whether it is to have a bowel movement or to urinate.

In English the word piss can be used as an expletive as in oh piss or piss on it, both expressions of disgust. But in Japanese it is used for swearing only in the expression *shonben tare* (damn you).

Tachi shonben (to piss in a standing position, meaning to piss in the street) is a notorious habit of Japanese men, especially when they get drunk. Many private homeowners who have been victimized by this habit post signs saying *shōben muyō* (no peeing here) on the walls outside their houses.

Shōben yokochō (literally, pissing sidestreet) refers to places where there are seedy but lively bars and, as a result, a lot of drunks with full bladders and empty inhibitions. An infamous *shōben yokochō* is located near the west exit of Shinjuku Station in Tokyo.

Tsure shonben or *tsure shon* is another popular habit among Japanese people. This means that, when someone goes to the bathroom, others will follow.

Shonbenkusai has two meanings. One is literally smelling of urine, and the other is immature or childish. The latter may be related to *ne-shōben* (bedwetting, with *ne* being sleeping). *O-nesho* is an affectionate shortened form for bed-wetting, whereas *o-morashi* is a somewhat contemporary synonym. *Morashi* comes from the verb *morasu* (to leak). A euphemistic equivalent is *futon ni chizu* (to draw a map on the futon). *Sosō* (blunder or carelessness) is another euphemistic expression for such behavior. A Japanese mother might say *mata* (again) *sosō shita no?* as a kind of mild protest when her child wets the bed.

O-nara is the basic Japanese word for a fart. *Nara* comes from the verb *naru* (to sound, ring, or strike). *He* is a slang synonym. The verb forms are *o-nara suru, he o suru, hē suru, he o koku,* or *he o hanatsu,* all of which mean to fart. *He* means nonsense or the easiest thing. *Hemitai* or *he no kappa* both mean nothing could be easier. *Hemitai-na yatsu* is a meaningless person. *Herikutsu* (literally, frivolous logic) is a false argument or fallacious reasoning.

Sukashippe is a noiseless fart, the *-ppe* being a euphonic change of *he*. *Saigoppe* (final fart) and *itachi no saigoppe* (a weasel's final fart) mean the final defensive when one is cornered.

Pū or *pū-pū* are mostly used by children. These are both onomatopoetic expressions that refer to farting. But use with care, as they do not mean the same as poo-poo in English, even though they sound the same.

There are several other onomatopoetic expressions for farting in Japanese, depending on the approximate note of the musical scale involved. When you pass wind in the case of loose bowels, for example, this is described as *pii-pii* (not the same as pee-pee in English). *Bū-bū* is used to describe a noisy fart, *pū-pū* is a moderate one, and *sū-sū* is a noiseless one. *Pu* or *putto,* on the other hand, are onomatopeias for light laughter or tittering.

Now let's move to the bathroom itself. *Gofujō* (being unclean) was often used among women before World War II to mean toilet or bathroom. But now it's rather old-fashioned, with only elderly ladies using it.

Kawaya (riverside shed) is another euphemism for toilet, as are *chōzu* (hand water), *tearai* (hand washing), *setchin,* and *habakari; Setchin* is said to come from *Setchō,* who was a Chinese Zen Buddhist who once served as a toilet cleaner at a temple. *Habakari* derives from the verb *habakaru* (to hesitate or be shy) and means both the toilet and the act of going to the toilet. Except for *tearai,* these words are rarely used nowadays.

By now you have probably noticed that the Japanese like to use the honorary prefix *o-* to make disagreeable or dirty things sound nicer or softer. Thus *o-tearai* and *o-toire* are currently the most popular terms for toilet. *Benjo* can be translated as lavatory, water closet, or even can. But the addition of *o-* makes it sound softer and more polite. *O-keshōshitsu* (powder room) is also commonly heard among adult women.

Kōshū (public) *benjo* or *kyōdō* (common) *benjo* both mean public convenience. By extension, the expression *kanojo wa kyōdō benjo* refers to a promiscuous woman, i.e., everybody's convenience.

Let's move on to bodily secretions. *Hana-kuso* is nasal mucus or, less politely, snot. *Hana* means nose and, written with different Chinese characters, the discharge from the nose. *Hana-mizu* (nose water) means a runny nose, and *hanatare* or *hanattare* are used to describe someone with a runny nose. *Tare* comes from the verb *tareru* (to drip or run down). *Hanattare* also means an immature kid, especially when you add *kozō* (kid), as in *hanattare kozō.*

Me-kuso (eye mucus), *me-aka* (eye dirt), and *me-yani*

(eye gum) all mean discharge from the eyes. The old saying *me-kuso hana-kuso o warau* (to laugh) can be translated as that's a case of the pot calling the kettle black.

Mimi-kuso is ear wax and *mimidare* is runny ears. *Ha-kuso* is dirt or impurities on the teeth. *Fuke* is dandruff. *Aka* is the combination of dead skin and dirt that accumulates when one doesn't bathe properly. Thus, the terms *aka-darake* or *fuke-darake* mean very dirty or filthy.

Heso no goma is the residue that accumulates in the navel, or what some people call bellybutton fluff. *Heso* is bellybutton, and *goma* is an ordinary word meaning sesame.

Tsume no aka means dirt under one's fingernail. The idiomatic phrase *tsume no aka o senjite nomu* (to drink brewed nail dirt) means to want to share the good luck of a superior at all costs.

Yodare (drool, drivel, slobber) refers to saliva running down the mouth unconsciously. Thus, *yodare-tarashi* would be a driveler. *Tarashi* comes from the verb *tarasu* (to hang down).

Yodare ga deru (to flow) and its synonyms *kuchi ni yodare* and *yodare tara-tara* can be used in three ways: to drool at something that looks delicious, to be anxious to obtain something, or to be looking at something very sexy. *Wā, oishisō, yodare ga desō* would be a typical thing to say when something appetizing is placed in front of you. *Yodare-kake* (bib) can be applied to adults who have been totally spoiled, as in the insulting expression *yodare-kake ageyō ka?* (shall I give you a bib?).

The words *hedo* (vomit) and the slang equivalent *gero* (puke) are commonly heard expressions. As for verbs, one can use *hedo o haku, hedo ga deru, gero o haku,* or simply *haku,* all of which mean to vomit. *Gero suru* is slang that also means to make a confession. Colloquially, there are several other verbs for vomitting, namely *ageru* (to throw up) and *modosu* (to return). *Ageru* actually means to lift up or raise. *Mukatsuku, muka-muka suru,* or *hakisō ni naru* mean to feel nauseated or sick enough to throw up. *Hakisō* or *hedo ga desō* are frequently used when something or someone is disgusting or nauseating.

Geppu is an onomatopoetic expression for a burp or belch and, written in different *kanji,* means monthly installment payment. There is a Japanese carbonized drink called *ramune* (from *remoneido,* or lemonade) and, when people drink it, they tend to burp. Given the Japanese penchant for play on words, the term *ramune* is also used to mean *geppu* as in monthly payment.

Shakkuri means hiccup. It is interesting that in English and Japanese alike, these words are both onomatopoetic and mimetic. *Shakkuri suru* means to hiccup. Be careful not to confuse it with *shakuri ageru,* which means to sob out or speak in a voice broken with sobs.

Kushami (sneeze) and *hakushon* (achoo) are also onomatopoetic expressions. When people ask you *kushami shinakatta?* (did you sneeze?), it's the equivalent of asking if your ears were burning. In other words, someone was talking about you.

Tsuba or *tsubaki* are Japanese words for spit or saliva, and *tan* is phlegm. *Tan o haku* or *tsuba o haku* are verbs meaning to spit. And *pe(p)* or *peppe* are onomatopoetic words for the action of spitting. When you say *tsuba o tsukeru* (to put saliva on something) or *tsuba-tsuke,* it means to mark a thing or person, especially a woman, for one's own. Colloquially this expression would translate as to have dibs on. *Ten ni tsuba suru* (to spit at the sky, or be daring) and *mayu-tsuba* (fishy) are derivatives of *tsuba.*

Kusai iki or *kōshū* both mean bad breath. *Kōshū* is an alternative way of saying *kuchi ga kusai* (smelly mouth) or *kusai iki* (bad breath). *Kō* is mouth and *shū* is odor or bad smell. When you want to be more precise, such expressions as *sakekusai* (smelling of liquor), *ninnikukusai* (reeking of garlic), or *tabako kusai* (stinking of cigarettes) are used. *Aitsu wa kuchi ga kusakute tamaranai* means I can't stand his foul breath.

Gekkei is the most ordinary term for menstruation, though it sounds rather awkward in Japanese because of the heavy "g" sound. *Tsuki no mono* (monthly phenomenon) and *tsuki yori no shisha* (messenger from the moon) are two rather charming euphemisms. The former is colloquial, and the latter is a literary expression. *Mensu* (from menses), *seiri,* (physiological phenomenon), and *seiri-bi* (menstrual period) are all rather formal terms. *Akai mono* (red thing), *are* (that), *hatabi* (flag day), *oshime* (on the rag), and *anne* (the name of a Japanese sanitary products manufacturer, derived from the famous scene in *The Diary of Anne Frank* in which Anne had her first period) are all more commonly used slang expressions. *Hatabi* comes from the design of the Japanese flag—a round red sun on a pure white background.

Emu (M), from the first letter of menstruation, is also used by young students. *Kame,* the romanized reading of the English word came, means for a woman to menstruate. *Tomato* (tomato) is also used. Among these expressions, *seiri, are,* and *anne* are the most popular.

5

Bad Personality, Attitude, and Behavior

(iya-na jinbutsu, kirawareru seikaku)

According to an October 1993 survey by Gillette Japan, the first in a list of traits of *kirai-na bosu* (unpopular boss) was *tanki* (short tempered). Next was *komakasugiru* (too strict), followed by *wagamama* (selfish, egocentric). Tops in the list for *suki-na bosu* (popular boss) was *yasashii* (sweet and gentle), the second was *kimae ga ii* (generous), and the third was *mendōmi ga ii* (looking out for others). Now, let us introduce some derogatory expressions for the personalities and attitudes of people, in addition to bosses, who are perceived to be *iya-na yatsu* (disgusting people), that is, *kiraware-mono* (people who are disliked by others) or *hanatsumami* (gross people).

Bad Personality

Here are some examples of *seikaku busu* (a bad personality). Adding *yatsu* or *ningen* after an adjective usually will give you a person with that characteristic. While *iya-na* is gross or disgusting, *iya-na yatsu* is a gross or disgusting person.

Waru-mono Group

People with bad personalities are most commonly called

73

waru-mono or more simply *waru,* both of which mean bad guys. The expression *akunin* is a more formal expression. *Akuma* and *oni* both mean devil, and are used for cold-blooded villains or frightening demons.

In 1994, a family in the Tokyo suburbs attempted to register their newborn baby with the name of Akuma, but the local ward office refused their request, saying that the child would resent his name when he grew up. The couple took legal action and won their case. Later, however, the parents changed their minds and gave the baby a more socially acceptable name. This incident caused considerable controversy around the issue of parents' right to name their child as they please. *Ninpinin* (evil one) or *reiketsukan* (cold-blooded), incidentally, are synonyms for *akuma* and *oni.*

Akutō means trash or refuse of society, and is a classic expression for a bad guy. *Kuzu* (rubbish) and *gomi* (trash) as in the phrases *ningen no kuzu, kuzu yarō,* or *gomi yarō,* are used to mean human debris. *Kudaranai yatsu* is a scumbag. *Harenchi ningen* is a shameless person. The word *hajishirazu* is similar; *haji* means shame and *shirazu* means does not know. *Garakuta yarō* is junk, *yakubyōgami* is a pest or odious person, *kiseichū* is a parasite, and *o-jamamushi* (literally, disturbing insect) is also a pest or disturbance.

Usotsuki Group

Usotsuki means fibber or liar, and *ō-usotsuki* is a big liar. *Horafuki* is a show-off. This comes from *hora* (fish story, tall tale) *o fuku* (to blow). *Hora* is actually a shortened form of *horagai* (conch or trumpet shell). *Fukasu* (literally, to puff or smoke) and *ōki-na koto o iu* (to tell a big thing) are synonyms.

Peten-shi is a shark or swindler. By itself, the word *peten,* which comes from a Chinese name, means fraud, deception, or swindle. *Inchiki yarō* is a hustler. *Inchiki* is often used in a teasing manner in ordinary conversation when you think someone is being sly or tricky.

Ikasama-shi is a tricky person, and *sagi-shi* is a crook. The *kanji* for *shi* means master or skillful person, but when it is used as a suffix it usually connotes bad sorts of people. *Yama-shi,* (literally, mountain master) is originally a vulgar word for a miner; later it came to mean a swindler. *Ikasama-shi* is related to gambling, and *sagi-shi* is an all-round word for a bad person. *Sagi,* by the way, is the legal term for fraud. *Haraguroi yatsu* is a black-hearted or evil-hearted person, a schemer. This expression comes from *hara* (belly) and *kuroi* (black), and is obviously similar to black heart in English.

Nijū jinkaku is a double personality, a Jekyll-and-Hyde. *Nimai-jita* (double tongue) is a double dealer, a duplicitous person. *Ura omote no aru yatsu* (literally, a man with front and back side) is a split personality. And *gizensha* (a person pretending to be honest) is a hypocrite. *Gizen* by itself means hypocrisy.

O-toboke is a person who plays dumb. *Ō-gesa ningen* is a person who talks big, an exaggerator. The *ō-gesa* here comes from *kesa,* a loose garment worn by Buddhist monks, and *ō-* (big).

Kuchisaki ningen is someone who is all talk and no action. And *o-shaberi* is a big mouth, a chatterbox. This comes from the verb *shaberu* (to talk or chat). *O-shaberi* is not always used in a pejorative sense; it can be also used to tease a talkative friend.

Kechi Group

Kechi means stingy or a stingy person, and it has several related terms. *Kechikusai* is petty-minded, and *kechinbō* is a a miser or skinflint. *Dokechi* and *shimittare* are terms used for miser, while *shimari-ya* is tight-fisted or thrifty. The verb derivative of *shimittare* is *shimittareru,* meaning to be reluctant to spend money. This is in turn derived from the verb *shimaru,* which means to be shut or closed. When one becomes offensively *kechi,* he or she is called *takari-ya* (a scrounge, sponge, or deadbeat) from the verb *takaru* (to pinch or squeeze). A *takari-ya* might make use of the verb *ogoru* (to treat) by saying *ogotte, warui na* (Treat me, okay? Thanks). *Gametsui yatsu* is a tightwad.

Keisan dakai and *dasanteki* mean calculating or selfish. *Keisan* is calculation or reckoning, and *dakai* is a euphonic change of *takai,* meaning alert. *Dasan* means calculation or selfishness.

A century ago, *sekoi* meant *warui* or *heta* (bad, no good); now it means *kechi* (stingy) or *sesekomashii* (fussy). *Sekoi* is acutally undergoing a revival among young people, as will be discussed in more detail later. *Kozakashii* is crafty or conceited, and *kozaiku suru yatsu* is man of cheap tricks. *Kozaiku* here means tricks or wiles.

Finally, when a *takari-ya* breaks the law, he is called *yusuri-ya* (a blackmailer). This term comes from the verb *yusuru* (to extort or shake down).

Wagamama Group

Wagamama is a common term meaning selfish or willful. *Katte kimama* and *wagamama katte* also mean selfish. *Katte* by itself means one's own way, and a person insisting on *katte* these days is not considered as bad as he used to be. *Hitoriyogari* is literally self-content, centering on one's own idea of what that contentment is. *Go-tsugō shugi* is opportunism. *Go-tsugō* here is convenience, and *shugi* is a suffix meaning -ism.

Wagamama as a personality trait often comes from being spoiled as a child, and many Japanese children, particularly little boys, are overindulged by their mothers. The words *amaeru* (to presume upon another's love, or play the indulged child) and its noun form *amae* are familiar to most people who have studied Japan. Dr.

Takeo Doi's bestseller *Amae no Kōzo (The Anatomy of Dependence)* stated that these notions are basic to the Japanese mentality, whether child or adult. Related to this is *amaenbō,* which is a mama's boy, and *amattare* and *dadakko,* both meaning spoiled brat. This latter comes from the verb *dada o koneru* (to fret, to be peevish or petulant), which, in turn, comes from *jitanda o fumu* (to stamp one's feet in frustration or anger).

Iikagen Group

Iikagen literally means good degree, but it is actually used to mean half-hearted or half-assed. *Iikagen* is a word that oten frustrates students of Japanese. How does a word that originally meant just right and well-balanced, come to have a negative connotation? It's even difficult for Japanese to understand the dictionary explanation. It goes like this.

The original meaning of *iikagen* was suitable degree; in other words, enough. Then it took on the meaning of only enough, not thorough, only so-so, and finally, unreliable. *Ii* is good and *kagen* is degree. So when you say *ii yu kagen,* it means bath water at a good temperature, *yu* being hot water. But when you say *aitsu wa iikagen,* it means he's unreliable. The reason for this change of meaning is perhaps that the Japanese feel that barely enough is really not very good at all.

Charanporan is used for an unreliable, irresponsible person, even worse than *iikagen*; this term comes from the sound of objects being thrown away and neglected. *Detarame* (nonsense) *ningen* is also a strongly derogatory term, and if someone is said to be *iikagen, detarame,* and *charanporan* all at the same time, then he is a totally despicable person.

O-tenki-ya (changeable as the weather), *uwaki ningen* (fickle person), and *kimagure-ya* (whimsical) all mean someone who is capricious and moody.

Otchokochoi (from the onomatopoetic *choko-choko*

used to describe small, fidgety motions) means scatter-brained as well as butterfingers. *Ukkari-mono* and *keisotsu ningen* are also used for a careless, rash person. *Ukkari* means carelessly, thoughtlessly, or heedlessly, while *keisotsu* is rashness or hastiness.

Asahaka (ningen) is a shallow or superficial person and *usuppera* is a close synonym. The *asa* in *asahaka* comes from the adjective *asai,* which means shallow or superficial, and *usu* is from the adjective *usui,* which means thin or weak (as in tea or a mixed drink). The addition of *-ppera* is for emphasis.

Ganko-mono Group

Ganko-mono is a stubborn or hard-headed person, and *ishibe kinkichi* is a synonym. *Ishi* here is stone, *be* is wall, *kin* is metal, and *kichi* is a common suffix in men's names. *Ishiatama* (literally, stone head) means hard-headed.

Gōjōppari is stubborn as a mule; a close synonym is *ijippari. Gōjō* here means obstinance or stubborness, and *iji* means temper or disposition. A person who is *shitsukoi* is too persistent, a pest.

Kanpeki shugisha is a perfectionist; *kanpeki* means perfection. *Majime ningen* is a real square, and the expression *kuso majime* refers to someone who is excessively serious or precise—in other words, anal retentive. *Korishō* means fastidious, and *kodawari ningen* is an excessively meticulous person. This kind of character trait, however, is nowadays regarded as rather desirable. *Kodawari* is an obstacle or obstruction. Finally, *katabutsu* means straight-laced.

Kawarimono Group

Kawarimono and *kawarimon* describe an eccentric or kinky person. Here are some related terms.

Iyami-na hito is a bitter person, and *hinekure-mono* is someone who is bitter or crooked. This comes from the verb *hinekureru* meaning crooked or twisted. *Amanojaku* is a perverse person. The word can be traced to a devil in old Japanese folk tales who was perverse about everything. *Kimuzukashii hito* is a difficult person. *Ki* here means mind, soul, or heart, and *muzukashii* is difficult. *Henkutsu* is an eccentric or a bigot. *Hesomagari* (literally, crooked or twisted bellybutton) is a perverse or obstinate person, while *tsumuji magari (tsumuji* is a whorl of hair on the head) means a screwy or cranky person. *Henjin* and *kijin* both refer to an odd or peculiar person.

Bukkirabō-na yatsu is a terribly blunt person.

Busutto shita and *aiso ga nai* describe a person who puts on a long face or lacks affiability, while a *butchōzura* is a sour or sulky face. *Inki-na yatsu* is a gloomy person.

Ingin burei-na yatsu is a person who acts with feigned politeness. Here *ingin* means politeness or civility, and *burei* means rudeness. *Kawaridane* is a peculiar figure or person. *Ningen girai* is person who doesn't like people, a loner. *Onna girai* is a woman hater or misogynist, and *otoko girai* is a man hater. *Kodomo girai* is a child hater.

Yowamushi Group

Yowamushi is a weakling or coward. It comes from the adjective *yowai* (weak), and *mushi* (insect). A similarly constructed term is *nakimushi* (crybaby), related to a Japanese superstition that there is a sort of insect inside people's bodies that affect feeling and thinking.

Okubyō-mono and *kowagari* mean coward. *Okubyō* is cowardice, and *kowagari* comes from the verb *kowagaru,* which means to fear. *Honenuki* means to have no spine. *Hone* is bone, and *nuki* means omission. *Koshinuke* is a similar term for a coward; *koshi* is the waist or the small of the back, and *nuke* comes from the verb *nukeru* (to fall out or slip off). *Make inu* is a born loser, from the verb *makeru* (to lose) and *inu* (dog).

Nanjaku describes a weak or effeminate person.

Shōshin-mono is an inhibited person. *Shōshin* (small heart) means timidity or cowardice.

Ikujinashi is a chicken, and *ijiketa* is to feel timid or defensive.

Makeoshimi is an unwillingness to own up to defeat, in other words, to cry sour grapes. This kind of person would be called *boyaki ningen* (a griper or grumbler), and might tend to have *higami konjō* (an inferiority complex). *Boyaku* means to grumble or complain, and *higami* comes from the verb *higamu* (to be biased or warped). *Konjō* is disposition or mind.

Bad Attitude and Behavior *(warui taido)*

Next, let's move on to people whose attitudes or actions are not too popular with others.

Deshabari Group

Deshabari is a nosy person, an intruder. It comes from the verb *deshabaru,* which means to intrude or meddle. *O-sekkaiyaki,* meaning a busybody or meddler, is a close synonym.

Zūzūshii and *atsukamashii* both mean impudent or presumptuous, while *zubutoi* means audacious or brazen. *Zu* or *zū* is an emphatic prefix, and *-butoi* is a euphonic change of *futoi* (wide, fat).

Tsura no kawa ga atsui (literally, skin of the face is thick) and *tetsumenpi* (literally, iron-face skin) both mean thick-skinned.

Rokotsu ningen (literally, bare to the bones person) and *akesuke ningen* (frank person) refer to someone who is too frank, conspicuous, or lewd.

Gami-gami Group

Gami-gami iu is an onomatopoeia meaning to chew out, nag, or scold. *Urusai* (annoying) can be used to mean shut up, and is commonly said in response to *gami-gami iu*. *Kogoto ga ōi (kogoto* literally means small complaint) means to give a good scolding. *Kogoto* are words used to chastise someone. *Hitokoto ōi* means one word too many.

Arasagashi is a fault-finder. *Urusa-gata* is also a fault finder, the annoyingly fastidious type. *Urusai* by itself is not always negative, by the way. *Kare wa sake ni wa urusai* means he is very particular about wine, implying he knows a lot about it.

Dokuzetsu-ya is someone with a sharp or barbed tongue. *Doku* here is poison, and *zetsu* means tongue.

Borokuso ni iu means to put someone or something down. *Boro* is rag and *kuso* is shit. Finally, *shitsugen-koji* is a person who habitually puts his foot in his mouth.

Ijiwaru Group

Ijiwaru is a nasty or mean person. It's a compound consisting of *iji* (mind) and *waru* from *warui* (bad, nasty). *Yowaimono ijime, gakidaishō,* and *ijimekko* all mean bully. *Yowaimono* is a weak person, and *ijime* comes from the verb *ijimeru* (to bully). *Gaki* is a vulgar word for a child or brat, while *taishō* is literally a military general. *Oyamano taishō* is literally king of the mountain; figuratively a bossy person. *Wanman* (literally, one-man) is a tyrant or boss with absolute authority in a company or group.

Me no ue no tankobu is a constant hindrance. This expression can be literally translated as a bump or knot above the eye.

Takabisha is an overbearing and high-handed person who talks down to others. *Taka* is high, and *bisha* (originally *hisha*) is a rook or castle in the chess-like game of *shōgi*.

Ibari-ya is an arrogant person who is up on his high horse. It comes from the verb *ibaru* (to swagger, be haughty).

Moretsu **Group**

Mōretsu ningen can be translated as eager beaver. By itself, *mōretsu* means violent or vehement. People who fall into this category would include *shusse shugisha* (status seekers, social climbers), *shigoto ningen* and *shigoto no mushi* (workaholics), *shigoto no oni* (work horses), *hataraki-bachi* (busy bees), and *kane no mōja* (money mongers). These days, many Japanese *mōretsu ningen* have literally worked themselves to death, a phenomenon called *karōshi*.

Senobi ningen and *takanozomi* are people who aim too high. *Senobi* means to stretch one's back, and *takanozomi* comes from *takai* (high) and *nozomi* (desire or hope).

Narikin means nouveau riche. It comes from a technical term in the game of *shōgi*. Just as a pawn is promoted to queen in chess, *fu* (similar to a pawn) in *shōgi* is promoted to *kin* (a gold piece) when it crosses a certain line in the opponent's territory. *Nari* is from the verb *naru* (to become). *Narikin,* therefore, means to be promoted to queen in a game of chess, or to become instantly rich. A similar word is *nariagari,* which means upstart.

Ichiryū are people who are first class or first tier; those who cannot attain this are *niryū* (literally, second rater or minor character), or *sanryū* (third rater). Even worse are the *dosamawari* (actors who play the small towns) or the *miyako ochi* (rustics). *Miyako* here means capital city, and *ochi* is from the verb *ochiru* or *ochinobiru,* which mean to fall or drop.

Nitemo yaitemo kuenai (yatsu) is a tough bird. This expression literally means even if you boil it, even if you bake it, you cannot eat it.

Umisen yamasen is an old fox. This expression comes from the legend of a snake that lived for 1,000 years in the sea *(umi)* and then 1,000 years in the mountains *(yama)*, becoming in the process *shitataka mono* (tough, experienced person). *Zurugashikoi* describes a person who is tricky. *Zurui* means sly or cunning, and *kashikoi* is also used in a positive sense to mean clever.

Gomasuri Group

The expression *gomasuri* (literally, a grinder for sesame seeds; figuratively an apple polisher or brown noser) can also be represented by the wringing hand motion one uses when grinding sesame seeds. Here are some similar words. *Yoisho ningen* is a flatterer. *Yoisho* is the expression Japanese use when they are lifting something heavy. *Chōchin mochi* (fawning type), *kaban mochi* (flunky), and *taiko mochi* (sycophant, flatterer) are all similar terms for *gomasuri* people. *Mochi* comes from the verb *motsu* (to hold or carry) and *chōchin, kaban,* and *taiko* mean lantern, suitcase, and drum, respectively. *Peko-peko yarō (peko-peko* is an onomatopoeia for the motion of nodding), and *iesu man*, both mean a yes-man.

Ketsufuki yarō is an ass kisser. *Ketsu* here is ass or rear, and *fuki* comes from the verb *fuku,* meaning to wipe. *Ayatsuri ningyō*, deriving from the verb *ayatsuru* (to manage), means a puppet.

Those who fawn on their bosses are *kageguchi yarō* (literally, shady mouth) or *iitsuke yarō* (informer or tattletale). Slang expressions such as *obekka* and *obenchara* (flattery to one's superiors) are also often used.

Kakkoman Group

Kakkoman is a newly coined word meaning someone who cares excessively about his appearance. *Kakko* here means shape or appearance. A related verb is *kakko (o) tsukeru* (to put on airs). *Kiza-na yatsu* or *kidori-ya* is an affected, snobbish, or showy person. Both *kiza* and *kidori* mean affectation.

Teisai ningen is someone who worries about appearances. *Teisai* means decency, form, or appearance.

Keishiki shugisha is a stickler for form, and *ko-yakunin* is a petty official who tends to *keishiki baru* (stand on ceremony). *Keishiki* in these expressions means form or formality, and *ko-yakunin* comes from *yakunin* (an official) and the prefix *ko-* (small). *Shittakaburi* describes someone who pretends to know all the answers.

Wazatoraman is a combination of Ultraman, a famous science fiction TV character, and *wazatorashii* *(waza to* means intentionally), and is used to describe unnatural or affected men. *Burikko* (excessively cute girl) is used for affected young women, a phenomenon we'll discuss in detail later.

Shibaigagatta means overly dramatic. *Shibai* is a play or drama. *Happō bijin (happō* is eight directions and *bijin* means a beauty) is everybody's friend. A close synonym for this is *iikaoshii*. *Iikaoshii* comes from *ii kao* (good face or smiling face) and *shitagaru* (to want to do).

Gehin Group

Gehin and *hin ga nai* both mean indecent or vulgar. The *hin* in these expressions means elegance or grace, and *ge* is written with the character meaning under or lower. *Gehin-na kotoba,* then, are vulgar words or gutter talk. *Gebita* and *gebirashii* are close synonyms. A feeling of vulgarity is definitely expressed with the *ge* sound.

Iyashii (mean) and *iyarashii* (disgusting) look similar to one another but, in fact, the *iya* in these two words are written with two different *kanji* characters. *Iyashii* (low or base) can also be used to describe a greedy person, especially someone who is greedy for food. *Iyarashii,* on the other hand, comes from *iyami* (disagreeable, offensive). *Iyami-na yatsu* is a sarcastic, disagreeable, offensive person, or a person with bad taste. *Iyamittarashii* is a derivative of *iyami,* and it is even more derogatory. *Iyarashii*, then, is a shortened form of *iyamittarashii*. It is also used to refer to sexual harassment. When some-

one says *iyarashii metsuki,* it means he's leering at me—
how disgusting!

Some other words used to describe sexual indecency
are *ogeretsu, sukebei, etchi, hasuppa,* and *shirigaru.*
Sukebei and *etchi* will be discussed further in Part Two.
O-geretsu is a word used by women for a lewd or
lecherous person. *Geretsu* is similar to *gehin,* with the
addition of the honorific prefix *o-.*

The term *hasuppa* comes from *hasu no ha* (*hasu* is
lotus and *ha* is leaves). Lotus leaves are big and look
rather magnificent as they float on the water. In the Edo
era, people thought this was somewhat representative of
uwaki onna (an unfaithful woman), *uwaki* (literally, floating mind) being fickleness. *Hasuppa no onna* is quite
similar to *uwaki onna* and *shirigaru onna.* In the latter,
shiri is buttocks or ass, and *karu* comes from *karui,*
meaning light, easy, or floating.

Akushumi means poor taste. *Aku* here is written with
the character for *warui,* meaning bad, evil, or wrong,
and *shumi* means taste or inclination.

Egetsunai describes a nasty person, while *gesu yarō* is
a cad. *Gesu* is a low-ranking official or a low-class person. The set phrase *gesu no kanguri* means a crooked or
suspicious person who will often groundlessly suspect the
worst of others. *Gesui* is a newly coined adjective derived
from *gesu.* *Gasatsu ningen* is a rough and rude person.
Gasatsu and *gazatsu* mean bearish or unrefined. *O-
somatsu* is shabby and stupid, *mittomonai* is shabby
looking, and *musakurushii* is messy. *O-somatsu* is commonly used by a hostess when she is complimented on a
meal. The guest will say *go-chisō-sama,* which means the
food was delicious. In a typically Japanese response, the
hostess will modestly demur by saying *o-somatsu-sama,*
meaning it was nothing much or it was not very tasty.

Yaboten Group
Yaboten is a person who is *yabo* (boorish, unrefined),

but with the added nuance of *ki ga kikanai* (stupid, senseless), *omoiyari ga nai* (unfeeling), and *sensu ga nai* (lacking in common sense). *Seken shirazu* describes a naive person. *Seken* here means the world or worldly affairs, and *shirazu* is a negative form of the verb *shiru* (to know).

Asahaka mono and *asajie* mean shallow wisdom. *Asa* here is written with the character for shallow, and *jie* is a euphonic change of *chie,* meaning wise or resourceful. A similar expression is *sarujie* (monkey's idea).

Tansaibō is single-minded, *bakashōjiki* is excessively honest, and *akimekura* is a blind fool or absent-minded person.

Pinboke (yarō) is to be out of focus or slightly senile. *Pin* here comes from *pinto* and means focus, and *boke* comes from the verb *bokeru,* which means to grow senile. *Pinto-hazure* is a more polite way of saying *pinboke.*

Onchi is tone-deaf, and *hōkō onchi* describes a person who has no sense of direction (literally, direction-deaf). *Onchi* comes from *on* (sound or music) and *chi* (foolishness).

Gutara Group

As already mentioned, *gūtara* is similar to *dame* and means good-for-nothing or laggardly. Some derivatives are *guzu, guzura,* and *motakō*, which describe a person who is *guzu-guzu* (slow and tardy), *mota-mota* (dawdling), and *niekiranai* (indecisive). *Mendōkusagari* is an idle or lazy person, and *mendōkusai* is something that's a pain in the neck. *Mendō* in these expressions is trouble or difficulty, and *kusai* means to smell or stink of.

Namake-mono is a lazy person. This expression derives from the verb *namakeru,* which means to be idle or lazy. The Japanese word for the sloth, an animal known mostly for hanging upside-down from trees, is also *namake mono,* though it is written with different characters.

Saboriman is a goof-off, *saboman* being a combination of the English words sabotage and man.

Darashinai and *shimari no nai* are close synonyms, meaning loose or slovenly. *Shimari* means tightness, firmness, or steadiness. *Darashi* is an inverted form of *shidara,* which means bad state or misconduct. *O-nimotsu* (luggage) is a person who is a big burden, and *ashi de matoi* is a drag. All of these people are *tsukiainikui* (difficult to get along with), *kattarui* (hard to deal with), and *tsukareru hito* (people who tire others).

Bukitcho **Group**

Bukitcho (or *bukiyō-na hito),* and its abbreviated form *buki*, mean clumsy or klutzy.

Hetakuso or simply *heta* is used to describe a person who is awkward at doing things. *Heta* means poor or unskillful, and *kuso*, as we have seen before, is a derogatory suffix meaning shit. *Kuchibeta* is a poor speaker. *Kuchi* here is mouth, and *beta* is a euphonic change of *heta* (poor). *Heta-uma* is a newly invented word to describe a person's whose artwork looks bad *(heta)* but actually has some unexpected merit *(umai).*

Tere-ya is a bashful type, someone who tries to cover his embarrassment. Many Japanese tend to be *hazukashigari* (shy or self-conscious), which is very similar to *tere-ya*. *Tere-ya* comes from the verb *tereru,* meaning to be bashful.

Koshi ga omoi is to have lead in one's pants or be a slow starter. *Koshi* here is the waist or the small of the back, and *omoi* means heavy. A similar expression is *nagatchiri*, used to describe a person who overstays his welcome. *Shiri ga nagai* is an adjective for this and literally means his ass is long. *Daikon yakusha* or just simply *daikon* is a lousy actor. This expression comes from *daikon,* a Japanese radish that is *shirokute futoi* (white and thick), and then from *shirōto* (amateur). It's interesting that in English an overzealous actor is described as a ham, which is also something to eat.

Jidai okure means out-of-date. *Jidai* here is a period or epoch, and *okure* comes from the verb *okureru* (to be late or slow).

O-mase is a precocious child, *okute* is a slow child or late bloomer, and *chie okure* is a retarded child. *Chie* here is wisdom, and *okure* comes from the verb *okureru*.

6

Animals

(dōbutsu kanren)

As is common in other parts of the world, Japanese use the names of animals to describe the appearance, as well as the character, of another person. Here are a number of such words.

We'll start with *inu* (dog). Although the dog has long been considered man's most faithful friend, most expressions related to this animal tend—puzzlingly—to be unflattering, whether in English or Japanese.

Banken (watchdog) can be understood in both positive and negative ways. A good watchdog is invaluable in protecting his or her master from physical harm. But an overzealous watchdog can attack for the wrong—often simply reflexive—reasons. *Bosu no banken* (the boss' watchdog) is an expression of criticism for such a person.

Kai inu ni te o kamareru (to have one's hand bitten by one's own dog) would be colloquially rendered into English as to bite the hand that feeds you.

Inu is sometimes used to mean *mawashi-mono* (secret agent) or *supai* (spy), as in *aitsu wa teki no inu da* (he's an enemy spy). When you say *inumitai ni kagimawaru* (to sniff around like a dog), it is the same as the English verb to dog, meaning to shadow. *Inu,* when it is used as slang, means cop, similar to the English usage of pig to refer disparagingly to a policeman. Furthermore, *inu* can be used to refer to someone disdainfully, as in *inu-chikushō* (you bastard).

Inu is also used as a prefix in two ways. The first is contemptuous as in *inu-zamurai,* namely, a stupid samu-

89

rai, *zamurai* being a euphonic change of *samurai*. The second way is to mean useless, as in *inu-jini* (to die in vain). *Inu-goya* (doghouse or kennel) means a small, dilapidated house. *Inu no tōboe* (the howling of a dog at something distant) implies a yellow dog or coward.

Inugui (eating like a dog) means sloppy or voracious eating, often accompanied by the onomatopoeic description *gatsu-gatsu*.

Inu to saru, or *ken-en no naka*, both of which mean the relationship between a dog and a monkey, mean to be at loggerheads or on bad terms with. *Inu ni hoshi*, literally a dog looking at the stars, implies lofty ambitions.

Although the cat *(neko),* like the dog, is a popular and well-loved pet, the general image of this animal is *zurui* (literally, sly or cunning; figuratively, catty or cattish). Again, most expressions related to this animal are unfavorable, be they in English or in Japanese.

In English, for example, a catcall is a sound made to express disapproval, caterwaul is to make the characteristic harsh cry of a mating cat or to quarrel like a cat, a cathouse is a whorehouse, and to be catty is to be slyly malicious or spiteful. We can, in fact, think of only one flattering term and that is pussy cat, said of someone who is gentle and kind.

The Japanese word *neko* (cat) in Japanese is said to come from the cat's cry, which sounds like *nē* or *nyā,* and the suffix *-ko,* used to describe something cute and small. In underground usage *neko* can mean the passive party in a lesbian relationship; we will write more about this later. It can also mean a geisha. This connection comes from the *shamisen,* a musical instrument made from catgut and often played by geisha.

Neko-nade goe (literally, the purring of a cat when caressed) means an insinuating voice. *Neko o kaburi* (a man wearing cat's skin) is a hypocrite, prude, or wolf in sheep's clothing. As a verb, *neko o kaburu* means to feign innocence. *Neko no hitai* (cat's forehead) refers to a very small place, as in the idiom *neko no hitai hodo no tochi* (a very tiny plot of land). *Neko-matagi* (literally, even a cat would step over it) means distasteful food, especially if it's fish.

Nekoze (cat's round shoulder), as we have already mentioned, is round-shouldered or a stooped back. *Neko kawai-gari* (to pet like a cat) is to dote on one's children or grandchildren.

Neko-jita (cat's tongue) is a person who doesn't like hot food (in temperature, not spiciness). Japanese tend to think that Westerners and Japanese have different senses of heat, and what is warm to a Westerner is only lukewarm to a Japanese. For their part, Westerners are somewhat offended by the Japanese habit of eating very hot noodles *(rāmen* or *soba)* with a loud, slurping sound (*zū-zū* or *tsū-tsū*). The idea is that gulping in air with the hot food cools it. Westerners would rather wait until the food cools on its own and eat it noiselessly *(oto o tatenai),* but the Japanese think this is pointless because the noodles turn soggy.

Neko-baba (cat's shit) is to pocket something secretly, embezzle, or misappropriate. It comes from the habit of cats burying their feces in the ground. The verb form of this expression is *neko-baba suru.*

Sakari no tsuita neko (a cat in heat) is a scornful expression used to describe noisy lovers or a promiscuous woman. *Dorobō-neko* (filching cat) is a cat burglar. *Bake-neko* (literally, goblin cat, or a cat disguised as a man) refers to an old woman who wears heavy makeup in an attempt to look young and beautiful. *Bakemono* or *obake* (monster) can be used to mean the same thing. *Neko no me no yō ni kawaru* (to change as a cat's eyes) means to make a chameleon-like change with less-than-honest motives.

Saru (monkey), *buta* (pig), *kitsune* (fox), *tanuki* (badger), *uma* (horse), *usagi* (rabbit), *nezumi* (rat), *shirami* (louse), and *tako* (octopus) are also commonly used to describe people, often in derogatory ways.

One can say *sarumitai-na kao* (or *tsura*), or simply *saru* for a person who looks like a monkey. *Mitai-na* is resembles or looks like, and *tsura* is a slang synonym for *kao*. The nickname *saru* refers not only to facial appearance, but to crafty or shrewd personalities as well.

Sarumane and *sarumane ningen* describe a monkey-see, monkey-do kind of person; in other words, an ape. An even more derogatory synonym is *etekō*.

In the Edo era, *saru* was used by criminals to refer to a low-class policeman. *Megane-zaru* is actually a specter temur or tarsier, a species of monkey with round, surprised-looking eyes. This term is used contemptuously to refer to a person who wears glasses.

In the Oriental zodiac *(jūnishi)*, the year of the monkey comes around every 12 years, and many Japanese send New Year's greeting cards that depict the famous hear-no-evil, see-no-evil, speak-no-evil monkeys with their paws covering their ears, eyes, and mouth. These three monkeys are known in Japanese as *san-en, san* being three and *en* an alternative pronunciation for *saru*. The top monkey *(mizaru)* puts his hands on his eyes, the second one *(iwazaru)* on his mouth, and the bottom one *(kikazaru)* on his ears. This is a very interesting pun on the word *saru. Zaru,* in this case, besides being a euphonic change of *saru,* is an old auxiliary verb used to make a negative statement. Thus, *mizaru* means I don't see anything, *iwazaru,* I won't say anything, and *kikazaru,* I don't hear anything.

The best-known rendition of the *san-en* in Japan is a wood carving on Yomeimon in the famous Nikkō Tōshōgū Shrine compound. It's said to be the work of Jingorō Hidari, a left-handed (thus, *hidari*) artist who allegedly lived in the early Edo era. The expression *san-en shugi*

(shugi is -ism) has a very negative connotation, implying a person who doesn't want to get involved in any unpleasantness or difficulty. The English equivalent would be a person who buries his head in the sand. Interestingly, Western children are taught the expression hear no evil, see no evil, speak no evil as a positive rule for life. A person who follows this teaching, in other words, is that admirable rarity who keeps his own counsel.

Pigs *(buta)* seem to suffer from a bad reputation almost everywhere, and Japan is no exception. The popular expression *buta ni shinju* (pearls before swine) is a translation from the New Testament. *Buta* in Japan is regarded as the dirtiest, fattest, ugliest creature of all. In reality, pigs may not be so bad, but *buta* still is used to describe a person who fits those negative stereotypes. In underground usage, *buta* means a zero or meaningless person. *Buta yarō* (pig creature) emphatically describes a disgustingly fat slob. *Buta zura* is a person with wide nostrils and thick lips, as well as a vulgar or dirty personality. *Buta bako* is the can or the pokey—a place where a suspect is detained.

Whatever people may think of pigs, pork is a popular dish in many countries. In the mountainous areas of Japan *shishi-nabe* or *inoshishi-nabe* (a stew made from boar's meat) is a popular and representative dish. Boars, however, have become increasingly difficult to obtain. Thus, this dish is now prepared with a domestically raised hybrid of the boar and the pig, called *inobuta.*

Kitsune (fox) and *tanuki* (badger) are used for people with *zurui* (sly) and *haraguroi* (evil) natures. *Tanuki* are regarded as less sly than *kitsune,* however, and *tanuki oyaji* is a cunning or wily old man in a somewhat positive sense.

Uma (horse) is not used to describe any particular personality traits, but *uma-zura* is the equivalent of horseface. *Uma ni kuwaseru hodo* is a common expression meaning to feed someone vast amounts of food—stuff one's face.

Ushi (cow) in Japan are thought of as slow. Thus, *ushi no yō-na* (bovine) is an adjective that often precedes the word *noroma* (a slow or sluggish person). *Gyūho* (literally, cow's steps) is a Japanese variation on filibustering, in which reluctant Diet members participate in legislative votes with excruciating slowness. *Gyū* is another pronunciation of the *kanji* character for *ushi,* and *ho* is step or stepping.

The rabbit *(usagi)* in Japan is regarded as gentle, modest, timid, and cute. There are no derogatory words related to the rabbit, except *usagi-goya* (rabbit hutch), which refers to the cramped housing in Japan. This word was coined after these conditions became well known outside of Japan, particularly in the West. Prior to this, such houses were described as *inu-goya*. *Usagi-chan* or *usa-chan* is an affectionate nickname for a cute young girl.

Nezumi (mouse) and the more derogatory derivative *nezuko* refer to a smallish, nervous person who is constantly darting to and fro. *Dobu-nezumi* is a sly, sneaky fellow (a rat). *Dobu* here means sewer. *Shirami yarō* is a lousy fellow. *Shirami* here is literally louse or vermin.

Also related to mice, there is *chūtarō,* which, though it sounds like a name, comes from the sound of a mouse squeaking *(chū-chū)*. Thus, *chūtarō* is an affectionate term for a mouse.

Sukan tako or simply *tako (yarō)* is a stupid guy. *Tako* is octopus. And, on a general level, *kedamono* and *animaru* mean animal, brute, or beast. *Kedamono no yō-na otoko* is often used to describe a man who exhibits bestial or brutish qualities.

PART

2

THE LANGUAGE OF SEX

sei kanren yōgo

Despite the fact that prostitution thrives under many guises and is carried on almost openly in Japan, the conservative government authorities and the police have continued to interfere to an excessive degree in the people's desire for more open sexual expression. This is especially true for the most typical four-letter word in Japan, *o-manko* (vagina or, vulgarly, cunt), and its verb form *o-manko suru* (to fuck). The use of this word in literature and the press is all but banned, and most Japanese are rather touchy about using it.

The definition of obscenity is tricky, and it varies from individual to individual, from society to society, and from time to time. But in Japan, the prevailing ideas about obscenity as opposed to the prevailing practices have led to some fairly ludicrous situations.

Way back in 1949, for example, there was an odd incident in which Eiichi Yamanishi used the expression *o-manko* in his translation of Norman Mailer's *The Naked and the Dead.* The Japanese police cracked down and forbade him to use it, but the American Occupation authorities overruled them. This, however, was really an exceptional case. Since then, conservative views have prevailed and only indirect expressions have been allowed by the police and other authorities.

There have been some efforts at rebellion and some noted court cases. In one such case, the well-known novelist Akiyuki Nosaka fought obscenity charges against his magazine *Half Serious,* which published the pornographic masterpiece *Yojōhan Fusuma no Shitabari,* thought to have been written by the famous novelist Kafū Nagai in the early part of the Shōwa era (1926–1989). *Yojōhan,* literally four and a half tatami mats, is used symbolically to mean a private room for lovers. With no particular plot, the story describes erotic love play and is full of language used on such occasions. During Nosaka's trials at both the Tokyo District and Tokyo High Courts, some of the nation's leading literary figures defended him, saying that the prosecutors' ideas about sex were far behind the times and that their suppression of Nosaka was uncivilized to the point of vandalism. Their arguments were fruitless. After two convictions, Nosaka appealed to the Supreme Court, which, in August 1980, ruled that *Yojōhan* is an illegal erotic work, thus denying the appeal and finalizing the guilty verdict. Nosaka and others were fined for the crime of selling obscene materials.

There have been other related incidents, such as the arrest and guilty verdict for the publisher and translator of *Lady Chatterley's Lover*. A 1957 Supreme Court decision in Japan found the D.H. Lawrence work obscene. As a result, the translator, English literature scholar Sei Itō, as well as the publisher, were fined. The book is still sold in Japan with the offending portions deleted. On the other hand, John Cleland's *Fanny Hill* and the controversial works of Henry Miller, such as *Tropic of Cancer,* have escaped the censor's stern eye.

The 1971 publication of Eugene E. Landy's *Underground Dictionary* in the United States probably came as a surprise to no one, given the country's liberal obscenity laws, albeit won only after many hard-fought court battles. But its 1975 Japanese translation—a far more elaborate publication than the original—by Katsuaki Horiuchi, is another example of the uneven application of obscenity regulations in Japan. For this work, Horiuchi, using 7,000 student-researchers, systematically collected, examined, and arranged for the first time a large number of Japanese underground words, many of which are banned elsewhere. The book was allowed to be sold as a "scientific study."

The Japanese obsession with showing pubic hair has also led to some silly contradictions. On the one hand, magazines portraying some of the most lurid sadomasochistic sex scenes imaginable are available to anyone capable of dropping a few hundred yen into a vending machine, while imported publications that show pubic hair—like Playboy and Penthouse—are systematically censored. An interesting sidelight to all this is that it is housewives and young students who are hired, as cheap part-time workers, to black out the offending portions. One must sympathize with these poor part-time workers who are subjected to such pornography on a daily basis.

Famous Western art masterpieces that show pubic hair have been prohibited from being imported and shown in museums. Perhaps the funniest example of the Japanese censors' attitude towards pubic hair can be seen in Stanley Kubrick's film *A Clockwork Orange*. In it, there is a scene in which three people run around naked. The scene was shot from a great distance and the film speeded up, so the viewer can barely see the characters, much less their pubic hair. But the censors ordered that the hair be blotted out. The result was three little flashing dots darting about the giant screen, as if disembodied, and served only to draw attention rather than divert it. It was laughable. For the police and customs' authorities, the only and the absolute criterion for obscenity is the appearance—or non-appearance—of pubic hair.

The struggle concerning obscenity between the side of the creators and producers, and that of the police and government authorities, intensified in the 80s. At the same time, society's attitudes about obscenity, freedom of speech, and sexual activity became more liberal. In this environment, in 1991, a black and white photo book by Kishin Shinoyama featuring actress/model Kanako Higuchi and containing many images showing pubic hair was published (ignoring the police), and sold very well despite its 3,800 yen price tag. Since then, many such books featuring famous actresses showing their pubic hair have been published legally. A male nude photo was also published in *An-An,* a popular magazine for young women.

In 1992 *La Belle Noiseuse*, a French movie that won an award at the Cannes Film Festival, was shown at more than 300 theaters with numerous pubic hair scenes intact despite the ban. This was reported by the press at the same time as a lift on the pubic hair ban.

In addition, the erotic *ukiyo-e* of the Edo period, which had been censored, finally were published in their complete form around 1987. Though each print was quite expensive, the 18th-century masterpieces of such artists as Utamaro and Hokusai finally reached the eyes of the general public.

As if floating above all this controversy, the sex industry in Japan is about as advanced as it is anywhere in the world. Porn theaters, for example, present *honban* (used in the entertainment trade to mean a take rather than a rehearsal) shows, featuring sexual intercourse between customers and performers, up to four times a day, though such shows are supposedly banned nowadays because of the AIDS threat. At the numerous *sōpurando,* pink salons, and other types of nightclubs around the country, male customers can engage in various types of sexual activities, including one-on-one or group sex, blow jobs and hand jobs, fettishes, homosexual sex, and S&M. In addition, adult toy and video stores abound.

Thus, Japan seems to be both sexually flooded and sexually repressed. Under these circumstances, coming to any sort of standardized definition of obscenity for Japan is going to continue to be a thorny issue for many years to come. Still, the struggle between the people's desire for more free expression and the authorities' wish to repress that expression has resulted in some relaxation of the rules, and most of the slang terms introduced below are now used openly in the evening papers and weekly magazines.

1

Sexual Organs and Private Parts

(hibu, chibu)

In the past, most Japanese used two rather inexpressive pronouns for the sexual organs, namely *are* (it, i.e., penis) and *asoko* (there, i.e., vagina). Other terms, and there are hundreds, have been avoided, so we'll introduce some of them here.

When young people become curious about the opposite sex and related matters, they often consult a dictionary in an attempt to put their feelings into words. In so doing, however, they will find rather boring, technical terms. Among them are *seiki* (sexual organs), *kyokubu* (the part), *inbu* (shady part), *chibu* (shameful part), *hibu* (secret or private part), and an old literary expression, *kakushi dokoro* (hidden place). One can specify which sex he is referring to by adding on to these expressions the prefix *josei no* (woman's) or *dansei no* (man's).

There is another group of words, easily found in the dictionary, that sound very lyrical in translation, but rather repugnant to the Japanese ear. They include *inmon* (shady gate), *gyokumon* (jewel gate) and *chitsu* (vagina), on the female side, and *inkei* (shady stalk), *gyokukei* (jewel stalk), and *dankon* (man's root) for men.

A more commonly used pair of words are *musuko* (son) and *musume* (daughter) meaning male and female sexual organs. *Segare,* which also means son, as well as *boya* (boy or son) are synonyms for *musuko*. Another

100

pair of words, wisteria and lily, namely *fuji* and *yuri,* are also used for male and female genitals. Obviously, this usage derives from the suggestive shapes of these two flowers.

Here are some words used to describe women's vaginas and related parts.

The most basic is *o-manko* (vagina or cunt). This term comes from *meko* and *me no ko,* which originally meant a girl. It then became *o-meko* by the addition of the affectionate or respectful prefix *o-,* and finally changed to *o-manko. O-manko* or *o-manko suru* also mean fuck or to fuck.

During the Edo period, *o-manko* was *bobo* or *tsubi* in Edo (present-day Tokyo), *o-meko* in Osaka, and *o-soso* in Kyoto. Even now, there are different names in the various local dialects in different prefectures. It is still *o-manko* in Tokyo and the Kanto district in general, and *o-meko* and *yachi* in Kansai. In Tohoku, in the northeastern part of Japan, *heppe* and *betcho* are used, while in Kyushu, the words are *bobo* and *o-soso.* When men get aroused they use these words, but women rarely do.

Wareme-chan (little crevice) and *koneko-chan* (little pussy cat) were created about 20 years ago. They were cute names used mainly in reference to little girls, but they didn't gain much popularity and are now almost extinct. *Koneko-chan* was also used to refer to a sexually attractive young girl in her teens or older. *Asoko* and *are,* however, are still the most popular words for private parts, and they are used by both sexes. Young people, however, tend more towards *kanto* (cunt) and the inverted word made from *manko,* namely, *kōman.*

Here are some other words used for the female organ: the very vulgar *manjū* (literally, bean-jam bun, or hair pie), the acceptable *josei-jishin* (literally, woman herself, used when referring to the sexual organs of a mature woman), *kannon-sama* (Goddess of Mercy), *himitsu no hanazono* (secret garden) or simply *hanazono, tanima* (valley), *tanima no yuri* (lily of the valley), *oku no in* (inner sanctum), and the vulgar *zakuro* (pomegranate).

Traditionally, the Japanese have used the clam shell *(kai)* to describe the vagina. Thus, *shijimi* (a very small clam shell) is used when referring to the genitalia of a prepubscent girl, *asari* (short-necked clam) for a girl who has reached puberty or a young woman, and *hamaguri* (clam) for an older, mature woman. Corresponding to these ages by color are *sakura-gai* (a delicate, pink shell—*sakura* being a cherry blossom), *aka-gai* (literally, red shellfish) and *karasu-gai* (literally, crow shellfish, or fresh-water mussel), which has a violet-black shell. Really large vaginas are called *awabi* (abalone), and old ones are called *uba-gai* (literally, old woman shellfish—or a kind of surf clam).

Other euphemisms include *iremono* (container), *saya,* (sheath), *ana* (hole), *yachi* (valley).

Though there is no scientific evidence to corroborate this theory, a small, tight vagina is supposedly better than a wide, loose one. There are many derogatory terms in Japanese for this. *Ō-ana* (big hole), *gaba-gaba* (an onomatoepoetic adjective for looseness), *buka-buka* (another onomatopoetic adjective, also used in reference to big shoes), *dekaman* (big cunt), *yuriman* (*yuri* is loose), and *taiheiyō* (the Pacific Ocean) are frequently used when referring to a large vagina. *Taiheiyō ni gobō* (burdock in the Pacific) or *taiheiyō ni kobune* (small boat on the Pacific) are typical idiomatic expressions used to describe the combination of a large vagina and a small penis.

Here are some terms for a so-called *meiki* (excellent box). *Atago-yama* (from a temple in Shiba, Tokyo, with many stone steps) is used to refer to a vagina full of pleats or folds inside. *Kazu no ko tenjō* (herring roe ceiling) is a vagina that has a bumpy or rough texture on the upper part. *Mimizu senbiki* (a thousand earthworms) is a vagina that feels as though there are earthworms squirming around inside. *Kinchaku* (money pouch) is one that is tight at the entrance. *Tawarajime* is a vagina that is tight at the entrance, middle and back *(tawara* is a bag for rice or charcoal, bound tightly at the top, middle, and bottom). Finally, *shiofuki* (spouting of a whale) is a vagina full of love juice *(tsuyu).*

The female organs are also differentiated as being *uwatsuki* or *shitatsuki,* the former kind having been regarded as excellent since ancient times. *Uwatsuki* is an upper-positioned vagina, which is easy to penetrate from the front, while *shitatsuki* (lower-positioned) has to be penetrated with the legs up or from the back.

There are also such expressions as *fukuman* (rich, happy vagina) and *pukuman* (rich, thick vagina). This latter term derives from the mimetic adjective *pukkuri shita,* meaning a round and swollen state. And recently, the terms *ageman* (literally, up-bringing vagina, or vagina of fortune) and *sageman* (vagina of misfortune) have come into use.

Dameman (bad vagina) as opposed to *meiki* are described with some of the following terms. *O-sara,* (dish or shallow pan) and *kawarake* (literally, unglazed earthenware, or hairless pussy) are disliked due to how they look. *Kusaremanko* means sick or smelly vagina. This term is derived from the verb *kusaru,* which means to decay. All of these big, ugly, bad vaginas are said to be *ōaji,* having little flavor in bed.

The pubic mound is referred to colloquially in Japanese as *biinasu no oka* (the hill of Venus) or *deruta* (delta). The word *dote* (mound or riverbank) is considered rather vulgar because of its "d" sound. When a woman has a rather high and full mound with distinctive pubic bones *(chikotsu),* one can say *(kanojo wa) dote ga takai.*

The anatomical words for vulva are *sho-inshin* (minor labia) and *dai-inshin* (major labia). Some rather vulgar synonyms are *hida* (fold) and *hira-hira* (fluttering thing).

The most colloquial, however is *kuchibiru* (lips); when you want to avoid confusion with the lips of the face, you can add the prefix *shita no* (the lower). *Hanabira* and its *kanji's* alternative reading *kaben* (petal), are two more beautiful expressions for the lower lips of the female organ. *Kanojo no kaben wa nurete ita* (literally, the dew was upon her petals, figuratively, she was wet) is a popular expression in erotic literature.

There are various words for the clitoris. *Tsubomi* (bud) is a beautiful colloquial expression, and *sane* (core) more vulgar. *Kashin* (heart of the flower) is rather literary, *inkaku* (shady core) is an unappealing anatomical word, and *mame* (bean) is a vulgar colloquialism. Other common expressions are *kuri-chan* (little clit), *kuritorisu* (clitoris), *botan* (button), and *beru* (bell).

There are numerous colloquial terms for the penis, *o-chinko, chinko,* and *chinpo* (dick, cock, penis) being among the most common. *O-chinko* originally came from the word *chinko* (small penis), used to describe a child's genitals. Variations include *chinboko* and *o-chin-chin*. The words *mara, henoko,* and *fuguri,* which have been used since the Edo period, are still commonly used.

Since *o-chinko, chinko,* and *chinpo* sound childish, there is a tendency to use *are* (that), *musuko* or *segare* (son), *penisu* (penis), or *dansei-jishin* (the man himself, a counterpart of *josei-jishin*). But when discussing little boys' penises, *o-chin-chin* is a rather affectionate and acceptable term, as in *kawaii o-chin-chin ne* (what a cute little penis).

Some other common words for the male organs are *ichimotsu* (that thing), *onii-san* (big brother), *naka-ashi* (middle leg). Such words as *yari* (lance), *sao* (rod), *kushi* (skewer), *katana* (sword), *banana* (banana), *matsutake* (a highly prized Japanese mushroom with a long stem and a round head), *aodaishō* (snake), and *teppo* (gun or pistol) are also popular in erotic literature.

Tama or *tama-tama,* meaning balls, refer to the male

testicles. *Kin no tama* (golden ball or balls) can also be used, but when *no* is omitted, it becomes very vulgar. *Kōgan* is testicles, and *fukuro* is bag, referring to the testicular sac.

Men whose sexual organs are long and thick are the objects of other men's envy the world over. Though most women say that the size of their partner's erect penis is irrelevant, men still obsess over this issue. In any case, here are some words used by Japanese when referring to a large penis: *kyokon* (huge root), *futozao* (thick rod), *taiho* (cannon), *dekachin* (big cock), *wazamono* (fine sword), *utamaro* (from the name of the famous *ukiyo-e* woodblock print artist who produced pornographic work depicting men with symbolically oversized and over-veined organs), and *uma-nami* (horse-like).

When referring to a small penis such expressions as *tanshō* (short and small), *hosomi* (slim-bodied sword) *sochin* (poor cock), and *inu-chin* (dog's cock) are used.

There are various opinions as to what is *jōmara* (a high-quality cock) or *meito* (excellent sword), but it is interesting that *kyokon* (big cock or well hung) has not necessarily been thought of favorably in Japan. Rather, an excellent penis seems to be a combination of *karidaka, sori,* and *kuromara. Karidaka* is a glans or head of a penis that resembles the head of a *kari* (wild goose); in other words, large and wide. *Sori* from *sorimara* is a towering curved penis. And *kuromara* is a well-experienced penis that knows how to please women. *Kuro* comes from *kuroi,* meaning black, and has the connotation of something that is accomplished or professional.

Kyokon is sometimes referred to as *dekachin* or *dekamara (dekai* is slang meaning big), but it also has the connotation of *baka no ō-mara* (stupid, big cock).

Here are some terms for *dame mara* (bad penis) or *sochin* (poor penis). *Kawakaburi* (a cock with lace curtains) and *komokaburi* (covered with a straw mat) are both used to describe uncircumcised penises. Japanese tend to dislike *hōkē* (foreskin) and usually have it removed, believing that this helps prevent disease and *sōrō* (premature ejaculation).

Oher slang terms for *dame mara* are *funyachin, funyamara, gunyachin* (all meaning worm or soft cock) *naemara, yakutatazu* (withered, useless penis), *handachi* (half mast), and *inpo* (impotent), a recently imported word. *Inpo no chinpo* is an impotent dick.

Let us move on to the female secondary sexual organs, the breasts. The word *mune* (breasts or chest) is an ordinary, non-sexual expression. *Oppai* is a near synonym derived from baby talk and can be used for both mother's milk and breasts, or for tits in a sexual sense. Variations of *oppai* are *paipai* and the slangy *paiotsu*. *Boin, deka-pai, miruku tanku* (milk tank), or simply *tanku*, all refer to big breasts. *Boin* is an onomatopoetic expression deriving from the swinging motion of the breasts. *Deka-pai* comes from the slangy adjective *dekai* (big) combined with the *pai* of *oppai*.

Nain and *pechapai* are antonyms for these terms, meaning small-breasted or flat-chested. *Nai* means nothing and *pecha* comes from *pechanko,* which means flattened or crushed. An English equivalent might be the old expression pirate's delight: a poor girl so flat-chested that she could be used instead of the plank pirates make their victims walk.

Chibusa is a more formal word meaning breasts. *Chikubi* is nipples. *Chi* comes from *chichi* (breasts), and *kubi* means neck.

In English, the word tits means both breasts and nipples. Similarly, in Japanese, *oppai* can be used to refer to both. *O-shaburi* (nipple or teething ring) is an expression used for nipples when engaged in some kind of love play. Nicer, however, is *sakuranbo* (cherry), which refers to the pink nipples of young girls. *Hoshibudo* (raisin) is used for the bluish-purple nipples of old women.

As sex play gets more serious the object is *kahanshin*

or the lower half of the body, more specifically *kafukubu* (the lower abdomen region). *O-shiri* or *o-ketsu* are ordinary, polite words for the buttocks and hips. If they're used without the honorific prefix *o-*, they sound slangy and rough—the Japanese equivalent of ass, can, or bum. Thus, women rarely say simply *shiri* or *ketsu*.

Ketsu is an alternative pronunciation of *ana*, which means hole. A large buttocks in Japanese is *ōki-na o-shiri* or, more vulgarly, *dekai ketsu*. *Oppai mo o-shiri mo ōkii* can be translated as she's really got tits and ass.

Kanojo wa shiri ga omoi (heavy) does not mean she has a big butt, but that she is lazy or sluggish. *Shiri ga karui* (light) *onna* or *shiri-garu onna* refers to a promiscuous woman or a woman with loose morals. *Shiri ga nagai hito* is a person who overstays his welcome. And *shiri ni shikareteru* (to be under pressure) means henpecked.

Ikketsu shugi (single-hole-ism) is a man who is faithful to one woman, (his wife) for his whole life. And *donketsu*, *biriketsu*, and *donjiri* all mean the tail end in any kind of game or contest.

Let's move on to pubic hair. *Mae* is a compound consisting of *ma* (eye) and *e* (towards). In underground language *mae* refers specifically to the private parts that are located on the front of the body. Common to both sexes, *mae no ke* (front hair) is the pubic hair. The most popular colloquial expression for pubic hair, however, is *asoko no ke*. *Inmō* literally means the hair on the shady part. *Mō* is an alternative pronunciation of the character for *ke*, which, incidentally, is the character used for the Mao in Mao-tse Tung. *Shimo no ke* or *shita no ke* are translated as the hair below, whereas *shimo no byōki* (lower sickness) means venereal disease.

Euphemistic literary expressions for pubic hair include *shigemi* (thicket), *kusamura* (bush), and *kageri* (shade). The trendiest word is simply *hea* (hair), and the *hea ronsō* (pubic hair controversy) continues around the issue of how much pubic hair can be shown in publications and films. As of the spring of 1994, pubic hair can be shown, so long as it is *wareme o misenai* (not showing the slit).

Most Japanese pubic hair is not *makige* or *kusege* (curly or kinky hair), but *chokumō* (straight), and the color is *makkuro* (jet black).

When one has rather thick pubic hair, it is described as *ke ga koi* (thick hair). Another ordinary expression is *kebukai,* which is a compound adjective consisting of *ke* and *fukai* (deep and dense). Slangy synonyms for this are *janguru* (jungle), *moja-moja* (thick, disorderly hair), *gowa-gowa no ke* (belly bristles), *fusa-fusa* (thick and straight), *o-shishi* (lion), *biibā-chan* (beaver), *anaguma* (badger), *kuma no yō-na ke* (literally, bear-like hair) or *kuma onna* (bear woman), and *tawashi* (scrub brush).

When a woman has sparse pubic hair, she is *ke ga usui* (thin). *Poya-poya* and *chobo-chobo* also refer to thin pubic hair. The slangy *paipan* means no hair at all, and is derived from a mahjong term that refers to the bare, white tiles used in the game. Some synonyms are *kawarake* (unglazed earthenware), *moya-moya* (thin), and *mumō* (no hair).

2

The Sexual Act

(seikōi)

Nowadays, regardless of age, the most popular expression for *seikōi* (the act of sex) is *etchi* (lewdness, dirty thing), with its derivative adjective *(etchi-na)* and derivative verb *(etchi suru)*. *Etchi* comes from jargon used by female students in the early 50s, and it has had, for a slang expression, a rather long lifespan. At first it meant a vulgar man, originating from the first letter of the word *hentai* (perverted). Later it was used in Seiichi Funahashi's novel *Shiroi Magyo* (*White Devil Fish*) and became a popular slang word.

Etchi doesn't sound as severe as *hentai* or *sukebei,* common terms for a lech, and now is used even by small children. It has also become a verb, *etchi suru,* which is the most acceptable way of talking about sexual intercourse or other sexual acts. It has wide use, such as *etchi-go* (lewd talk), *etchi-bideo* (pornographic video), *etchi-bon* (dirty book), *etchi (-na) hanashi* (sex talk), and *etchi-na eiga* (porno film). *Etchi* has indeed become a national slang word and is even used by large newspapers.

Common usage would be *etchi-na koto shinai de* (don't be so lewd), or *kinō kare to etchi shichatta* (I had sex with my boyfriend yesterday).

Some other words for sexual intercourse include *hameru* and *hame-hame suru* (literally, bury it, or fuck), *dashi-ire* (in and out), *nuki-sashi* (stroke), *sōnyū suru* (to insert), and *koshi o tsukau* (to use one's hips or waist).

One characteristic of the Japanese language is its widespread use of onomatopeia. Some onomatopoetic expressions for hot and heavy intercourse are *ban-ban yaru* (to bang), *zubo-zubo yaru* (to thrust or ram noisily), *zuba-zuba yaru* (to pile drive), *busu-busu yaru* (to pierce), *gui-gui yaru* (to push up), and *zun-zun tsukau* (to use a pestle).

For softer sex, you can use the expressions *suka-suka yaru* (to thrust softly), *kunyu-kunyu suru* (to fuck with a soft grinding action), or *peka-peka suru* (shallow fucking). *Hongoshi* is literally real waist movement. *Nuki-sashi naranai* comes from *nuki* (pulling), *sashi* (sticking in), and *naranai* (cannot do). The original meaning refers to the fear of being seen while having sex, i.e., what should we do if we're caught in the act—just go on or stop? The expression is also used as an adjective to describe something pressing, urgent, or imminent.

Other synonyms for *etchi suru* include *karada o awasu* (to unite both bodies), *itadaku* (to take or receive), *mi o makasu* (to yield the body to), *ajiwau* (to taste or savor), *mono ni suru* (literally, to make a thing one's own, acquire), *saigo made iku* (to go all the way), *saigo no issen o kosu* (to cross the final border) and the slangy *yatchau* and *komasu,* both meaning to frig. *Yatchau* comes from the verb *yaru,* and *komasu* literally means to give or to do with one's will. Additionally, *ireru* and *insāto suru* both mean to put it in, insert, or enter.

Among terms that should only be used by men are *issen majieru* (to fight a battle), *itadaku* (to take or score), *te o dasu* (to fiddle with), *te o tsukeru* (to lay hands on), *hairu* or *ireru* (to enter or to put in), and *okasu* (to rape).

The female counterparts—Japan still being a highly male-dominated society—are always passive in form, such as *yaraseru* (to let a man do it), *mi o makaseru* (to give oneself to), *ageru* (to give), *ukeireru* (to accept or receive), *mi o hiraku* (to offer oneself to), and *okasareru* or *yaraseru* (to be raped).

Buchikomu (to ram) is a slangy verb meaning to throw

or strike something violently. It can also be used to describe the action of a man forcing himself into a woman. *Nejikomu* (to screw it in) and *tsukkomu* (to poke it in) are similar to *buchikomu*. The verb suffix *-komu* connotes the use of force.

Here's a typical exchange two young women might have.

Doko made itta no? B? C? (How far did you go with him? B? C?)

Un! Mada A made! (No way! We only went up to A!)

Among the younger generation, the letters of the English alphabet, namely, A, B, C, D, and E, mean the various stages of sexual relationships. Just as with the English terms first base, second base, and so on, A refers to kissing, B to caressing the breasts or light petting, half C (pronounced *hāfu shii* or *hanbun shii)* to heavy petting, C to intercourse, D to pregnancy, and E to abortion. They are used as a way of avoiding direct expressions, and are still used among high school students (though not as much as they used to be in the 70s and 80s).

A newer description is *wan, tsū, surii,* where *wan* (one) is to kiss, *tsū* (two) is to touch, and *surii* (three) is to have sex. When the police are questioning juvenile delinquents or suspected young troublemakers, it is said that they now use these terms rather than the words for kissing, petting, and intercourse.

As for the A stage, the terms *kisu* (kiss) or *kisu suru* (to kiss) are understandable among people of all ages. *Kuchizuke* (literally, mouth touching) is also used, in a more literary sense. The latest expression is *chū suru, chū* being another onomatopeia for kiss.

Pettingu is now regarded as a Japanese word. There are alternatives, *ichatsuku* and *icha-icha suru,* which mean to flirt with, fondle, or be lovey-dovey. *Mune ni sawaru* (to touch the breasts) is a very straightforward expression, also used to describe a typical form of sexual harassment. If you want to be rather vulgar, you can use the term *momi-momi suru* for touching the breasts. *Momu* is a verb meaning to massage and, when doubled for emphasis, implies sexual behavior. Even dirtier-sounding are the verbs *ijiru* or *ijikuru* (to play with the finger). The object of these latter two is not necessarily the breasts.

The old Japanese for *hāfu shii* or heavy petting is *chichikuriau,* which means to pet or caress one another. There is no connection with *chichi* of the breasts, although many Japanese themselves are under the mistaken impression that there is. According to the authoritative *Kojien* dictionary, the expression is onomatopoetic, coming from the sounds of petting. *Dakiau* (to embrace), *betatsuku,* and *beta-beta suru* (to flirt with) all refer to heavy petting as well.

Verbs associated with heavy petting can vary from the simple *sawaru* (to touch), *ijiru* or *masaguru* (to finger or grope), to the more descriptive *kosuru* or *sasuru* (to stroke or massage), *nigiru* or *nigi-nigi suru* (to grasp), *shigoku* (to stroke or rub), *jirasu* (to tease), *tsumamu* (to pinch), and *yubi o ireru* (to insert a finger).

Somewhere between *hāfu shii* and C, though perhaps closer to C, we come to oral sex. *Shikkusu nain,* the English 69, refers to simultaneous oral sex. Fellatio is *shakuhachi,* from the so-named Japanese flute. The act of fellatio is *shakuhachi o suru* (to play the flute). *O-fera,* from the English fellatio, is popular among young people.

Conversely, cunnilingus in Japanese becomes *hāmonika* (harmonica or mouth organ). So, *shakuhachi to hāmonika no gassō* (a flute and harmonica ensemble) is synonymous with *shikkusu nain*. Verbs such as *nameru* (to lick), *taberu* (to eat), *picha-picha nameru* (to lap), and *shaburu* and *o-shaburi suru* (to suck or lick) all refer to oral sex. *Ōmatabiraki* is spread-eagle, a position often adopted in oral sex. *Kunni,* from the English, is popular slang.

Oral sex usually leads to sexual intercourse, so we're

now quite safely within C. When one feels horny, some of the most common expressions are *mō gaman dekinai—kimi* (or *anata*) *ga hoshii* (I can't stand it any longer—I want you). *Gaman* is a commonly used word for endurance or perseverance. Other more common euphemisms include *konya wa sabishii* (I feel lonely tonight) and *watashi no apāto ni yoranai?* (won't you drop by my apartment?).

The most popular and direct expression, however, is simply *shitai* (I want to do it) from the verb *suru*. *Yaritai* from the verb *yaru* means the same thing, but it's regarded as a male expression. *Are ga shitai* (I want to do that), *kimi to yaritai* (I want to do it with you), *ii koto shitai* (I want to do a nice thing), and, more directly, *kimi* (or *anata*) *to netai* (I want to sleep with you) are all euphemisms for I want to have sex with you.

Other colloquial verbs are *are o suru* (to do that), *nani o suru* (to do that thing), *itasu* (to do), and *neru* (to sleep with). One gentler expression is *aishiau* (literally, to love each other, or to make love). In addition, there are expressions such as *ikenai koto suru* (to do something no good or wrong), and *warui koto suru* (to do something bad), which also mean to have sex.

But the absolutely most basic (and base) word is *o-manko suru*, which should be used with great caution—never in public—and only with one's sexual partner or spouse. As is typical in Japanese, there are numerous words coined from *o-manko*. *Giriman* is marital duty or obligatory love-making with one's wife. *Giri* is the Japanese word for obligation. *Tama ni wa giriman shinai to mazui yo*, then, would be translated as your wife will be frustrated unless you service her once in a while. *Tetsuman* is all-night fucking. (An all-night mahjong session, by the way, is also called *tetsuman*.) *Asaman* and *hiruman* (*asa* is morning, and *hiru* is noon or daytime) mean morning fuck and daytime fuck or matinee, neither of which is very popular as yet in Japan.

Jōji is a love affair. When used as a verb, it means to have sexual intercourse or to have an affair, as in *jōji o motsu.* Some other literary euphemisms include *kankei* (relation or relationship), *sei kankei* (sexual relationship), and *nikutai kankei* (carnal relationship). *Fukai naka* (deep relationship) and *ii naka* (good relationship) can both be translated as intimacies. The noun *majiwari* and the corresponding verb *majiwaru* refer to intercourse. *Itonami* (business or performance), *himegoto* (secret relationship), and *nuregoto* (wet relationship) are some more words for love-making.

Now we'd like to introduce a few words referring to the first sexual experience *(hatsu taiken).* In Japan, as is the case most everywhere in the world today, the age of *hatsu taiken* is gradually getting younger. A female virgin is *shojo,* and a male virgin is *dōtei. Shojo o ushinau* (to lose one's virginity), *shojo o ageru* (to give one's virginity), *shojo o ubau* (to steal a girl's virginity), and *onna ni naru* (to become a woman) are other expressions for the first experience. A man's first sexual experience can also be called *fude oroshi. Fude* is a brush made of hair used in Japanese calligraphy; here it is a euphemism for penis. *Oroshi* means first-time use. The bridal night is *shoya,* and the consummation of a marriage is referred to as *toko iri* (literally, bed entry).

The first sexual experience of the year is called *hime-hajime.* The day for this activity in the highly structured and rigidly scheduled society of Japan is said to be January 2, though we're sure there are a few cheaters out there somewhere. The *hime* in this expression can be construed in three ways: *o-hime-sama* is princess, *himegoto* is a secret deed, and *himei* is a scream. *Hajime* means the beginning or the first. It has been reported in the press that some women's rights groups have taken exception to the term *hime-hajime,* claiming that it is discriminatory against women. Why, they ask, can we not use the term *tono-hajime* (*tono* is prince, lord, or gentleman) when the initiative is taken by the woman? Perhaps the best solution would be to call it *toko-hajime* (the first bed).

Teenagers in Japan are becoming increasingly sexually active. The Japanese call such activity *momoiro yugi* (pink pastime) or *hi-asobi* (fire play). The police solemnly call it *fujun isei koyu* (impure heterosexual conduct).

As a result of increased *fujun isei koyu*, more and more young girls are getting pregnant. The polite, formal word for pregnancy is *ninshin. Ninshin suru* means to be pregnant. Colloquially one can also say *kodomo ga dekita* (to have made a child) or simply *dekita* or *dekichatta. Haramu* means to conceive.

As for the panting and moaning of love-making, there are expressions such as *ano koe* (that voice), *ano toki no koe* (the voice at that time), and *nami-goe (nami* means wave, and here it refers to a voice that rises and falls like waves on the shore).

In addition, *aegu* is to pant and sigh, *aegi-goe* is a panting voice, *yogari-goe* means the voice of pleasure, *naki-goe* means a crying voice, *nakidasu* is to shriek out, *wameku* is to scream or screech, and *sūhā* (from *sū-sū* and *hā-hā*) is an onomatopoeia for panting and gasping. Thus, cheap pornographic movies are referred to as *sūhā-mono*.

During the act, some of the most common utterances are *aa ii* or *ii wa* (it's good), *motto yatte* (do it more), *motto fukaku* (deeper), and *motto tsuyoku* (harder). You get the picture.

The common expression for coming or having an orgasm is *iku,* which means to go. In the Japanese way of thinking, when one reaches a climax, the mind goes away from the body. *Ki o yaru* literally means to send out one's mind. Another expression is *tengoku e iku* (to go to heaven). Japanese women who are on the verge of having an orgasm will sob out *mō iku! Itte* (come) and *ki o yatte* (spend it) are imperative expressions. When a woman says *kite* (come), it means put it inside me.

Other synonyms for *iku* are *shinu* (to die), *shinda* (to have died), *shisshin suru* (to be in a trance), *shoten suru* (to go to heaven), *bakuhatsu suru* (to explode or blast off), *fukujōshi suru* (*fukujōshi* literally means death riding), *hateru* (to end), *nobori tsukeru,* (to climax), and *doku-doku yaru* (to come gushingly).

Sometimes women pretend to have an orgasm, and there are expressions for this in Japanese, too. *Iku furi o suru* is to play or pretend, with *furi* meaning false show or pretense. *Itta furi o suru* means to pretend to have come.

Kanjita furi o suru is to pretend to enjoy. And *engi suru* and *o-shibai suru* both literally mean to put on a play. *Engi* and *shibai* both mean a play. Another technique for pretending is *sumata*, in which the penis is inserted between the legs instead of into the vagina. This position is allegedly very popular in the sex industry in Japan now because it's less risky than actual intercourse.

There are 48 styles of sexual positions, called *shijūhatte uraomote* (48 styles, front and back), and numerous variations. Their poetic names are also noteworthy. Since they are difficult to describe and translate into English, we will introduce just a few.

Honte is the orthodox man-above position, which includes the missionary position; this is also called *honmadori. Agehahonte* (swallowtail butterfly), *ajirohonte* (fishing net style), and *sekireihonte* (wagtail) are minor variations on *honte,* mainly having to do with whether the woman's legs are around her partner's waist, buttocks, or thighs.

Chausu (literally, handmill for tea) is the woman-above position, referred to as coffee grinder or meat grinder in English. There are many variations. *Ushirodori* is the rear-entry position, and *yokodori* is the side-by-side position. *Ushiro* means rear, and *yoko* is side.

Mukudori and *tomoe* are 69 or simultaneous oral sex positions. *Tomoe* is a perfect circle. Nowadays, as we have said, *shikkusu nain* (69) is commonly used as well.

Here are some expressions used when one is close to climax. *Motto yatte, motto tsuite* is fuck me harder. *Tsuku* means to push or drive. *Sansen isshin* (after three shallow moves, thrusting once deeply), is a popular sexual technique. *Torokeru* is to melt, and *torokesō* means melting or it feels like I'm melting. *Oku ni ataru* is literally to feel it deep inside.

Kibun o dasu is to get excited. *Nureru* is to become wet or lubricated. Some onomatopoetic expressions for being wet include *gusho-gusho* and *bisho-bisho* (flooded or oozy), *nuru-nuru* (slippery), and *gusshori nureru* (dripping). Love juice is called *tsuyu* or *o-tsuyu*. *O-tsuyu ga ōi* describes a woman who is very wet.

Atsui mono (hot thing) means semen. So do *miruku* (milk) and *yoguruto* (yohgurt) because of the similarity in appearance. In order to keep the *yoguruto* from spurting in the wrong place, the Japanese commonly use condoms (*kondōmu* or *kon-chan*). Some more contemporary synonyms are *sukin* (skin), *gomu* (rubber), and *sakku* from the Dutch *roede-zak,* meaning rubber sack.

When the usual sexual outlet is denied, people often turn to *masu* or masturbation. *Shiko-shiko* is an onomatopoetic expression meaning push-push or fuck, but it can also be used to mean masturbation with a slow, but steady, hand action. *Senzuri* and its more slangy inverted form *zurisen* also refer to male masturbation. These words come from *sen kai kosuru* (to rub or jerk a thouand times). It's interesting that female masturbation in slang is called *manzuri* (rub off). *Man* as a numerical unit that means ten thousand, but it can also be thought of as an abbreviation of *manko* (vagina).

The most common related verb is *masu-(o)kaku* (to jerk off), which comes from *masutābēshon* (masturbation) and *kaku* (to stroke). The verb *kaku* alone has the meaning of to jerk off or jack off. Thus, when a person indulges excessively in masturbation, others might jeeringly call him *kaki-sugi*, *-sugi* being a suffix meaning too much or excessive. *Jika hatsuden suru* (literally, to self-generate electricity) means to beat the meat.

Other rather euphemistic expressions are *hitori asobi* (to play with oneself), *tenagusami* (finger or hand play), *nigi-nigi suru* (to grip), and *o-supe* (hand job or blow job), which comes from a special service offered at *sōpurando* (massage parlors).

There are, of course, a number of rather pedantic expressions that don't sound very good in Japanese, such as *ji-i, jitoku,* and *shu-in. Ji-i,* which is a medical term, literally means self-consolation; figuratively, playing with oneself. *Ji-i o suru* is the verb form. *Jitoku,* now rather archaic, can be literally translated as self-abuse. And *shu-in* is a compound word made up of *shu* (hand) and *in* (indulgence or going to excess). It can be translated as solitary vice.

Tobashikko (literally, who-can-shoot-it-further game) is the equivalent of circle jerk. Boys will be boys the world over.

3

Homosexuality

(dōseiai)

Because the Japanese still expect everyone to marry and have children, regardless of their sexual orientation, most Japanese will tell you that they don't know any homosexuals. What this really means, though, is that they don't know that they know any homosexuals, or, if they do, they are playing the old *honne/tatemae* game again.

In any case, there are plenty of Japanese words for homosexuals, homosexuality, and related practices. The official word for homosexuality is the rather literal *dōseiai,* which means same sex love. It can be used both for male homosexuals and for lesbians.

The most common and colloquial expression for a male homosexual, however, is *okama.* It comes from *kama* (iron pot or pot for cooking rice). *Kama* was first adopted as a slang synonym of *ketsu* (ass) or *ketsu no ana* (anus). *Kare wa okama (da)* thus means he's a homosexual or he's gay. *Kare wa kamakke ga aru* can be translated as he has homosexual leanings. In this expression, *-kke* means tendency or inclination.

In English the word queer has been used to describe male homosexuals. In Japanese, too, people might say *kare wa hen da* or *aitsu wa okashii,* both meaning he looks queer or strange. *Okama bā* is a gay bar. The most popular *okama bā* area in Tokyo is Shinjuku 2-chome.

Other contemporary expressions for male homosexuals are *homo* and *gei,* both borrowed from the English. *Homodachi,* coined from *homo* and the *dachi* in *tomodachi* (friend) is used for one's male homosexual lover.

119

Recently, there has been a dramatic increase in hormone injections and sex change operations, resulting in *nyū hāfu* (new half). *Shii mēru* (from the English she-male) is also heard, but the expression *nyū hāfu* is more popular at present. Thanks to operations and injections the breasts grow, the male organs atrophy, and some *nyū hāfu* even undergo *tama-nuki* or *sao-nuki* operations and have artificial vaginas constructed. *(Tama-nuki* means an absence of balls, and *sao-nuki* is an absence of the rod.)

Kagema was used in the Edo era to describe a young homosexual prostitute who served at banquets. *Kagema* literally means shady room, perhaps because what took place behind the bright banquet hall was shady business in a shady room. It has been reported that *kagema-jaya* (gay tea houses) thrived during the Edo era—a relative equivalent to today's gay bars.

Going back to current expressions, *okama, homo, gei,* and *danshoku* are all quite popular. The last one is the most formal and literally means color (or lust) with a male. Color-related words, as will be described more fully below, are often used figuratively in Japanese to refer to sexual matters.

Some verbs used to describe acts of male homosexuality are *okama o horu* (to dig), *homoru* (a shortened form of *homo-suru*), *gei to asobu* (to play with a gay), and *danshoku ni fukeru* (to indulge in pederasty). *Kiku o tsumu* (to pluck a chrysanthemum) is a rather poetic term. *Kiku* (chrysanthemum) symbolizes the anus, and *tsumu* is to pick or pluck.

Among *okama,* there is the male role *(otoko-yaku)* and the female role *(onna-yaku).* In underground terms the former is called *tachi* and the latter *neko* or *anko.* *Tachi* comes from *kabuki,* where performers are divided into two types. *Tachi-kata* (literally, standing section), means actors and dancers who perform standing up, and *ji-kata* (literally, ground section) refers to the orchestra and chorus, who are sitting. *Tachi* and its verb *tatsu* also mean erection and to erect; thus *tachi* was adopted in homosexual jargon to mean the so-called dominant male partner. The expression *ne-tachi* refers to a man who behaves as a woman except in bed. And *neru to tatsu mono nāni?* (what is it that stands up when you lie down?) is a favorite joke to mean a man's penis. The female, or *neko* role comes from *neru-ko* (sleeping or lying part) and *anko* comes from *aneko* (younger sister or young girl).

Here are some words for lesbians. A counterpart for *okama* (male homosexual) is *onabe,* but this term is not used much anymore. In Japanese, people say *nabe kama* to mean kitchen utensils, as well as symbolic things that a bride needs to get married. While *kama* is a pot, *nabe* is a pan. But the most popular expression is *rezubian* or *rezu,* as in *ano ko wa rezu da* (that girl is a lesbian).

Esu (S) is an abbreviation of the English sister and refers to the early stages of lesbianism, usually during high school. *Eru* (L) from lesbian is also used euphemistically.

Kai-awase literally means putting two shells together, a game played in the old days, but as slang it is used to refer to lesbian conduct.

Ainame (mutual licking) refers to women's 69 or simultaneous cunnilingus. *Tomogui* (devouring each other) and *mesu-mesu* (female and female) are synonyms.

Rezukke is a typical adjective used to describe a woman with lesbian tendencies, while *rezuru* is the verb for engaging in lesbian activities. In underground terms, a lesbian who plays the masculine role is called *tachi* or *o-tachi* (butch or bull dyke), the same as male homosexuals. Its counterpart is *neko* or *o-nene*, for the partner who takes the female role. *Tachi* indicates the standing role and *neko* the lying part.

Lesbians sometimes use *seigu* (sexual tools), more colloquially referred to as *otona no omocha* (adult toys).

Harigata is an archaic term for dildo; some more modern expressions are *baiburētā* or *baibu* (vibrator) and *dendō-kokeshi* (motor-operated *kokeshi* doll). You will understand why the word *kokeshi* (wooden doll, a product of the Tohoku region) came to be used in this way if you look at the back of one of these dolls some time; it looks like an erect penis. Needless to say, it's not just lesbians who use *otona no omocha*. Stores selling such sexual paraphernalia are easy to find in the seedier districts of Japanese cities and major towns.

4

The Ejaculation Industry

(shasei sangyō)

A prostitution prevention act *(baishun bōshi hō)* was passed in 1956, making prostitution illegal in Japan after April, 1958. In reality, however, unless a woman is forced into prostitution or girls under 18 years old are involved, there is no enforcement, and this law is often called *zaru hō* (a law full of loopholes). Though we're discussing the sex industry here, the etymology of *zaru hō* is both interesting and relevant. If you try to scoop up water in a *zaru* (bamboo basket), all the water will drain through, rendering the effort meaningless. Thus, the expression *zaru hō* means a powerless or useless law.

Before this law was passed, prostitution was authorized in particular districts of every city in Japan. These licensed quarters—or quarters for license, if you will—were called *yūkaku* (playing quarters), *iro-machi* (literally, color district, or sex district), and, after World War II, *akasen* (literally, red line) or *akasen kuiki* (red-lined district). These latter two expressions come from the fact that the police circled the pleasure quarters with red lines on their maps. All of these terms can be translated as red-light district.

Among the *yūkaku* of old, Yoshiwara in Tokyo, Shimabara in Kyoto, and Nakamura in Nagoya were particularly famous.

Sangyōchi and *nigyōchi* were other pleasure districts where geisha were available for dissipation and eventually prostitution. *Sangyō* literally means three kinds of businesses: *geisha oki-ya* (geisha house), *ryōri-ya* (Japanese restaurant), and *machiai* (dating house). The *nigyōchi* consists of only the first two. Akasaka, Yanagibashi, Tsukiji and Shinbashi in Tokyo, as well as Ponto-chō and Gion in Kyoto, were famous geisha districts.

In those days, *baishun-yado (baishun* literally means selling spring, and *yado* is an inn), *inbai-yado* (house of prostitution), and *aimai-yado* (literally, ambiguous house) all referrred to whorehouses or brothels.

Despite nearly four decades of prohibition of prostitution in Japan, the business is still thriving. There are many variations on the way it is practiced, and it flourishes quite openly. In fact, we could say that Japan is a *baishun ōkoku* (prostitution kingdom).

The sex industry is referred to as *shasei sangyō* (ejaculation industry), and it employs more than 50,000 women nationwide. The women who work in *sōpurando, fasshon massāji,* and *pinku saron* described below often earn more than 10 to 15 thousand dollars a month, tax-free. In the past, most women in the sex industry were over 30, but since 1985, the lure of quick money has attracted numerous young women in their 20s called *shinjinrui* (new type of person). This phenomenon will be discussed in detail later.

Just as there are various types of prostitution and ways of engaging in the business, there are also many words for prostitute in Japanese. The most widely used and popular term is *baishunfu,* which is also a legal term. *Baishun* (selling spring) implies the sale of something fresh and beautiful, and *fu* is written with the character for woman.

Inbaifu literally means selling or seller of obscenity and refers both to prostitution and prostitutes. *Shōfu* is a general expression for a prostitute of any type. *Inbaifu,* for its part, has the connotation of a low-class hustler. The term *yasu-inbai* is also very common, and it means a cheap pro.

Machi no onna (street girl) and *yoru no onna* (night

girl) are also commonly used terms for street walker or hooker. One can also simply say *sutoriito gāru* (street girl or street walker). In acutality, there aren't very many street walkers in Japan any more, except in some of the seedier areas. The sex industry, as we will amply document below, has gone, if not underground, at least indoors.

Yoru no himegimi (night princess) is a rather polite variation of *yoru no onna*. *Yoru no chō* (literally, night butterfly), on the other hand, refers to a bar or cabaret hostess; these women do not necessarily prostitute themselves. *Hitoyo-zuma* or *ichiya-zuma* (literally, one-night wife; colloquially, one-night stand) are other euphemistic terms.

Geisha (officially *geigi*) are usually not prostitutes. *Gei* is translated as accomplishments, and *geisha* originally meant a woman full of accomplishments. But later, it came to connote a girl who appeared at expensive banquets to play music, sing, dance, and entertain guests, sometimes also providing sexual services on occasions when a client would offer a sizeable sum of money. *Geiko* and *maiko* refer to young geisha. In Kyoto tourists delight in seeing glimpses of *maiko* (literally, dancing girl) walking to their next job.

After a certain age a geisha usually becomes a kept woman *(kakowaremono, mekake,* or *o-mekake),* living off a former patron. The latter two words come from *me o kakeru, me* being eye, and *kakeru* meaning to cast. *Kago no tori* (caged bird) is another expression for a kept woman, not necessarily a geisha.

Jorō was commonly used for prostitutes before the prostitution prevention act was passed. It is said that *jorō* came from *jōrō,* which meant noble woman or court lady in the very old days. As Japanese language tends to be extremely polite, even in reference to prostitutes, the honorific *o-* is often added to create the word *o-jorō*. In the days before prostitution was banned, the terms *jorō-*

ya (whorehouse) and *jorōkai* (going to a brothel) were commonly used.

Those of you who have attended *kabuki* performances have probably seen the famous *oiran* plays. *Oiran,* a now archaic term, means a high-class prostitute in the *yūkaku* or *kuruwa* (both mean pleasure quarters) during the Edo era. The etymology of this word is quite interesting. It is said that the younger prostitutes called the older ones *oira ga nē-san* (literally, our elder sister—*oira* meant I or we in the language of Edo). This phrase, in turn, was shortened to *oiran.* The *oiran* wore luxurious kimono and were exorbitantly expensive to procure. They were the *kōkyū baishunfu* (high-class call girls) of the day.

Jorō were forced to speak a special language called *kuruwa kotoba* (pleasure quarters language), in which, for example, *watashi* (I) became *wachiki* and *de arimasu* or *desu* (auxiliary verbs for to be) became *de arinsu.* The reason for *kuruwa kotoba* is simple. Many of the *oiran* were sold by their impoverished rural families and sent to Edo. This practice was called *miuri* or *jinshin baibai.* (*Miuri* means sale of the body, and *jinshin baibai* is human traffic.) In order to cover up rustic speech patterns, which might have offended wealthy and sophisticated customers, a special dialect called *kuruwa kotoba* was invented. One can still see touristy *oiran* shows in Tokyo's Yoshiwara as part of organized sightseeing bus tours.

During the postwar Occupation, Tokyo's Yūrakuchō district was one of the most popular hangouts for street girls who were trying to solicit business from American soldiers. These girls were called *pan-pan* or *pan-pan gāru.* The etymology of this term is uncertain, but one of the more popular theories is that when a man wanted a street girl, he would clap his hands making a sound like *pan-pan.* The derogatory *pansuke* was also used. These words are now archaic, except for *panma,* which combines *pan-pan* and *anma* (masseuse). Men on business

trips often call on the services of *panma*, and there are
any number of seedy hotels in Japanese cities that are
eager to accommodate them.

Baita (literally, selling woman; colloquially, whore) is a
very disdainful expression for a prostitute that is also
heard when one really wants to insult a woman. For
example, a cuckolded husband might scream at his wife
kono baita, dete (i)ke! (get out of here, you whore!).
Abazure (hussy, hooker) can also be used in place of
baita. Finally, there is the expression *puro,* which is said
to come from prostitute or professional and is now used
as a general term to mean a professional woman in the
sex industry.

When women such as office girls, housewives, or
college students engage in sex services on a part-time
basis in order to make extra money, they are called *semi-
puro*.

Nowadays, the prostitution business is thriving in new
guises, such as *sōpurando,* pink cabarets, and nude
shows. *Sōpurando* (abbreviated as *sōpu)* are perhaps
the most popular form of commercialized sex in Japan,
and they are located not only in major cities, but in
smaller cities as well.

When *sōpu* first started appearing in Tokyo's Yoshiwara
area, the existing establishments were called Turkish
baths (*Toruko*). In 1984 they were re-named *sōpu* in
response to heavy criticism from Turkish citizens who
considered the name *Toruko* an insult to Turkey and its
people. But no matter the name—the routine is still the
same, and many evening papers have special columns
describing *sōpurando* around town, their prices, ambi-
ence, and services provided.

The basic routine in a *sōpu* goes like this. The customer selects a girl from a photo display. He pays the
admission charge at the front desk and the girl he has
chosen welcomes him into a private room. The admission charge is roughly a third of the total. The balance is

paid to the girl after she does her job, which is quite different from the advance payment that's the rule in the West. The total price is, on average, 30,000 yen. If the service provided is really outstanding, though, the customer may give the hostess a tip or bonus.

Services offered are determined by individual *sōpurando,* and, of course, some variations on techniques can be introduced by the hostesses themselves. At inexpensive *sōpu,* there are no fancy bathing techniques, and each customer is allotted only 50 minutes or so. At the very expensive *sōpu,* which charge 50,000 to 80,000 yen, the customer will be treated to a bath, oral sex, and sexual intercourse. Then he can rest some with Scotch or brandy and go on for a second round. At such *sōpu,* a hostess will spend up to two hours with a customer. At medium-priced establishments, in the 35,000 yen range, the time is a bit shorter—about an hour and a half.

Due to the threat of AIDS, *nama honban* (literally, raw performance; figuratively, "bareback riding") has gradually fallen from favor and has been replaced by *gomu-tsuki* (sex with a condom; *gomu* here means rubber, and, by association, condom, and *-tsuki* is a suffix meaning with) or *sukin shiyō* (skin-use, or condom) services. *O-miyage* (literally, souvenir; in this context, sexual disease) means a sexually transmitted disease from a prostitute. Many Japanese believe non-Japanese more likely to have AIDS, and most *sōpurando* have, in recent times, become off-limits to foreigners regardless of race.

Although *sōpurando* regulations are occasionally tightened, they are subject to little real enforcement. Thus, they are really nothing more than good old-fashioned prostitution with the protective cover of a few bubbles. The girls, probably to everybody's relief—theirs and the customers included—are off the streets, but still plying the same old trade. The *sōpurando* districts scattered about the nation are the modern equivalent of the old *akasen kuiki* (red-light districts). It is said that there are more than 1,500 *sōpurando* in Japan, employing some 20,000 hostesses. And the services provided are said to be much more relaxed, cleaner, and amusing than in the old whorehouses.

At whorehouses in the past, a prostitute wouldn't really let down her hair during her first meeting with a customer. This first encounter was called *furi* (casual) or *ichigen* (first sight or first appearance). *Furi* comes from the verb *furari to yoru,* which means to drop by casually. The second time was called *ura* (literally, reverse side). *Ura o kaesu* (literally, turn over) meant to go to a certain prostitute for the second time. This expression came from *rakugo* theater, in which each performer sits on one cushion. When the performer leaves the stage and another comes to take his place, the cushion is turned over. The third time was called *najimi* (literally, familiar customer or regular customer).

At a present-day *sōpurando,* a hostess will treat her customer as a welcome guest from the first encounter. Why the difference? In the old days, prostitutes served under a kind of bondage system. They couldn't be freed until they had worked for a certain period of time (*nenki*—period of service). And even then, they were often exploited by their bosses. Every prostitute had a sad story to tell. The famous playwright Chikamatsu Monzaemon often wrote on these themes, and his work can be seen even now at *kabuki* theaters. Today, on the contrary, hostesses at *sōpurando* are in the profession of their own free will. The *sōpurando* owner's take is not particularly high, and the girls can earn a great deal of money if they work hard, although there are many who are exploited by *himo* (literally, string; figuratively, pimp).

A *honban* (literally actual performance, as opposed to rehearsal; in this case, intercourse) course, for example, usually costs about 30,000 yen. If a hostess receives two-thirds of this, and services three to five customers a day, she can easily earn some two million yen a month. After a year or so of this, she may retire to marry, nobody being any the wiser.

The most famous *sopurando* zone in Japan is Tokyo's Yoshiwara (which has 170 *sopu*), traditionally a red-light district. This is followed by Shinjuku in Tokyo, Ogoto in Ōtsu on Lake Biwa, Kanatsu-en in Gifu, near Nagoya, Hori-no-uchi in Kawasaki, Fukutomichō in Yokohama, Sakaecho in Chiba, Susukino in Sapporo, Fukuhara in Kobe, and Nakasu in Fukuoka, with nearly 50 *sopurando* in each. Because of the severe competition, each *sopurando* tries its best to develop new techniques. As a result, *sopurando* have become veritable wonderlands for innovations in sex and modernized prostitution.

A technique called *awa odori* (literally, bubble dance) is said to be the key to the thriving business of the *sopurando*. This technique is said to have been invented about 20 years ago by a hostess in Kawasaki, who washed her client with her bubble-covered body on an air mattress—making special use of her breasts and vagina—instead of a sponge. Within a year, this technique spread throughout the rest of the country.

Many other innovations were soon to follow. *Tokei* (literally, watch or clock) is a hostess-astride position, in which she turns her body around like the hands of a clock. *Nirinsha* (bicycle) is threesome (two hostesses, one client), and *toroika* (troika) and *sanrinsha* (tricycle) mean foursome, though by the time a customer wants to indulge in this, he may find it too expensive. *Furu kōsu* (full course) now comprises *awa odori, sōname* (kissing all over the body, including—of course—*shakuhachi,* oral sex), and *honban*.

It can be inferred that in Japan, these techniques are not often tried at home. Thus, *sopu* have gained inordinate popularity among middle-aged men.

With the stiff competition that exists in the prostitution business in Japan, however, even creative and unusual techniques may not be enough. Some *sōpurando* cater to various fantasies and have their hostesses dress up as *suchuwadesu* (stewardesses), *ama* (nuns), *jogakusei* (schoolgirls in sailor blouses), *kangofu* (nurses), *banii gāru* (bunny girls), *ninja* (black-clad spies from olden times), and *hanayome* (brides).

Sōpurando are implicitly part of the prostitution industry. But, for convenience's sake, it is construed that the business deal is negotiated in private, behind closed doors, between a hostess and her client. Therefore, the sophistry goes, it's not really prostitution. So anybody with the money can get just about any service he desires, secure in the feeling that the authorities will let well enough alone.

Another form of prostitution is the *pinku saron* (pink salon), abbreviated as *pinsaro,* where hostesses entertain the customers by going down on them and by allowing themselves to be touched. This special service always ends with a hand job or blow job using a condom and *oshibori* (wet hand towel). Occasionally, there is even intercourse in the woman-astride position. The time allotted for each customer is usually only about 30 or 40 minutes, but the hostesses are very skillful and can almost always satisfy in the given time.

The routine goes like this. Once the customer is seated, the hostess brings him a drink and has a brief conversation with him. Then, she unzips his fly, washes him with an *oshibori* and gets on with her business. Everything goes on in such a dark, noisy, atmosphere that there is little chance of being disturbed by other guests—everyone, after all, is being kept busy in similar fashion. In fact, the customers are kept so well-occupied that their beer is often left untouched.

Pinku saron usually open around 5 P.M. and, a few hours earlier if you're in the neighborhood, you can see the sanitary suppliers bringing in enormous quantities of *oshibori* and taking the used ones away. Fees at a pink salon run from 6,000 to 10,000 yen, including a can of beer and some *o-tsumami* (literally, things to be picked up and relished; figuratively, snacks or hors d'oeuvres). This moderate pricing attracts middle-aged and young men of modest means.

There used to be quite a number of housewives making part-time money as hostesses. While they were hard at work, so to speak, their children were cared for at nurseries in the salons. Now, the hostesses tend to be young girls, including college students.

More than ten years ago, there were drinking establishments called *kyatchi bā* (catch bars). Such places in Shinjuku's Kabuki-chō were the subject of considerable journalistic interest because of numerous troubles between the customers and *bōryokudan* (violent gangs) who ran the bars.

These places were called catch bars because touts called *pōtā* (porters) would catch *kamo* (literally, ducks; colloquially, suckers) and persuade them to come into certain bars where they would unknowingly be charged prohibitive sums. Once the poor saps had entered, hostesses would surround them and order cola and fruit juice without asking permission. One pitiable fellow was charged 120,000 yen for three *mizuwari* (whisky and waters), three coke highballs, and a dish of hors d'oeuvres. Others have been charged 50,000 to 60,000 yen for a few drinks.

These bars were also called *buttakuri bā* (rip-off bars). This phrase comes from the verb *buttakuru,* meaning to rob. According to the police, the porters would keep their eyes peeled for three types of people: drunks, men who seemed undecided about where they were going, and travelers apparently from the countryside. Increased anti-gang activity by the police, however, has led to the demise of these bars, one by one.

Next, we will introduce the nude show or strip show. In

Japan, all the major cities have big nude theaters; in the Kanto region, there are said to be at least 30 and they are open every day from 11 A.M. to 11 P.M.

Sutorippu shō (strip tease or nude shows) started in Japan after World War II. At that time, shows were limited to baring *oppai* (breasts). Little by little, though, dancers became increasingly bold, showing their lower halves ever so briefly.

Every new technique and trick in this business has come from the Kansai region, where the competition is severe. One such technique is *toku-dashi* (special performer/performance), which appeared there some 30 years ago. Such performers were paid more than three times what an ordinary *odori-ko* (dancing girl) would have received because they risked arrest by performing *zen suto* (totally nude shows). From there, they began to go farther and show more. *Opun* (open) and *sakasa bui* (inverted V) refer to opening up the vagina with the fingers. Bed shows featured masturbation. Also, *nyūyoku* (taking a bath) shows were popular in the summertime.

Gaijin (foreigner) shows began in 1965, the year after the Tokyo Olympics, again in the Kansai region. At that time, people were so eager to see *kinpatsu* (blond hair) that some Japanese strippers dyed their hair, both on their head and in the nether regions.

Twenty years ago, *rezu* (lesbian) shows appeared. A *rezu* show is also called *shiro-shiro* (literally, white-and-white; actually, woman-and-woman), while *shiro-kuro* (black-and-white) refers to a show performed by a man and woman.

Next to appear, along with the escalation of techniques, were *tengu* or *kaiten beddo* (revolving bed) shows. A *tengu* (goblin) is an imaginary monster with a very long, red nose that is said to live deep in the mountains and be able to fly. A *tengu* mask made of soft plastic was first used in a bed show in the early 70s in

Kansai. It fascinated the audience to see the performer plunging the long red nose into and out of her vagina.

Still, these techniques were not enough. The next idea was the *namaita* show. Up until this time, the audience had been forbidden to touch the performer or her clothes. But all this changed in the mid-70s with the *namaita* idea. This was the first time members of the audience were invited up on the stage to touch and fondle the strippers. It is said that the term *namaita* comes from two expressions. One is *nama de itazura suru,* combining *nama* (raw), and *itazura suru* (to be naughty). The other is an inversion of the idiomatic *manaita no ue no koi* (literally, carp on a chopping board), which means I am at your mercy. In the *namaita* shows, customers were allowed to touch the dancers' private parts either with their hands (after being cleaned with an *oshibori*), or with a *tengu* nose or other artificial phallus. Five years later, in 1979, the strippers began to masturbate customers on stage and finally, in the early 80s, *honban* shows were introduced.

A visit to one of these establishments at that time was really quite amusing. The customers would often do *jan-ken-pon* (paper, scissors, rock) for the girl, with the winner leaping up on the stage and stripping—usually to his socks and wristwatch. Those who succeeded in reaching orgasm—despite the scrutiny of the assembled audience—were warmly applauded; those who didn't were left to scrabble off the lighted stage with their clothes amid sniggers and ribald comments.

There is also a show called *hanadensha* (literally, floral tram; euphemistically, sexual trick show). This was named after flower-bedecked floats which ran on festive occasions but carried no passengers. The thought behind this allusion was simple: they let you see it, but won't let you ride. *Hanadensha* was commonly practiced by geisha of old, who would cut bananas, smoke cigarettes, lay eggs, or write letters using *fude* (brush) with their vaginas.

In the late 80s, *honban* shows in strip theaters disappeared due to police raids, but professional *shiro-kuro* shows and *hanadensha* are still around.

In the 80s, the ejaculation industry was enhanced by the arrival of *fasshon herusu* (fashion health) or *fasshon massāji* (fashion massage parlor), abbreviated FH, FM or *herusu*. Since their introduction on late-night TV shows as trendy businesses, the popularity of these services has been boosted by young women who have flocked to them, drawn by opportunities for no-intercourse, high-paying jobs. Since they offer *ippon nukeru* (one shoot) at a third of the price of *sōpurando*, they are patronized often by young men; unlike *sōpu,* however, the services at FH are limited to 69. More recently, in the 90s, the *imēji kurabu* (image club) has emerged. This kind of establishment specializes in staging sexual harassment and other fantasy scenarios, but like FH, FM, and *herusu,* provides only oral sex.

Among the new arrivals on the sex industry scene is the *esute kurabu* (sexual esthetic massage club for men), which have increased in number dramatically in the past two years. These male-oriented esthetic clubs offer a strained at best relation to esthetics, featuring anal finger-fucking by young women.

Sado-masochism has also become popular in the 90s, and many *sado-mazo kurabu* or *esu-emu kurabu* can be found in the Roppongi and Shinjuku areas of Tokyo. The women who play the sadist roles are called *jo-ō-sama* (literally, queen). Queens give *dorei* (slaves) various forms of *o-shioki* (discipline) using implements including ropes, whips, candlewax, and enemas. Customers wishing to play sadistic roles use ropes, whips, and *baibu* (vibrators) to *ijimeru* (torment) the women in masochistic roles, called *emujo* (literally, M-women). This costs from 25,000 to 30,000 yen for about 70 minutes, and these clubs are said to be frequented in the middle of the afternoon by executives, lawyers, and politicians who are under particularly great stress. Since no sexual intercourse is involved, *esu-emu kurabu* are not under the jurisdiction of the prostitution prevention act.

Nyū hāfu kurabu that feature homosexual sex have also recently appeared. Homosexual sex—even if it involves a male prostitute—is not subject to the prostitution prevention act, so these clubs are also allowed to operate relatively undisturbed.

Despite the fact that such explicitly obscene shows, along with *sōpurando* and *pinku saron*, are tolerated, if not quite condoned, by the government, production and sales of hard-core pornographic pictures are still tightly regulated.

It is now legal to show pubic hair in magazines and there are special publications devoted to that purpose. *Hea nūdo* (hair nudes) are, in fact, currently very popular. Prior to the 1990s, however, this was strictly forbidden. Instead, there was the so-called *biniiru-bon* boom from the mid-70s to the mid-80s. *Biniiru-bon* or *bini-bon* (literally, vinyl-covered books) made their first appearance in 1973 after a long cat-and-mouse struggle with the censorship laws. They openly carried pussy and split-beaver shots, obscured only by tiny see-through panties. These books usually contained 64 color pages and were sold at two to three times their actual production cost. They were distributed directly from the publisher to the retailer, cutting out any middlemen and making handling them very profitable.

Police in Tokyo occasionally raided publishers of *biniiru-bon* porno, making arrests, but offenders were usually released after paying fines. Most *yakuza*-related publishing companies were organized just to put out one or two such books; they were then quickly dissolved, so they were very hard to catch. Thus, pornography remained a profitable underground industry for the *yakuza*. The mid-80s finally saw this industry come grinding to a halt, as large-scale police raids confiscated hundreds of thousands of contraband books and ran publishers out of business.

At the end of 1980, the sex industry enjoyed a new fad called *nō-pan kissa* (no-panty tearoom). The idea was to have coffee shop waitresses go around serving with bare breasts, extremely short skirts, and no panties, or only *pansuto* (pantyhose). The phenomenon was trumpeted on TV programs, magazines, and evening papers, and was a hit for while with horny men of all ages. Due to the high price of the coffee, however, and perhaps the customers' sense of shame at peeking under skirts, this phenomenon lasted only six months.

After the demise of the *nō-pan kissa*, *aijin banku* (literally, lovers' banks) appeared. *Aijin banku* were basically prostitution clubs, where a high entrance fee was charged, and young women who had registered with the system were introduced to clients. Machiko Tsutsumi, the owner of one famous club called *Yūgure-zoku,* appeared on TV and advertised heavily. She made an *arakasegi* (fast buck) and achieved enormous riches in a two-year span, but was arrested under the prostitution prevention act. *Aijin banku* disappeared in 1984.

Illegal prostitution organizations known as *dēto kurabu,* or DC (date clubs), continue to bloom, however. There are large numbers of stickers advertising these date clubs stuck on public phone booths near train stations, and it is quite easy to call and arrange to meet a woman at a love hotel. The newest service provided by this kind of date club is sending a requested girl to a customer's house or apartment by car. Her male manager or pimp waits somewhere in the vicinity until she's finished.

This sort of prostitution is called *shutchō sābisu* (visiting service) or *takuhai sābisu,* which means delivery service to one's home. *Taku* is an abbreviation of *jitaku* (one's house), and *hai* is from *haitatsu* (delivery). *Taku-haibin* or *takkyubin,* is an express courier industry that has enjoyed a great deal of popularity in the last 20 years.

Demae, or delivery (as in pizza, etc.), is also used to describe this kind of call girl service. These date clubs, like fashion massage parlors, employ young women from all over the world. The price is around 20,000 to 30,000 yen for 90 minutes. There are frequent police raids, but they are almost always an ineffective *itachi gokko,* or vicious circle.

Similar services for the ladies are not as widespread, but they do exist. The latest such service, run by the *yakuza,* are the *shutchō hosuto kurabu.* Host clubs in Japan feature attractive young men who cater to female customers' every whim and desire, including, if the price is right, having sex with them. Many of these women are middle-aged and tired of being ignored by their husbands; on the other hand, some are soapland hostesses. *Shutchō hosuto kurabu,* is about the same as the *shutchō* service described above, but with the genders reversed.

Men who work in *shutchō hosuto kurabu* can have sex all they want and make money doing it. Naturally, there are many applicants for these jobs, and the key to getting hired is paying a large sum of money to the *yakuza* who organize the business. Worse, the *yakuza* can do all sorts of things to get rid of a *hosuto* once he has outlasted his usefulness. They might hire a *sakura* (decoy), or a *tsubushi-ya* (crusher, smasher). Posing as a customer, she will make up reasons to criticize the host's services. He'll then be accused of losing a very important customer, be fired, and be forced to pay damages to boot. According to a recent police report, some 30,000 victims have paid a total of 15 billion yen in the nine years since this tricky business first made its appearance in Hiroshima. The victims seldom take legal action, and the *yakuza,* realizing this, take full advantage of their victims.

In 1982, riding on the wave of the video equipment boom, *pinku bideo* (x-rated videos) appeared. These videos have come to be called *adaruto bideo* (adult videos), or *ēbui* (AV), and scores of new videos are released every month.

Most AVs have *bokashi* (obscuring) signals on the genitals, but there are *chō-usukeshi* (extremely lightly erased) videos, in which genitals and acts of sexual intercourse are almost completely visible. Just as in the U.S., these can be rented at local video stores. *Chō-* in this expression is a prefix meaning super- or ultra-, *usu* is short for *usui* (thin, weak), and *keshi* means erasure or obscurement, as in *keshi-gomu* (eraser). There are also *urabideo* (underground videos), which show everything quite explicitly and are sold through *yakuza*. These days, *AV gyaru* (adult video girls) appear quite openly as main guests on late-night TV shows.

Some more vocabulary related to pornography in Japan: *Ero-hon,* which refers to both pornographic picture books and obscene literature, comes from the English erotic book. *Ero-shashin* refers only to pornographic photographs. *Wai-bon* is literally obscene book, *wai* being the Chinese character for obscene, and *bon* being a euphonic change of *hon* (book). *Aka-hon,* or *aka-bon,* originally comes from the red *(aka)* covers used for pornographic books in the Edo era, and is still used to mean pornography.

Shun-ga are a type of *ukiyo-e* woodblock prints famous for their especially graphic pornographic images. *Shun-ga* literally means spring pictures, and the word *shun*, or spring, appears in several other amorous terms, as well. *Shun-pon* is a widely-encompassing term for pornographic literature, subsuming *shun-ga* and also including dirty texts. *Baishunfu,* literally women who sell spring, are prostitutes. *Shunjo,* or spring emotion, refers to sexual excitement.

Some other terms for pornographic literature used in the Edo era were *kōshoku-bon* and *makura-zōshi.* *Kōshoku* is sensual or erotic, while *makura* is pillow. *Zōshi* is a euphonic change of *sōshi,* which is roughly equivalent to book. Also among the older expressions is *makura-e* (literally, pillow picture), which is near in meaning to *shun-ga*.

In current usage, the most popular and contemporary expression is *poruno* as in *poruno suki?* (do you like pornography?). When a certain item of pornography is banned from sale, it is called *hakkin(-bon)*. *Hakkin* is an abbreviated form of *hatsubai kinshi* (sale prohibited). It is possible to publish *hakkin* pornographic books by marketing them as scientific texts and using genre names such as *seisho* (literally, sexual book). Ironically, a homonym for this word means Bible, which could cause a great deal of confusion.

As for pornographic movies, we can say *ero-eiga, pinku eiga,* and *poruno eiga.* The Nikkatsu Production Company's *roman poruno* (romantic porno films) series, which included such titles as *Koi no Karyūdo (Hunter of Love)* and *Mesuneko no Nioi (Smell of the She-Cat),* are typical of this genre. The availability of erotic films like these has decreased with the advent of adult videos.

5

The Language of Seduction

(kudoki no kotoba)

When young men and women set out in search of sexual conquest, they often seek to flatter and seduce, especially in the preliminary stages. Japanese, like other languages, has plenty of phrases for these purposes. Here are some terms used especially by young people on the prowl.

Naui or *nau-na* were once very fashionable adjectives used in praising a woman or girl. They come from the English now. Thus, *ano ko wa naui* means she's trendy, not only in fashion, but in thinking as well. Some men think that if a girl is flattered by this, it follows that she will be relatively easy to seduce. If she looks a little offended by the description, it just might be better to forget about her and look toward more fertile pastures. *Naui gāru* is a trendy gal. But this expression is rarely used nowadays.

Ikasu, which means pretty good or wonderful, is the causative form of the verb *iku,* to go. *Ikashite iru* and *ikashiteru* are derivatives of *ikasu* and mean to be wonderful. *Ikeru,* the potential form of *iku,* is also used to convey a pleasant meaning. Japanese people often use the expression *kono sake wa naka-naka ikeru* (this *sake* tastes pretty good).

Saikō (literally, highest) is number one, or tops, used both as an adjective and noun as in *kanojo wa saikō* (she's tops). The emphatic expression *ano ko wa saikō ni ikasu* (or *ikashiteru*) would mean that girl is dynamite (or a knockout).

Gunbatsu, an inverted form of *batsugun* (outstanding), is a synonym for *saikō.* It comes from the verb *gun o nuku,* which means to come out on top of the group or to lead the pack. *Gun* is group, and *batsu* is an alternative way of pronouncing the Chinese character for *nuku,* which means to surpass. Thus, *gunbatsu* means excellent. *Kanojo wa batsugun* can imply that she is good looking and/or she's good in bed.

Kakko ii and *kakko ga ii* mean both to look good and dress well. Nowadays, it's also used to praise someone's behavior or way of thinking. Thus, it's the most common word for praising someone regardless of age and sex.

Kakko means appearance; *ii* is good. When you limit the meaning of *kakko ii* to the face, then it means good-looking. But the latest interpretation of this word, with its streetwise variations *kakko ii, kakku ii,* and *katcho ii,* not only means to have a nice figure or to be good-looking, but to be wonderful in anything. Sometimes, these expressions are also used in a slightly jeering manner, as when one says oh great! in a tone of voice that implies just the opposite. *Naui, ikasu, saikō,* and *kakko ii* can be used by both males and females to refer to either sex.

Nikui is the latest synonym for *ikasu* and *kakko ii* among young people. It usually means hateful, but used in the way described above, it means awfully good or irresistibly good.

Sugoi is another popular term which is often used to imply the opposite of its own meaning. The word originally meant dreadful, awful, or terrible. But when one says *sugoi bijin,* it means a smashing beauty, while *sugoi hansamu* is terribly handsome. *Sugoi* in this sense really means wonderful. Men often use the rougher variation *sugē* instead.

On the other hand, the pat expression *wa! sugoi! ya da!* is used by about 90 percent of young Japanese girls to mean wow, that's really awful!

Kawaii (cute, pretty) is a word commonly used by men

when praising a woman's looks, as in *ano ko wa kawaii* (she is pretty or cute). Variations, such as *kawwaii* or *kawayui* are often used by young girls to describe anything cute. *Kawairashii* is another word for *kawaii*.

When you use the word *kawaii-ko-chan,* which was fashionable in the 60s, it refers to a cute girl. It is used by men as in *kinō kawaii-ko-chan to neta* (yesterday I slept with a cute young girl). This phrase, however, is rarely used nowadays. It might be heard among middle-aged women at host bars where young boys cater to their every whim and fantasy. When a customer at such a bar sees a particularly appealing host, she might say *ano kawaii-ko-chan o yonde* (call that cute boy over here).

Oishisō-na onna (good-looking woman or woman who's good enough to eat) might be thought of as a contemporary substitute for *kawaii-ko-chan,* especially among young people. *Oishii* used by itself as an adjective means tasty or nice, and appears in such phrases as *oishii baito* (good part-time job).

Shibireru (literally, to be numbed or paralyzed) is one of the latest terms in fashion. It can be used to describe either a person or his behavior when deeply impressed or fascinated. Its past tense form, *shibireta,* or its past perfect *shibirechatta,* are frequently used as in *sugoi, ano ko ni shibireta* (wow, I'm really into that girl). You can also use the interjection *shibireru* to mean wonderful, terrific, or fascinating. And, when you say *shibireru hodo no bijin,* it means a bewitching beauty.

Shibui and its inverted variation *bushii* are also currently popular among young people as words of praise. When *shibui* is used for the color of clothes, it refers to quiet, tasteful, or plain colors. When it goes too far and the colors become too quiet or muted, this is called *jimi.* Now, when one says *shibui,* the more emphatic *shibūi,* or the inverted *bushii,* they are almost equivalent to *kakko ii.*

Antonyms for *shibui* are *kiza* and *hade*. *Kiza, kiza-na,* and the inverted colloquialism *zaki* come from the verb *ki ni sawaru,* which means to grate upon someone's nerves. People have shortened this term to *kiza,* which means offensively affected or showy manners. Thus, *aitsu wa zaki da* and *kiza-na yatsu* both mean he's a showoff. There are a lot of synonyms for *kiza,* including *kidotteru* (to be affected) and its derivative *kidori-ya* (prig, snob), *unuboreteru* (to be conceited) and its derivative *unubore-ya* (snooty), *butteru* (pretentious), and *mieppari* (showoff). Other words that young people use to describe affected stylishness are *ikigatteru* and *tsuppatteru.*

The term *hade* (showy or gaudy) comes from a way of playing the *shamisen,* the traditional three-stringed instrument. The orthodox way of playing the *shamisen* is called *honte,* while an unorthodox way is called *hade.* This term later came to be used to describe dressing in bad taste for one's age. Nowadays, it's used by young people to mean gorgeous in a good sense, since recently people have begun to dress and act more elegantly. This is especially true since the 1960s, when a phenomenon called the *pēkoku kakumei* (peacock revolution) occurred in Japan. Before that, it had been considered unseemly, especially for men, to pay too much attention to dressing lavishly or individualistically.

Hade-zuki or *hade-gonomi* both mean a showy or expressive person. *Hade ni yarō* in male language and *hade ni yarimashō* in female language are quite popular expressions used when people go out drinking or partying to mean let's have fun or let's party.

A contemporary expression with a contemptuous connotation of being too showy or always wanting to be the center of attention is *medachitagari.* It can be used as in *ano ko wa itsumo medachitagaru* (she always wants to be in the limelight) or *aitsu, medachitagari-ya da* (he likes to be the center of attention). These expressions come from the verb *medatsu,* which means to be conspicuous.

Pikka-pika was once a very fashionable onomatopoetic expression for shining. It comes from *pika-pika hikaru* and *pika-pika suru,* both meaning to shine, to glitter, to flash, and to sparkle. The term *pikka-pika no jūhassai* is the rough equivalent of Sweet 16—actually, in this case, Sweet 18. Another expression, *hana* (flower) *no jūhassai,* can be rendered into English as a blossoming 18-year-old. *Kanojo wa ima pikka-pika no sutā* means she is really a shining star, although this expression is rarely used these days.

Gingiragin and *gin-gin* are two more now-fashionable words meaning sparkling. They come from the onomatopoetic expressions *gira-gira suru* and *kira-kira suru,* both meaning glaring or glittering. Related to these are two more onomatopoetic terms, *kin-kira* (followed by *no,* plus a noun) and *kin-pika,* which mean glittering tackily, as in *kin-pika no yasu-mono* (cheap tinsel or glittering trinket).

Gingira and *gingiragin,* on the other hand, are used in a more powerful sense. When used by young people, for example, *gingira no kanojo* means an eye-catchingly attractive woman. Also, you may have observed trucks that are decorated by their drivers with fancy lights and decorations. These are described as *gingiragin* (decked out). Some of the more extreme drivers spend millions of yen to decorate their trucks.

Gin-gin is used in the same way as *saikō.* If one asks *kanojo wa dō datta?* (how was she?), the answer might be *gin-gin da yo* (she was tops), referring either to her performance in bed or on the dance floor. You can also use this expression to mean to the limit or to the utmost as in *ore wa gin-gin ni tsupatte ita* (I resisted everything to the absolute end). *Gin-gin* in this case probably comes from *gingiragin* and *giri-giri* (to the limit). *Giri-giri no nedan,* for example, refers to the rock bottom price.

The expression *gin-gin ni o-mekashi* means decked out or dolled up. *O-mekashi* comes from the verb *mekasu* (to primp or to doll up).

Kimatteru is another fashionable expression used to praise someone's fancy way of dressing. *Kyō wa kimatteru ne* translates into wow, do you ever look good today. *Kimatteru* is a form of the intransitive verb *kimaru*, meaning decided. Thus, *kimatteru* (and its transitive form *kimeteru*) mean being decidedly well dressed.

These terms are used when young people go out on the *hanto* (hunt) for romantic companionship. You may have noticed young people on the street trying to pick up members of the opposite sex by saying such things as *ne, ocha nomi ni ikanai?* (hey, want to go have a cup of tea?), or *disuko ni ikanai no?* (how about going to a disco?). This is called *gāru* (girl) *hanto* or *boi* (boy) *hanto*, depending on the gender being hunted.

6

Other Sex-Related Expressions

(seiyōgo)

Hotaru in an ordinary conversation means firefly, but it is now used to mean a motel, because of the neon signs that flash hotel names through the night. It's a rather apt coinage when one thinks of its phonetic similarity to the word *hoteru* (hotel). *Rabu hoteru* (literally, love hotel), *onsen māku* (the symbol used to denote a hot spa), *sakasa kurage* (an upside-down jellyfish—an upside-down jellyfish resembles an *onsen māku*), *tsurekomi(-yado)* (literally, bring-a-friend-in inn), and *doya,* an abbreviation of *yado* (inn), are all synonymous with *hotaru*.

Sukebei, as we've mentioned earlier, is a very popular term meaning lewd or lewd person. It's become so popular, even among some non-Japanese that it is commonly used in such porn havens as Times Square in New York or the Eros Center in Hamburg. Touts, eager to attract customers, will shout such things as *otō-san* (hey, pops) *sukebei ne* (you're horny, eh) to Japanese men passing by.

The *suke* in the *sukebei* was originally *suki,* meaning to like (women). The *-bei* was commonly used until the early Meiji era as a suffix in common male given names, such as Tarobei and Saburobei. It means sentinel.

Sukebei or, more colloquially, *sukebe,* dates from the Edo era and can be applied to either a man or woman, as either a noun or adjective. By itself, it means what a lecher you are. *Sukebe otoko* (man), *onna* (woman), and *ningen* (character) are also heard frequently. *Sukebe konjō,* meaning greedy thinking, or trying to push one's luck, is a popular expression used by both men and women. *Sukebe banashi* is dirty talk. And *sukebe jijii* is a dirty old man (the kind who waits for little girls in the park). One can be both *nonbei* and *sukebei,* as in *kare wa sukebei de nonbei* (he's a dirty-minded drunk). Despite the fact that *sukebei* is quite adaptable as a personal name, no one seems anxious to give it to their children.

Wada heisuke also sounds like an ordinary person's name. But, when read in an inverted order and with a slight euphonic change, it becomes *sukebe da wa. Wada heisuke* was once often used by young girls to avoid using the direct expression.

Iro, the word for color in Japanese, has sexual connotations. And, given the Japanese penchant for playing on words, it's not surprising that *ero* can be substituted for *iro*. It can also be used in place of *sukebei*. These three expressions (*iro, ero,* and *sukebe*), in fact, have become almost interchangeable in modern usage, with *ero* leading the popularity polls as a prefix borrowed from the European languages (erotic, etc.) and thus more up-to-date and fashionable. Thus, we have such terms as *ero-banashi* (dirty talk) and *ero-jijii* (dirty old man).

Iro in Japanese has many meanings, including color and sensual pleasure. *Iro-iro na* means many kinds, or various. *Iro-gonomi* or the more ribald *ero-gonomi* means horny or libidinous. The *-gonomi* here is from *konomi,* meaning one's liking or inclination. It is written with the character for *suki,* which means liking or fancy. A related pair of adjectives, thus, are *onna-zuki* and *otoko-zuki,* which can be interpreted as woman-crazy and man-crazy, respectively.

Stronger than these are *onna-gurui* and *otoko-gurui,* the *-gurui* here being a derivative of the verb *kuruu* (to go mad or become insane). *Onna-gurui* means philandering or woman-chasing, and *onna-gurui o suru,* to philander.

Conversely, *otoko-gurui* means wantonness or promiscuity on the part of a woman, and *otoko-gurui o suru* is for a woman to behave licentiously.

Iro-kichigai (*kichigai* is madness or insanity) or *shikima* (*shiki* is another way of pronouncing the character for *iro*) mean lech or Don Juan, or, when used in reference to a woman, a nymphomaniac. *Iro-ke* is sex appeal. *Kanojo wa iro-ke ga aru* means she's sexy or she's got sex appeal. *Iro-goto* is a love affair. Adding the suffix *-shi,* which means master or practitioner, yields the term *iro-goto-shi,* a lady killer. *Iro-otoko* and *iro-onna* mean sexy man and sexy woman, respectively, and are commonly used to mean boy- or girlfriend, as in *anata no iro-otoko* (your boyfriend) or *boku no iro-onna* (my girlfriend). *Iro-ppoi yume* (*-poi* means tinged with, and *yume* is dream) is a wet dream. This can also be pronounced *emmu.*

Since we're on the topic of lasciviousness, this might be a good time to relate the sad story of Japan's own Peeping Tom: the turtle with the protruding teeth.

It seems that, during the latter part of the Meiji era (1868–1912), there was a buck-toothed and *sukebei* fellow by the name of Kamejirō Ikeda. He was so drawn to the sight of naked women that he often peeked into the women's section of the public bath. One night, old Kamejirō became so out of control that he followed a woman home and raped her. In the publicity that attended his crime and punishment, Ikeda became immortalized as the Peeping Tom of Japan.

Kamejirō, Ikeda's given name, can be divided into *kame* (turtle) and *jirō* (second son). *Deba,* or *deppa* colloquially, means buck teeth. When we put the two parts together as *debakame* or *debagame,* we recall Kamejirō Ikeda and all the other buck-toothed turtles who have followed in his trail. Note, though, that *debagame* is never used to refer to women in Japan. Women, so the thinking goes, have little interest in men's naked bodies.

A person of either gender who is curious about other people's private affairs and peeks into their windows or invades their privacy in other ways, is guilty of *nozoki* (peeping), a synonym for *debagame*. *Nozoki shumi no hito* (*shumi* is tendency or hobby) is a person who is curious about other people's private lives (often middle-aged women).

The following Japlish (Japanese-English) abbreviations have all been made popular nationwide by the evening tabloids, which carry with gleeful abandon ads for and articles about the sex industry: *rorikon* (Lolita complex); *minisuka* (mini-skirt); *panchira* (a quick glimpse of the panties); *tii-bakku* (thong panties); *wanren* (a girl's hair style in which the hair is of one length); *toragura* (transistor glamour, for small and glamorous girl); *terekura* (telephone club, which arranges for date calls from women—a modern form of prostitution); *kyabakura* (a cross between cabaret and night club, sometimes featuring shows with young girls); and *imekura,* the image or fetish clubs described earlier.

In addition to these, there are some sex-related expressions, unique to Japan, that have become quite common.

Oyako donburi, from a Japanese dish that uses chicken and egg (*oya* is parent, and *ko* is child), means a case in which a man has slept with both a mother and her daughter. This term also now means incest between mother and son or father and daughter.

Mara kyōdai refers to men who have had sex with the same woman. *Mara* is cock, and *kyōdai* means siblings.

Harachigai refers to children of the same father, but of a different mother. *Hara* is the abdomen or belly and *chigai* means different. A synonym for this is *hatakechigai* (different field). *Tanechigai* is different father, same mother. *Tane* means seed.

Rōdo-shō (roadshow) means to do it in the middle of the road or to have sex in a park. The traditional slang synonym for *rōdo-shō* is *ao-kan* (outdoor fucking). This comes from *ao-tenjo* (blue heaven) and *kan* (violating a woman). Because of the lack of privacy in small Japanese homes and the fact that many people, particularly in the cities, don't have cars—not to speak of cars with roomy back seats—this is a rather common practice in Japan and provides voyeurs with endless fun.

Nozokiya are among the three groups of people in Japan who habitually dress in black. The other two are theater stagehands and *ninja.* The term *nozokiya* comes from the verb *nozoku (*to peep) and the suffix *-ya,* meaning person.

Esu-efu (S.F.) is not an abbreviation for science fiction, but for sex friend. Thus, *kanojo wa boku no esu-efu* means she's my sex friend.

Rukkusu (looks) refers to a person's facial appearance. Young Japanese also tend to use *feisu* (face) as in *ano hito wa rukkusu ga ii* or *feisu ga ii,* both meaning that a person is good-looking.

Bokkusu (box) is now used in Japanese to mean female genitals, just as in English. From this comes *aisu-bokkusu* (icebox) for a frigid woman. In this connection, it's very funny to see what are called *hotto bokkusu* (hot box) at Japanese restaurants. The manufacturer obviously had no idea what the term means in English slang, but, in case you're wondering what it is in Japanese, *hotto bokkusu* are used to keep *oshibori* (hot towels) warm.

Barikeido (barricade) refers to a cock teaser. On the other hand *sase-ko (-chan),* which comes from *saseru* (to allow to do), is an easy make. The male counterpart, a so-called easy rider, is *yari-o,* from *yaru* (to do). The *ko* and *o* in these two expressions are typical female and male name suffixes.

PART

3

UNDERGROUND AND YAKUZA-RELATED LANGUAGE

angura, yakuza kanren

The Japanese *yakuza,* which means gangster(s), have become almost as famous as their colleagues in the Mafia, as both pursue their dark ends out of sight of most *katagi* (honest, respectable folk).

The word *yakuza* has its origins in a card gambling game called *oicho kabu* or *sanmai garuta.* Players use three cards numbered from one to ten. The highest possible score is attained when the sum of the numbers of the three cards ends in a nine, such as when a player is holding a two, three, and four, or six, four, and ten. Combinations ending in zero, such as five, six, and nine, are the lowest. Of such combinations, an eight, nine, and three is considered the worst of all. In Japanese, the characters for eight, nine, and three can be pronounced *ya, ku,* and *san,* or *za,* respectively. Put them together, and you have *yakuza,* a real loser. In the Edo era, people used this term to refer to useless, meaningless things.

Colloquially, softened expressions for *yakuza,* such as *yā-sama, yā-san,* and *yatchan* are most often used. *Yā-sama* (an abbreviated form of the euphemistic and cautious *yakuza-sama*), *yā-kō* (a contemptuous way of saying *yakuza*), *sujimon,* and *kumi no mono* are frequently used as colloquial synonyms for *yakuza.* According to *yakuza* themselves, they invented the word *yā-sama* to describe *tekiya* gangsters, which we will discuss later. *Sujimon* is a shortened form of *sono suji* (that group or that family) *no mono* (member). *Kumi,* euphonically changed to *gumi,* is often used in the names of *yakuza* groups, as in the notorious Yamaguchi-*gumi.* Some synonyms for *kumi* are *kai* (association), as in Tōsei-*kai,* and *ikka* (family) as in Anegasaki-*ikka.*

A contemporary synonym and legal term for a *yakuza* group is *bōryokudan. Bōryoku* means violence or rowdiness, and *dan* is gang or group. *Bōryokudan,* thus, can be translated as criminal organization. *Bōryokudan-in* is the common term for gangster. The police call them *maru-bō,* from the recent custom of putting a circle *(maru)* around the *kanji* for *bō* in *bōryokudan.*

During the Edo and early Meiji eras, *yakuza* made their living by gambling. *Bakuchiuchi* (gambler), *toseinin* (drifting gambler), and *gokudō-mono* were used as synonyms for *yakuza* in those days. A person bitten too hard by the gambling bug may become *monnashi (yarō),* a penniless (person), someone without a pot to piss in. The *mon* here is written with the character for an old monetary unit. Such people are often the target of *shakkintori* (the debt collector).

Today, though, with gambling strictly regulated by law, *yakuza* have to be resourceful in coming up with other illegal sources of income. Similar to their Mafia counterparts, the *yakuza* have formed many big crime syndicates called *bōryokudan* (violent groups), and engage in both legal and illegal commerce, which we will describe later.

A police survey in December, 1990 found 3,300 *yakuza* organizations in Japan with 88,600 members. Their numbers, however, belie their influence. According to an expert on the *yakuza,* the total gross income of the crime syndicates in Japan in 1986 was estimated at at least seven trillion yen. Moreover, his estimate doesn't reflect earnings from violence in civil cases. (By comparison, the figure released by the Presidential Advisory Commission for underworld income in the U.S. in 1987 was $106 billion.)

Kakusei-zai (stimulant drugs) are the number one source of illegal income for the *yakuza,* accounting for about half of their revenues. This is followed by: *nomi-kōi* (illegal bookmaking); *tobaku* (gambling and betting); *fūzoku-han* (immoral activities, including some kinds of prostitution); porno *bottakuri* bars, *sōkaiya* (company nuisance); *shoba-dai* (territory money); and, *saiken toritate* (collection of bills). Beyond these activities there

is a huge grey area secretly tied up with powerful politicians and big businesses. Recently, this illicit union of
politicians and gangsters has given birth to some major
scandals.

Among such scandals, the biggest one was the recent
Kōmintō Incident. In 1987, the *Kōmintō* (Emperor's
Subject Party), a right-wing fascist group, created persistent disturbances against Noboru Takeshita, who was
then a candidate for prime minister. Takeshita asked the
late Susumu Ishii, head of a large *bōryokudan,* the
Inagawa-*kai,* to intervene on his behalf. Ishii succeeded
in getting the *Kōmintō* to quiet down, and Takeshita
became prime minister. No one knows how much Ishii
was paid, but the scandal shows beyond doubt that there
is a *yakuza* presence at the highest levels of Japanese
politics.

There are many *ingo* (argot terms) used by the police
and those in the underground world, which even Japanese knowledgeable in the field don't know. To most
people, these terms sound very much like *chinpunkanpun*
(gibberish). Here, we will limit ourselves to introducing
some phrases that may be familiar to some readers
through detective or *yakuza* dramas on TV or in the
movies. For example, police jargon such as *teguchi*
(modus operandi), *ashidori* (literally, trace of the suspect;
figuratively, the route that the suspect used to flee),
harikomi (stakeout), and *hotoke* (literally, Buddha; figuratively, a murder victim), are now common words.

Among *yakuza* jargon, *nawabari* (territory), *geso*
(footgear), *gase* (sham or lie), *sakura* (dummy), *shari*
(rice), *doya* (inn), and *neta* (article, commodity) are in
common use.

*Narazu-mono, gokudō-mono, gorotsuki, buraikan,
akutō,* and *yota-mono* are all terms for various types of
undesirables and are regarded as synonyms for *yakuza
(-mono).* The obsolete term *narazu-mono* comes from
the expression *dō ni mo naranai* (nothing can be done;

a person/situation is hopeless). Therefore, it means a hopelessly bad person. *Gokudō-mono* is from *gokudō* (wicked, profligate); *gokudō musuko* means prodigal son. *Gorotsuki* comes from the verb *gorotsuku,* which means to hang out or loiter. Originally a freeloader, it now implies a bad person, particularly a ruffian with no fixed abode, or homeless person. *Buraikan* is similar to *gorotsuki* with overtones of unreliability. *Bu* means no or not, *rai* is reliable, and *kan* is person: these parts combine to mean a drifter. This term, however, has become dated, and is rarely heard today.

Aku-tō is a compound made from *aku* (bad) and *tō* (group or political party). It refers either to a group of bad people or an individual. *Waru-mono* (literally, bad fellow) and its shortened form *waru* are synonyms for *aku-tō.* In contemporary usage, both *aku-tō* and *waru* can be used rather lightly, like the English rogue. *Aitsu wa waru da* means watch out, he's no good in a playful sense.

Yota-mono comes from the *yota* that means idle talk or nonsense and implies that someone is a good-for-nothing.

Yakuza, yota-mono, and *gurentai* are the most fashionable words, but there are many more euphemistic expressions for undesirable types. *Machi no dani,* for example, means street vermin; *dani* is a tick. *Hanatsumami,* which refers to a disgusting fellow, comes from the verb *hana o tsumamu* (to hold one's nose). *Ningen no kuzu* means human trash. You can also simply say *kuzu,* which means rubbish, trash, or scum. *Shakai no teki* can be literally translated as public enemy. *Kirawaremono* means a disliked or hated person, while both *gokutsubushi* and *mudameshigui* mean idle, useless person. *Goku* is grain and *tsubushi* is wasting. *Muda* means a good-for-nothing or a waste, while *meshigui* is literally rice-eater. When these parts are assembled into *mudameshigui,* we get a term suggesting that someone is so useless that even feeding him is a waste of food.

1

Yakuza Organization

(soshiki)

In the gangster world, strong feudal rules *(okite)* that require absolute obedience to the boss of the family are still dominant. It is said that when the boss says white is black, his followers all agree. *Oyabun* is the most popular term for the boss. *Oya* is parent, and *bun* is status. *Oyabun* can be translated as godfather or don. The term *oya,* when used in connection with gambling, refers to the keeper of the bank in a game. Synonyms for this include *kashimoto* (banker) and *dōmoto* (dealer). *Oya-dama* (chief) and *o-kashira* (literally, head) have been used in the past to describe a boss of a *yakuza* group. Nowadays, however, these terms are somewhat out-of-date, although Japanese still use *oyabun* sometimes in playful conversation.

Contemporary *yakuza* groups are extremely well organized—so well organized, in fact, that they have formed corporations and similar groups. In such organizations, the boss is called *kumichō* (literally, group leader) or *sōchō* (literally, president). Followers of the *oyabun* are called *kobun* (literally, followers), *teshita,* or *teka.* The latter two expressions both mean under the control of. Upon receiving a cup of *sake (sakazuki)* from the boss at an initiation ceremony, the follower enters into an *oyabun-kobun kankei* (follower-leader relationship) with the boss. Large *kumi* (underworld organizations), can have thousands of followers, while the smallest groups might claim only three or four. The big *kumi* comprise many smaller ones, also called *kumi,* under their influence. An organization as a whole is often called *ikka* (family or group), similar to mafia organizations in the West.

Among the *kobun,* a ranking member is called *kanbu* (executive). *Daikanbu* (*dai* means big) can be translated as big executive. *Daikanbu* are called *aniki* (elder brother or elder pal) by lower-ranking followers. *Anii* and *o-anii-san* are variations of *aniki.* These terms are also used to mean gangster.

Aneki (elder sister) does not mean a high-ranking female follower. *Ane-san, anego,* and *aneki* all refer to the boss's wife, even though she may be far younger than many of his followers. A female boss is also called *ane-san. Samanii* (an inversion of *nii-sama,* or elder brother), *aniki bun* (a sworn elder brother), *samanē* (an inversion of *nē-sama,* or elder sister), and *aneki-san* (wife of a boss) are related terms.

Aniki and *aneki* are also ordinary colloquialisms used to mean elder brother and elder sister, respectively.

Ranking below the *aniki* are the *otōto,* or *shatei,* meaning younger brother. Of all the *kobun,* the lowest-ranking ones are called *shitappa* or *sanshita* (subordinates or underlings). *Sanshita* refers to a person who is three ranks below. Variations include *sanshita yakko* and *sanshita yarō.* To these near-slaves go tedious chores like lookout duty *(mihari)* and shadowing or tailing *(bikō).* *Hashiri-tsukai* (errand boy) is a synonym for *sanshita.* Sometimes these low-ranking gangsters will move up in the world; *haku o tsukeru* (literally, to gild) is the term used for this, meaning to achieve a higher rank in a *yakuza* group.

Gurentai refers to young street gangsters. It is derived from the verb *gureru,* which originally came from *hama-guri* (clam). The etymology of *gureru* is very complicated, and even most Japanese people don't know it. When you invert the two shells of a clam, naturally their edges cannot meet. This discrepancy was called *guri-hama,* which is the inverted way of pronouncing *hama-*

guri. This word was created more than 500 years ago to indicate discrepancies in daily life. This, then, evolved into *gurehama,* from which the verb *gureru* was created.

Gureru has three meanings: to go wrong, to become abnormal, and to turn bad. *Gurentai,* which is made from *gureta* (the past tense of *gureru*) plus *tai* (group or corps) refers only to the third meaning. It is a collective word, but you can use it as a singular, as in *aitsu wa gurentai da* (he's a hoodlum). Minor members of gangster groups are also often called *chinpira,* which means an insignificant person who thinks a great deal of himself and behaves that way. This word is often used to refer to juvenile delinquents and punks.

Yakuza syndicates have now spread their influence even to the nation's high schools and junior high schools, where they recruit future members. *Banchō* is a juvenile gang leader in a junior high or high school. It has been reported that gangs in junior high schools have threatened fellow students in attempts to extort money to buy and play computer games. Female *banchō* are called *suke-ban. Suke* is a *yakuza* word for girl or woman, and *ban* is a shortened form of *banchō. Suke-ban* groups have been rumored to force other girl students to engage in prostitution.

Yakuza bosses, as well as local politicians, are often called *kaoyaku* (boss of the territory, or local boss). *Kao* is face, and *yaku* is office or post. A related expression, not *yakuza*-specific, is *kao ga hiroi* (literally, his face is wide or broad), meaning that a person is well known. *Kaoyaku,* naturally, are eager to keep their reputations as clean as possible so as not to lose their widely known faces. *Kao ga tatsu* (literally, his face is standing upright) means to save one's face. A *kaoyaku* will guard carefully against *kao o tsubusareru* (to have one's face smashed) and *kao ni doro o nurareru* (to have one's face splattered with mud), both of which mean to be humiliated.

As with gangsters in other countries, each *yakuza*

organization has its own territory *(nawabari)* where a boss and his group can enjoy supremacy. The term *nawabari* originally comes from the act of stretching a rope *(nawa)* to determine the boundary of a piece of land. Later, it came to mean the territory of a *yakuza* gang or of a gambler. Nowadays, it has become popular in journalistic usage to describe any kind of influential territory. For example, *nawabariarasoi (arasoi* means dispute or struggle) means turf war.

Another expression for territory is *shima. Shima* originally meant and still means island. But it was also used to denote a limited area, such as the pleasure quarters, and then a *yakuza's* territory. The difference between *nawabari* and *shima* is that you can use the former in ordinary conversation as in *oi, ore no nawabari o arasu na yo* (hey, don't muscle in on my turf); but when you hear *oi, ore no shima o arasu na,* the speaker is definitely a gangster.

What exactly goes on in a gangster's *nawabari? Yakuza* get territory money or *shoba-dai. Shoba* is the inverted form of *basho* (place or territory), and *dai* is fee or charge. Other argot terms for *shoba-dai* are *kasuri* or *mikajime* in the Kanto region and *mori-ryō* in Kansai. Bars, cabarets, massage parlors, restaurants, snack bars, movie theaters, hotels, motels, and pachinko and game parlors, all belonging to the category of business referred to as *mizu shōbai,* are easy marks for the *yakuza* when demanding their territory money. *Kasuri* comes from the verb *kasuru* (to squeeze); *mori-ryō* is from the verb *mamoru* (to guard) and *ryō* (charge, fee).

The territory money is paid because if any violence should occur in an establishment, the customers won't want to come back, and business will suffer. Thus, the owners usually acquiesce and pay what's demanded of them. To the *yakuza's* way of thinking, they are merely collecting protection money so that the *mizu shōbai* establishment won't be victimized by yet another rival gang.

The term *mizu shōbai* comes from the words *mizu* (water) and *shōbai* (trade or business). Water is hard to shape, hard to catch. When you say *shōbu wa mizumono,* it means you cannot forecast the result of a match or bout—it's a gamble. *Mizu shōbai* businesses, then, are particularly vulnerable if they're involved in some unpleasantness, and this makes them vulnerable to the *yakuza,* who offer them protection with one hand but threaten them with the other.

Sources of Income *(shikingen, shinogi)*

Yakuza call the means of securing their livelihood *shinogi,* which comes from the verb *shinogu* (to endure). As a rule, the organization will protect and feed its members and take care of them when arrested, but a gangster's daily earnings rise and fall according to his own skill, cunning, and luck. Even so, he is required to hand over a certain portion of his income to his boss.

Territory money is one form of *shinogi,* but, according to the best estimates, the drug trafficking business is the major source of *yakuza* income, generating almost half. Despite the enormous sums of money earned in illegal drugs, or perhaps because of them, strong regulations against such substances persist in Japan. There are not a great many terms in Japanese to describe these substances. *Kusuri* (drug or medicine) and *yaku,* which is another pronunciation of the *kanji* for *kusuri,* are general terms for all kinds of drugs, including narcotics *(mayaku),* stimulants *(kakusei-zai),* LSD, marijuana, and amphetamines. The most commonly used stimulant drug in Japan is called *hiropon.*

Peichū is a narcotic drug addict, while *ponchū* is a stimulant drug addict *(pon* is an abbreviation of *hiropon).* The feeling of being high is called *raritte iru* or *raritteru* because people in this condition cannot properly pronounce the "r" sounds of *ra, ri, ru, re,* and *ro. Roretsu ga mawaranai* (literally, articulation doesn't come around; figuratively, cannot speak distinctly) is another popular idiom used when people can't talk properly, either because they have had too much to drink or because of having taken drugs.

It's a coincidence that drugs, or *yaku,* in Japan are handled by the *yakuza,* although there is no etymological connection between these two words. A person who handles the drugs commercially is called *bainin* (peddler). *Bai* is selling, and *nin* is person. Originally, this term merely meant a merchant, but today most Japanese would associate this term with a drug pusher.

Apart from drug trafficking or smuggling *(mitsuyu),* gangs are involved in many seemingly legal businesses, which we will go into later. Some of their more traditional activities, and the words that describe them, follow here.

Dorobō is an elided form of *tori ubau* (literally, take and rob), and it means thief. *Nusumi* and its legal counterpart *settō* mean theft. The gangster word *nobi,* which also means theft, comes from *shinobikomu* (to creep into). A derivative form, *nobishi,* is another rough term for *dorobō.*

Koso-doro means surreptitious thief. It is a compound word combining *koso-koso suru,* a mimetic expression for to sneak, and *doro,* from *dorobō.* A *kaihō-doro* is the kind of thief who robs drunks while pretending to take care of them.

There are quite a few terms for various types of theft. *Gōtō* and its underworld version, *tataki,* both mean robbery or burglary. *Tataki* (literally, knocking) comes from the technique of knocking on the door before breaking into a house. There is also an association with burglars who beat up their victims.

Arakasegi, arashigoto, oshikomi, and *oshikomi-gōtō,* are synonyms for *tataki* and *gōtō. Ara* is tough and *kasegi* means earning, while *shigoto* is work. *Oshikomi* comes from the verb *oshikomu* (to break into a house).

The verb *inaoru* (to change one's appearance or become violent) can be combined with *gōtō* to get *inaori gōtō* which means a situation in which a thief has been detected and become violent. *Dorobō ga inaotta* means a burglar has become violent. It is also used when a burglar visits a house pretending to be a salesman or telegram carrier.

Other uses of *gōtō* abound. *Pisutoru* (pistol) *gōtō* means hold-up. *Ginkō gōtō* refers to a bank robbery, and *jidōsha* (car) *gōtō*, is a robbery in which a getaway vehicle is employed. *Tsuji-gōtō* means highway robbery in the literal sense. *Tsuji* is street corner. *Oihagi* (highwayman) is a slang synonym for *tsuji-gōtō*. *Oi* comes from the verb *ou* (to chase), and *hagi* from the verb *hagu* (to deprive of or strip of). And, speaking of high-speed robbery, *kuruma dorobō* is a car thief.

Okibiki is luggage theft, whereby a person's bag is taken and another one, which looks the same but contains nothing of any value, is put in its place. *Oki* means putting or placing and *biki* is drawing away. Pickpocketing is *suri*. *Suri* comes from the verb *suru,* which means to pickpocket. An underworld equivalent is *matchan,* a play on words. *Suru* can also mean to strike or rub. Thus, when one lights a match, is it *matchi o suru.*

Kyōkatsu is a legal term for blackmail or intimidation. It has several vulgar synonyms, including *yusuri, katsu-age,* and *takari. Katsu-age* is a compound word derived from *kyōkatsu* and *makiageru* (to seize), and it means to extort money. *Takari* is a form of the verb *takaru,* whose usual meaning is to flock together. Now it is used when gangsters surround a victim and force him to hand over his money. *Takari* is also frequently heard in colloquial conversations meaning to force a friend to pay a bar bill.

The only legal forms of gambling in Japan are: gov-

ernment-sponsored *keiba* (horse racing), *kyōtei* (motor-
boat racing), *keirin* (bicycle racing), *ōto reisu* (motorcycle racing)—*ōto* here comes from *ōto-bai,* meaning
autobicycle—and *takarakuji* (lotteries sponsored by the
national and local governments). But that doesn't mean
much. *Bakuchi* (gambling) is another illegal source of
income for the *yakuza.* Betting is routinely practiced
when playing *hanafuda* (a type of card game), *mājan*
(mahjong), *saikoro* (dice), *kake* (private pool betting),
poker, and roulette.

The *yakuza* have nothing to do with these sorts of
private betting pools. But they do run organizations for
betting on professional baseball games. *Yakyū tōbaku*
(betting on baseball) is quite popular especially in the
Kansai region. Dealers telephone customers to obtain
their bets, and gangster organizations sometimes go so
far as to influence outcomes by threatening individual
baseball players.

Yaochō originally comes from the word for
greengrocer's shop *(yao-ya)* and the nickname of a
greengrocer, Yaochō, who lived in the early days of the
Meiji era. Yaochō used to play *go* (the national board
game of Japan) with an ex-sumo wrestler. Even though
Yaochō was by far the more skillful of the two, the results
always came out even because Yaochō intentionally wasn't
playing his best game. Thus, the word *yaochō* came to
mean fixing a competition. *Yaochō* is frequently seen in
sumo, horse racing, and bicycle racing.

Two ways to make money out of gambling are pro-
moting and cheating. The Japanese word for a gambling
promoter is *dōmoto* (sponsor). The *dōmoto* (who are
yakuza) collect *shoba-dai* or *terasen* (literally, temple
money) not only for baseball games, but also for betting
on cards and dice games. The commonly used word
terasen has its origins in the fact that, during the Edo
period, gambling often took place on the grounds of

temples and shrines, which were regarded as sacred areas. In return for their tacit permission, the religious organizations received a commission.

Ikasama(-bakuchi) means a prearranged swindle. *Ika-sama-shi* (swindlers) will plot together *(guru)* to cheat an easy victim (*kamo,* or duck). *Kamoru* (to victimize), a verb derived from *kamo*, is used today in ordinary conversation.

Sitting ducks, of course, often lose in gambling. *Suru* means to lose in general, and *bakuchi de suru* is to lose money in gambling. *Chara* is used as a general slang term for being equal with no debt or loan, as in *kore de chara* (this makes us even).

The *yakuza* in Japan are deeply involved with betting on horse racing. In Japan, the only legal horse race gambling is run by the national and local governments. But sometimes, when a bettor finds that it's too much trouble to go to an official government pool ticket window, he opts to place his bets elsewhere by telephone. And that's where *yakuza*-controlled *nomi-ya* come in.

Nomi-ya ordinarily means a bar or tavern, often with a red lantern hanging outside. But when this term is used in connection with horse-race gambling, it describes a person similar to a bookie, someone who figuratively swallows *(nomu)* his clients' orders at his own risk. The *nomi-ya* doesn't actually place the bets that are ordered; rather, when his clients lose, he wins, and vice-versa. Obviously, he depends on them to lose most of the time; but even on the off-chance that a client makes a killing or *ō-ana* (literally, big hole), the *nomi-ya* cuts his losses by setting a ceiling for the payoff. The legal term for what *nomi-ya* do is *nomi-kōi*. As one might expect, when people place losing bets and then try to get out of paying, there are all sorts of pressures *yakuza* can bring to bear to get them to think again.

Also under the sway of the *yakuza* are the *yosō-ya* (literally, forecasters), who sell their tips on the races.

Sōkaiya or *kaisha-goro* (*goro* comes from *gorotsuki,* or ruffian) both mean company nuisance, and this is another way the *yakuza* make their living. The former expression comes from *kabunushi sōkai* (general meeting of stockholders), which, in Japan, are usually completed within 30 minutes. *Kabunushi sōkai* are not opportunities for the stockholders to better understand the company's situation, as they are in Europe and America. They are really only formalities carried out by the company to comply with the law. Executive board members think that the shorter the general meeting, the better. They only hope that no troublesome questions will be asked. And this is where the *sōkaiya* come in.

Sōkaiya often buy a few stocks to be qualified to attend the meeting, then disrupt it until the company agrees to pay them off. Usually, they go to the company before the meeting and ask for money. Most companies will pay if the amount asked is within tolrerable bounds. At the same time, the company asks the *sōkaiya*'s assistance—for more money, of course—in keeping the honest, and sometimes noisy, stockholders' mouths shut when the company has some problem or scandal it doesn't wish to explain. Thus, it is the companies themselves that encourage the existence of the parasitic *sōkaiya.* If, during one of these meetings, a shareholder should want to inquire about some scandal or wrongdoing on the part of the company, the chairman of the meeting will ignore him while the *sōkaiya* shout and clap their hands. The meeting will then end noisily within a few minutes. This kind of meeting is called *shan-shan taikai, shan* being the sound of clapping hands, and *taikai* being a general term for a mass meeting.

Aside from the occasional income they derive from sabotaging shareholders' meetings, *yakuza*'s major source of funds from corporations is from monthly patronage or support money (often called *sanjo-kin*). *Yakuza* seeking such income are called *kaisha-goro* (parasites on a company). Company officials who refuse to pay this tribute will be harrassed by *sōkaiya* until they cave in. *Kaisha-goro* who make use of their own publications, magazines, and newspapers to harass and blackmail, are called *shuppan-goro, zasshi-goro,* and *shinbun-goro,* respectively.

As we mentioned earlier, a large bloc of funds is allocated by local and national authorities to improve living conditions for residents of *buraku* (outcast) villages. The *yakuza* saw that such antidiscrimination projects would be a good source of income. Despite the fact that they were not from such areas, they claimed to be *dōwa dantai* and obtained public funds by blackmailing. They were called *dōwa jiken-ya* or *ese-dōwa*. The word *dōwa* is an abbreviation of *dōhō ichiwa, dōhō* being brethren, and *ichiwa* meaning peace or harmony. *Jiken-ya* is troublemaker, and *ese-* is a prefix meaning false or spurious.

Yakuza now infiltrate every aspect of the economy, touching even the lives of very ordinary folk. People who live in Japanese apartment buildings *(manshon),* for example, have reported trouble in the past with the *kakuchōdan* (men who attempt to sell newspaper subscriptions through force and intimidation). *Kakuchō* means expansion or expanding, while *dan* means group. In Japan, newspapers are mainly sold by subscription. Thus, it is crucial for the newspaper owners to secure more subscribers in order to sell advertising. As a result, a so-called *shinbun sensō* (newspaper war) rages, employing *kakuchōdan* as foot soldiers. The *kakuchōdan* are paid a piece rate, so they have to be aggressive and pushy (a sales technique called *oshi-uri*) to get subscriptions.

The *kakuchōdan* work only at selling newspaper subscriptions along with tickets to baseball or soccer games. They often use kitchen implements such as *nabe* (pots) and *kama* (kettles) as gifts for housewives in their sales campaigns. *Interi ga tsukuri, yakuza ga uru shinbun* (newspapers written by the intelligentsia and sold by *yakuza*) is what one weekly magazine had to say about this situation. *Kakuchōdan* are a relatively new development in the business activities of the *yakuza,* however, and there are still many honest salesmen in the newspaper industry.

Sara-kin is another recent business field for the *yakuza*. *Sara-kin* is an abbreviation for *sarariiman kinyū* (financing for white-collar workers). *Sara-kin* companies loan small amounts of money to individuals lacking strong credit, at usurious interest rates. Not only white-collar workers, but housewives and even students borrow from them. This kind of business has become more and more widespread over the past 15 to 20 years, and their average interest rate is more than 30 percent a year. It's very easy to borrow from them and equally hard to return the money.

The forerunner of the *sara-kin* boom, *kane-kashi* (money lending or money lender) was called *kōri-kashi* (loan sharking). People in this business also charged exorbitant interest rates, called *to-ichi* or *to-san*. *To-ichi* (literally, one to ten) is an abbreviation of *tōka de ichi-wari,* meaning ten percent for ten days. *To-san* is 30 percent for each ten days.

Sara-kin is a modern, organized business. When people badly in need of money borrow from such a company and fail to return the sum plus interest within a given period, they will be called upon by a *toritate-ya* (collector), who may call as often as ten times a day, even going so far as to visit the victim's home or office with persistent and violent threats. The victim then may borrow money from another *sara-kin* to pay off the first debt. Thus, it becomes a vicious cycle, as the debt rapidly burgeons. This is called *sara-kin jigoku* (usury hell), and borrowers are often forced to quit their jobs and sell their property. In the most extreme cases, some commit suicide. The newspapers often carry tragic stories about the victims of *sara-kin* companies.

Sara-kin, however, is just the tip of the iceberg of *yakuza* business activities. Gangster *jiken-ya* are involved in three types of activities.

One shady business at which the gangs excel is one in which *yakuza* take advantage of some financial scandal within a company and buy cheaply a large amount of its stocks. They then force the company to buy the stocks back at a high price. Sometimes the *yakuza* simply take over the company. This kind of maneuver is called *nottori* (takeover) and the person or people who carry it out, *nottori-ya.*

The second type of *jiken-ya* specializes in intervening in real estate disputes, taking advantage of eviction cases, boundary disagreements, or trouble arising in connection with the transfer of real estate. They offer their unwelcome services as negotiators, often usurping the property in question, and, to make matters worse, sell it without permission by drawing up a false contract. This kind of *jiken-ya* is called *jimen-shi* (land swindler, *jimen* being land). Some readers may be familiar with this type of scam from Jūzō Itami's film *A Taxing Woman's Return.*

Jimen-shi have been called *jiage-ya* since the bubble economy days of the late 80s. At that time, not only banks and security firms, but also general corporations with huge profits to spend, made frenzied investments in land, buildings, and stocks, and land prices skyrocketed. Large corporations used *jiage-ya* belonging to *bōryo-kudan* or *yakuza* groups behind the scenes to threaten land owners to sell *(jiage)* their property at well below market price. There were numerous horrible incidents such as houses being demolished in the middle of the night by bulldozers, the helpless family members standing by in their nightclothes. At that time, the total land value of Japan exceeded that of the United States, size disparity notwithstanding.

The third type of *jiken-ya* intervenes in disputes arising from traffic accidents. They force both parties to reach an out-of-court settlement and get commissions from them. In this case, the *jiken-ya* is called *jidan-ya* (compromise maker).

Pakuri-ya and *sarubēji-ya* are two more types of *yakuza*. The former comes from the verb *pakuru* (to snatch or swipe) and the latter from the English word salvage. The *pakuri-ya* will victimize a company that is in financial difficulty, urging it to draw a promissory note *(tegata)*, and pledging to use the note to obtain cash to help it out of its troubles. The *pakuri-ya* then discounts the note for cash and disappears. When the note comes back to the company for payment, the company is in an even worse position than before.

Pakuru (to snatch) originated from *pakutto taberu* (bite at, snap at), where *pakutto* is a mimesis for biting. Like the English verb to snatch, *pakuru* is also used to mean the apprehension of a criminal, as in *satsu ni pakurareta* (he was grabbed by the cops).

The *sarubēji-ya* tries to snatch the note back from the *pakuri-ya* by force and, if he succeeds, demands a huge commission. Often there are fights between *pakuri-ya* and *sarubēji-ya,* many of which are staged since they are members of the same gangster group working hand-in-hand to victimize floundering companies. This phenomenon is called *hitori futayaku* (double role).

As a result of constant pursuit by the police, and having achieved a certain level of wealth, *yakuza* groups have increasingly been forced to ply their shady trades in what look like legitimate businesses. They establish affiliate companies under guises including those of *shōji gaisha* (trading companies), *doken-gyō* (construction and engineering contractors), *fudōsan-ya* (real estate agencies or realtors), *kōgyō gaisha* (entertainment promoters), or *geinō-sha* or *purodakushon* (either meaning production companies for show business). Nowadays, it's common to use a more modern sounding name, such as *geinō purodakushon* (entertainment production).

Yakuza-run *shōji gaisha* engage in various business activities, such as lending money and running bars, cabarets, restaurants, coffee shops, motels, theaters (often of a sleazy sort), and *pachinko* parlors. (*Pachinko* is a kind of Japanese pinball game.) It's really very difficult to know whether such establishments are run by *yakuza* or not unless some trouble occurs.

The *shōji gaisha* that are run by the *yakuza* might be called jacks of all evil trades. Even worse are the *yūrei gaisha* established by the *yakuza*. A *yūrei gaisha* (literally, ghost company) will buy a commodity without paying or by issuing a promissory note. By the time the note is due, the *yūrei gaisha* will have gone out of business. The commodity that has been purchased is then sold to the *batta-ya* or *tatakiuri-ya* (merchant who sells hot goods at bargain prices). *Batta* means grasshopper or locust and *tataki-uri* is literally selling on the street with a pounding noise. The verb *tataku* (to hit, of which *tataki* is a conjugation) is also often used to mean beat down the price.

The *yakuza*-run *doken-gyō* are often called *doken-ya* or *furyō doken* (bad contractors). Such firms force companies to sign contracts for some construction or engineering work. These contracts are drafted to contain unreasonable conditions, and the *yakuza* realize astronomical profits.

Some *yakuza* groups make their major income from brokering temporary jobs in harbor work, mining, and construction. A *tehai-shi* (boss) will offer *furōsha* (vagrants) the opportunity of work and remuneration. Then he will take them to the site of the job boxed up in a so-called *tako-beya* (octopus pen) and subsequently treat them as slaves. This sort of business is not confined to Japan, as you will recall from the Marlon Brando movies *On the Waterfront* and *The Godfather*.

Kusare'en (literally, bonds so thoroughly rotten that they cannot be divided into good and bad portions, or at all) also exist between the *yakuza* and the entertainment industry. There are many ways for the *yakuza* to approach entertainers, but the main reason for their success is that show business can so easily be disrupted by violence. Once bonds are forged, the entertainers find themselves under the control of the *yakuza kōgyō-shi* (impressario). When this happens, the entertainer can't refuse to give any *yakuza*-arranged performance, no matter how undesirable the venue.

Some notorious production companies even take a generous squeeze for themselves out of the entertainer's payment. This kind of shakedown is called *pin-hane* (kickback). *Pin-hane* comes from the expression *pin o haneru* (to skim some off the top). *Pin* originally comes from the Portuguese *pinta* (point). Later, it came to be used to mean number one, because a single spot on a die is equal to one, and finally, to refer to the top. The transitive verb *haneru* expresses a sweeping, snatching action of the hand. *Atama* (head or top) *o haneru, atama-hane* or *uwamae* (outer skirt of a *kimono*) *o haneru* all mean the same thing.

Tekiya

A major splinter of *yakuza* groups are the *tekiya* or *yashi,* who engage in shady peddling activities, black marketeering, and the street stall business. Nowadays, the boundary between *yakuza* and *tekiya* is becoming more blurred, as each of them increasingly gets into lines of business that used to be reserved for the other.

The Japanese have many festival days *(en-nichi* or *o-matsuri)* at the various Shinto shrines and Buddhist temples around the country. On such occasions, street stalls are set up in the precincts of the shrine or temple and on the nearby streets. The vendors at such stalls are called *en-nichi-ya*. Though most of these stalls are temporary, some have become permanent institutions. The world-famous *Naka-mise* at Asakusa Kannon in Tokyo, for example, contains hundreds of such stalls.

In most cases, the temporary stalls and their allocation *(shoba-wari)* are controlled by the *tekiya* or *ya-shi* leader. No one can sell any goods in the precincts of the shrine or temple or on the nearby streets without their personal permission. Their permission, of course, can be bought by paying *shoba-dai*. There are usually lots of stalls at fairs and festivals, but many of them sell *yasu-mono* (cheap or inferior articles), which break in a day or two. In some cases, though, one can find some nice traditional items, like *take-tonbo* (bamboo dragonfly), a lovely children's toy.

Apart from fairs and festivals, there are many kinds of street vendors at the *sakariba* (bustling areas), such as Shinjuku, Ueno, and Shibuya in Tokyo. They are called *roten-shō*. *Roten* means open-air (shop), and *shō* is a merchant or vendor. They usually conduct their business in makeshift stalls or *yatai* (a movable stand on wheels). Street vendors who use *yatai* are also called *yatai*. The areas that can be serviced by *roten-shō* or *yatai* are controlled by the *tekiya* boss. Sometimes the *tekiya* themselves may be running the stalls. *Oden-ya* (Japanese stew vendors), *rāmen-ya* (Chinese noodle vendors), and *yaki-imo-ya* (roasted sweet potato vendors) are among the more commonly seen *yatai*. If you want to differentiate between a vendor on wheels and an ordinary shop, you can add *yatai-no* as in *yatai-no rāmen-ya*.

Once *banana-uri* (banana vendors) flourished in every big city in Japan as a type of *roten-shō*. More than 30 years ago, bananas were imported on a quota basis *(wariate-sei)* and were expensive. Some were put on the market illegally by the *tekiya,* and *banana no tataki-uri* (auction sale of bananas) was seen everywhere in Japan. *Tataki,* as we have mentioned, means striking or beating. Here, it was the sound of a can beating on a stand. Often the dialogue between vendors and bystanders would become quite amusing and people would be urged to buy with a laugh. Nowadays, though, *banana-ya* and their humor are gone, replaced by taciturn vendors selling everything from pets to pornography. These various articles are called *neta* in *tekiya* patois (*neta* is an inverted form of *tane,* or seed). Thus, *netamoto* (*moto* means origin or source) in gangster language refers to the distributor, namely the *oyabun* (boss).

In the entertainment districts of some of Japan's larger cities, there are *yatai* vendors selling *hotto dokku* (hot dogs), *tōmorokoshi* (grilled corn), and *tako-yaki* (a kind of pancake mixed with small pieces of octopus) near the entrances of train stations. They, too, need to get the illegal permission of the *tekiya* to ply their trade at a particular location, as well as the legal consent of the police. Nowadays, *yatai* have become very modernized, using station wagons with their own electric generators *(jika-hatsuden)* instead of the traditional portable carts.

The *tekiya* also control the fortune tellers, called *eki-sha* or *uranai-shi,* who sit at small stands on the street. *Eki-sha* are among the nation's most popular consultants for matters related to people's fortunes or personal concerns. *Uranai-sha* usually examine the hands of their guests, especially the *tesō* (the lines on the palm) to read their fortunes. These diviners are called *tesō-mi* (palmists). *Eki-sha* also often use divining rods made of bamboo. Young people, especially girls, like to visit them to seek advice regarding *nayami* (problems) or *mi no ue banashi* (personal affairs or circumstances) that they would never otherwise talk about, even with their mothers. In this way, *eki-sha* often play the part of a psychoanalyst, a much-needed service in today's Japan.

2

Underground Jargon

(angura ingo)

Yakuza Jargon, Police Terms

Contemporary *yakuza* have an extensive secret jargon, or *ingo*. In fact, a pamphlet entitled *Ingo-shū* is published occasionally by the Tokyo Metropolitan Police Office (MPO). This pamphlet, which the MPO printed to help policemen understand the language used by juvenile delinquents, lists no fewer than 700 underworld terms. These are divided into four categories: traditional *ingo,* or traditional, well-established terms; new words and usage; place names and numbers; and *bōsō-zoku* (motorcycle gang) argot.

Before introducing some of the words contained in the pamphlet, we shall classify *yakuza* language into five categories: inverted words or inverted pronunciation, such as *naon* instead of *onna* (woman or girl) and *bonzu* instead of *zubon* (trousers); abbreviations, such as *satsu* for *keisatsu* (police); real jargon and vulgarisms, including such terms as *deka* instead of *keiji* (investigator) and *kisu* instead of *sake* (rice wine); conventional expressions with new underground meanings, as in *oyaji* (daddy) to mean policeman; and loan words from foreign languages such as *dorinku* (drink) to mean *nomi-kōi* (illegal bookmaking).

Let's start with underground expressions for the police, who are the greatest enemies of the *yakuza*. One of the most popular slang terms for policemen in the underworld is *o-mawari* (fuzz). *O-* is a respectful prefix and *mawari* comes from the verb *mawaru* (to go around or to patrol). The word *o-mawari-san* is used commonly in ordinary, polite conversation.

Satsu, as we mentioned above, is an underworld expression for both police and policeman. On the rare occasions that underworld characters might want to express some affection for the police, they might say *satsu no danna, danna* being master or gentleman. The term *oyaji* (daddy) would express the same sentiments.

In the United States, perhaps the most commonly used derogatory term for policeman is pig, an expression often heard during uprisings and demonstrations in the 60s and 70s. In Japan, the equivalent is *inu,* which means dog. The term is commonly employed by thieves, *yakuza,* and members of the *sayoku* (left wing). The dog is said to have been the first domesticated animal *(kachiku)* in the world, and it is known to be very faithful to its master. Because of this undying fidelity, the dog would never betray or turn on its allies. Thus, *banken* (watchdog) is used in Japanese to describe someone who is merely a watchdog for his master or boss. *Ban* means watching and *ken* is a different way of pronouncing the character for *inu*. The expression *kenryoku* (power or authority) *no banken* refers to the police or the military.

Another meaning of the word *inu* is spy or agent, as a dog is apt to sniff around *(kagi mawaru)* in everybody's business. *Inu* is also used to express disgust for something that is thought to be meaningless.

Pori-kō is another insulting word for policeman. It combines *porisuman* (policeman) with the derogative suffix *-kō*. *O-ma-kō* (cop or fuzz) is a similar word using *o-mawari* (policeman). *Aka* (red) is one of the latest *yakuza* words implying policeman. *Ita-kō* is yet another new word, coming from *itachi* (skunk), and, again, the insulting suffix *-kō*.

The most common legal term for policeman is *keisatsukan*. This word, however, is rarely heard except on formal occasions, and no one would really use it in ordinary conversation. Instead, they might say something like *keisatsu o yobe* (call the police!) or *hyaku-tō-ban shiro* (call 110!). *Hyaku-tō ban,* or 110, is the emergency number to call throughout Japan. Apparently, it was chosen because it's easy to dial and remember in emergencies. This is similar to 911 in the United States.

Another popular and interesting underground expression for policeman is *deka*, which is used when referring to a detective *(keiji)*. It is an inverted and shortened form of *kakusode,* which means square sleeves. In the Taishō era (1912–1926), detectives wore Japanese *kimono*-style uniforms with square sleeves. At that time, criminals began to use the word *kakusode* as a synonym for a policeman. *Deka* and its variation *deka-chō* (chief detective) were popularized as journalistic slang by NHK television's popular program *Jiken Kisha* (City Desk Reporter). Today, reporters and *toppu-ya* (muckrakers) often use the term *deka-chō* or, more politely, *deka-chō-san.*

Shifuku (plain clothes) is a word used for detectives. These officers wear ordinary street clothes on the job instead of the Western-style uniforms *(seifuku)* donned by regular policemen.

Mappo and *mappō* are argot terms for a policeman in uniform. The etymology of these words, however, is unknown. *Mappo no ojō* is for a policewoman, *ojō* being an abbreviation of *o-jō-san* (young lady). *Ahiru* (duck) has come to be used frequently as a derogatory reference to a uniformed policeman who walks his beat slowly, ducklike, as if to emphasize his authority.

Let's move on now to expressions that police themselves use in referring to cases *(yama)*. *Gaisha* is police/journalistic slang for the victim. It is a shortened form of the ordinary word *higaisha* (victim). In police language, *maru-hi* or *maru-gai* are synonyms for *higaisha* or *gaisha*. *Maguro* (tuna) is the body of a person run over by a train.

Yakitori (grilled chicken) is a fire fatality. Either of these can be called *hotoke* (Buddha or dead). *Hotoke ni naru,* then, means to be dead or to die.

Aka inu (red dog) and *akai uma* (red horse) both mean arson; *akai neko* (red cat) is both arson and fire. *Ami* (literally, net) is a police term for dragnet. *O-kyaku* (literally, guest) is a victim, and *kunoichi* is a woman. The term *kunoichi* derives from the fact that the character for woman can be broken up into hiragana *ku, katakana no,* and the *kanji* for *ichi* (one). *Kona* (literally, powder or flour) is heroin. *Kobu,* which means lump or tumor, is used to mean a child, and *kobu-tsuki* is a common word to mean a woman with a child or children to feed.

Police work often involves searches *(gasa-ire)* of places under suspicion. *Gasa* is thought to be either an inverted abbreviation of *yasagashi* (house search) or to come from the onomatopoetic *gasa-gasa* (rustling sounds).

Hoshi refers to a suspect or criminal offender. It's a shortened form of *zuboshi* (bull's eye). Thus, there are expressions such as *hoshi o ageru* (to arrest the offender) and *hoshi ga wareru* (to mark a suspect). Note, however, that when you say *zuboshi* in an exclamatory way, it means right on, just like the English bulls-eye!

O-miya-iri (literally, entering into a shrine; figuratively, unsolved mystery) is a popular term among police and journalists when the police investigation of a crime is unsuccessful. It means the police are baffled, and comes from *meikyū* (labyrinth), *mei* being a different pronunciation for the ideograph for *mayou* (to be lost), and *kyū* being an alternate reading for *miya* (palace, shrine, or any big building where one can easily get lost). Among ordinary people, the expression *meikyū-iri,* rather than *o-miya-iri,* is the common term used to describe a baffling case.

When making an arrest, police sometimes need an *o-fuda,* or an arrest warrant. *Fuda* here literally means card.

Sho, short for *keisatsusho,* is police station. Police have been accused of using violent *gōmon* (torture) on a suspect in the process of investigation. The suspect, unable to endure, will confess, or *hakujō suru, jihaku suru* (the *haku* in these expressions is written with the character for *shiro* meaning white, suggesting coming clean), or *mōsu* (to talk). This is also referred to as *doro o haku* (literally, vomit mud—the *haku* here is not the character for *shiro,* but one meaning to vomit), or *gero suru* (literally, vomit). A related expression is *doro o kaburu* (literally, to put mud upon one's own head), where one becomes *migawari* (a substitute who takes the blame for the crime of the *oyabun* or *anikibun* and goes to jail for him). This is a common practice among gangster organizations everywhere.

Criminals are eager to run away from their hideouts, or *yasa* (an inverted form of *saya,* which means sheath) before arrest *(teire). Nigeru* is a verb meaning to escape; *tōbō suru* and *tōsō suru* are formal versions with the same meaning. *Takatobi* literally means flying high, but it is also used to mean to skip town. Its verb form is *takatobi suru.*

The adjective *yabai* is a slang term describing the feeling a criminal has when he feels in danger of being apprehended by the police. It comes from the now-archaic noun *yaba* (inconvenience). People use this adjective often in ordinary conversation to mean risky, troublesome, or embarrassing.

When a criminal detects (*kanzuku* or *kagitsukeru*) that the police are on his trail, he will naturally get ready to take off. In such a case *nagai tabi* (long journey) or *tōi tabi* (far journey) is applied. The verb *zurakaru* is another slangy expression meaning to go on the lam. An even more informal euphemism for skipping out is *tonzura suru.* An ordinary word for this is *yonige* (nocturnal flight). *Fukeru,* normally used to mean to be boiled or to be steamed, is slang for to fly off, while *jōhatsu suru* (to evaporate) is an expression that describes the contemporary phenomenon of disappearing, suddenly and without a trace, from one's family, friends, and job.

Sugata (figure) *o kuramasu* and *yukue* (whereabouts) *o kuramasu* are colloquial phrases meaning to hide oneself and to cover one's traces, respectively. *Kuramasu* in these expressions means to disappear. *Senpuku* is a bookish expression for concealment or escaping into hiding. *Mi o kakusu* (literally, to hide one's self; figuratively, to be in hiding) takes place, of course, at a criminal's hideout—called, in ordinary conversation, *kakurega*.

The hideouts of left-wing activitists are specifically called *ajito*. This expression comes from the Russian word *agipunkt,* which originally meant agitation headquarters and later underground headquarters.

When a suspect fails in his attempt to evade the police, the expressions *nengu o osameru, yaki ga mawaru,* and *doji o fumu* are used, meaning to bungle. *Nengu* means yearly land tax, and *osameru* means to reap one's due. *Yaki* means tempering, as in tempering a sword, and *mawaru* in this case is to spread. When a sword is overheated, it loses its sharpness. The phrase *yaki ga mawaru* means to become dull or lose one's edge. In other words, a criminal might be more alert and not so easily caught if he were younger. *Doji* is an expression for *shippai* (failure) and is always accompanied by the verb *fumu* (to step). The idiomatic phrase can be translated as to screw up. There are many theories as to the etymology of *doji.* One is that it came from *tochiru* (to make a mistake); another is that it originated from the term *tsuchi* (dirt, earth) *o fumu* or *tochi* (piece of land) *o fumu,* either of which conjures up the image of stepping out of the *dohyō* (wrestling ring) in a sumo match, which automatically means that the wrestler has lost.

Once a criminal has blundered and is arrested, he is, as a matter of course, imprisoned. *Musho* is slang for either jail or prison. It is an abbreviation of *keimusho,* an ordinary word for prison and is used in such expressions as *musho-iri* (thrown into the slammer) or *musho gurashi* (prison life). *Buta bako,* which literally means pig box, can be conveniently translated as pokey. It is used either for a police cell or jailhouse. The alliterative expression *buta bako ni buchikomu* is a typical idiomatic phrase used when someone is thrown into jail. The verb *buchikomu* is used when people throw or strike something violently.

Prisoners or jailbirds *(shūjin)* everywhere spend a lot of time thinking about life outside. *Shaba* is a vulgar antonym for *musho* and means the outside world. It originates from a Buddhist term meaning the earthly world as opposed to the celestial world. It later came to refer to a freer world than that found in prisons and, by extension, in the army and whorehouses. Prisoners often say *shaba no kūki ga suitai* and *shaba no meshi ga kuitai* (I want to breathe outside air, and I want to eat outside chow, respectively), both of which mean I want out of here. The opposite of *shaba no meshi* is *kusai meshi* (stinking food); *kusai meshi o kuu* (to eat stinking food) is an idiom for serving a prison term.

Occasionally a prisoner will attempt to break out or escape from jail *(datsu-goku* or *rō-yaburi). Rō, goku,* and *rōgoku* all mean prison, and *yaburu* is to break out. *Shima yaburi* in the Edo era meant jail-breaking. *Shima* (island) in this case refers to an island of exile like Hachijōjima or Sadogashima, two penal islands in Japan. Legitimate release from prison is referred to as *shussho.*

A person who has a criminal record is called *zenka-mono, zen* being past or previous, and *ka* being a criminal charge. *Mae* (before) is an underground slang term for shady past, while *mae-ari* refers to an ex-convict. *Mae* is written with the same *kanji* as *zen,* and *ari* comes from the verb *aru* (to have). The expression *fudatsuki* (on the black list) is often used to mean a habitual criminal *(joshūhan)*.

When a *yakuza* big shot *(ō-mono)* is released from prison, his gang will celebrate his return. Such a celebration party is called *shussho iwai, iwai* being a celebration, usually congratulatory in nature. If the *ō-mono* thinks he was imprisoned because of an informer's tipoff, he'll be sure to look into the matter. He might start by giving the suspected informer the cold shoulder, or *hijideppō*. A synonym for this is *hijitetsu o kurawasu* from the motion of elbowing someone to show dislike. When he is convinced of the informer's guilt, he will decide to strike. *O-rei-mairi* is a popular slang expression for this. The word comes from the tradition of paying a visit of thanks *(o-rei)* to a shrine or temple when one thinks a god has helped him. *Mairi* comes from *mairu,* the humble verb for to go or to come. When a gangster actually pays a retaliation visit, he uses the set expression *kari o kaesu* (to settle a debt or to pay a bill).

There are several underground expressions for the informer *(mikkokusha)* and his information or tips *(mikkoku).* When an informer rats on someone in his own *yakuza* gang, he is called *uragiri-mono* (rat) from the verb *uragiru* (to betray). *Tarekomi,* from the verb *tarekomu* (to inform), is a popular slang term for squealing. *Sasu* (to prick) and *barasu* (to divulge or reveal) are other slang verbs meaning to rat. From the police's standpoint, *tarekomi* is a kind of *urikomi* (selling) act.

When an *uragiri-mono* is discovered in a *yakuza* group or family *(ikka),* he has to be punished or rubbed out according to the rules of the family *(ikka no okite).*

As with gangster organizations everywhere, not only betrayers but also gang members who bring shame upon the boss are chastised as examples *(miseshime)* to others. *Shimatsu* (literally, disposal or settlement) is a typical expression for such retribution. This term takes two forms: *shimatsu o tsukeru* and *shimatsu suru*. The former means to fix or punish someone. The latter appears in ordinary conversation meaning to put something in order. In its darker incarnation, though, it's used to mean to kill someone. *Kata o tsukeru* and *keri o tsukeru* are two more verbs meaning to settle or put an end to a matter.

Once it's been decided that payment must be meted out to a certain gang member, what kind of settlement is mandated? *Kesu* (to rub out) would be the solution in the most severe cases. In slightly less serious instances, *yubitsume* (cutting off a finger, usually the little one) is required. This punishment, still fashionable in *yakuza* circles, is carried out by the offender himself.

Yaki o ireru refers to various types of corporal punishment. *Yaki,* as we mentioned previously, comes from hardening or tempering a blade. This expression means to teach a lesson to or crack down on. *Shigoku* and its noun form *shigoki* mean to train hard or to put through the mill. These expressions are also used when referring to extremely heavy sports training in school, as well as torture.

Kawaigaru is a sarcastic expression meaning to treat someone with adoration. *Itaburu* is to torture or discipline someone. Extreme *itaburi* is *naburi goroshi* (torture to death).

Shioki (punishment or execution) is now somewhat out-of-date, but it can sometimes be seen in titles of period adventure dramas (*jidai geki* or *chanbara eiga*) on TV, such as *Shioki-nin (The Executioner)*, with their swaggering *samurai* and simpering ladies. When you add the honorific prefix *o-* to this word to make *o-shioki,* it becomes a commonly used motherly colloquialism meaning to punish a child.

A rather square expression, *seisai,* is used to mean punishment or sanction under the law. Colloquially, it's also used for private punishment or what might be called vigilante justice. It's more or less synonymous with *rinchi* (lynch).

Fighting Phrases *(kenka yōgo)*

Yakuza or *bōryokudan* are specialists in the art of violent fighting (*kenka* in ordinary terms, and *goro* in underground slang). As a result, they tend to be hired as *yōjinbō* (bodyguards) or *koroshi-ya* (hired killers) by people in need of such services. *Yōjinbō* is a combination of the words *yōjin* (precaution as in *hi no yōjin,* which means fire watch) and *bō* (bar or bolt). Originally, it was used as a synonym for *shinbaribō,* which is a bar used to fasten a door. Today, however, it refers to a bodyguard, or other kind of "enforcer." *Koroshi-ya,* referring to a professional killer or trigger man, comes from the verb *korosu* (to kill). *Hittoman,* from the English hit man, is also used.

There are other slang terms meaning to kill someone. They include *tatamu* (to fold), *barasu* (literally, to disjoint), *yaru* (literally, to do), and *kesu* (literally, to wipe out). A close equivalent to this latter in American gang language would be to rub out. A gangster might say, for example, *aitsu o tatanjae* (kill him). *-Chimae* or *-chae* is a contracted form of *-te-shimae,* which means to do something thoroughly.

Han-goroshi, which literally means half-killing, is to beat a person to a pulp. Gangsters frequently use such verbs as *nosu* or *nobasu* (to extend or knock down), *tatamu* (to fold) *buttobasu* (to strike or beat), *bunnaguru* (to strike hard), *yattsukeru* (to beat up), and *itaime ni awasu* (to make a person cry with pain) when referring to beating up or injuring a person. *Yaki o ireru* can also be used in this connection, meaning to perform a group lynching. *Bōryoku* (violence or force), *bōryoku kōi* (an act of violence), *bōkō* (violence, usually rape), *shōgai* (injury), and *satsujin* (homicide, murder) are all legal terms for these antisocial deeds.

The *yakuza* are very fond of *kenka,* which is a general term for both quarrel and fight; the verb form of *kenka* is *kenka o suru.* In Japanese, you can buy and sell a fight. When you say *kenka o uru* (sell), it means to pick a fight, while *kenka o kau,* (buy) means to rise to the bait.

Kenka originally meant to be noisy with loud voices. If you want to specify that you mean a verbal altercation, you can say *kuchi* (verbal) *genka, genka* being a euphonic change of *kenka. Ii-ai* is a similar expression, meaning to have words with someone. *Koron* (bickering) and *nonoshiri-ai* (to abuse one another) are some other expressions for verbal quarreling. The expressions *naguri-ai no kenka* (coming to blows) and *tokkumiai no kenka* (scuffle) refer to physical fights.

Both *ō-genka* and *hade-na kenka* mean serious quarrel or serious fight, such as disagreements between parents and children *(oyako genka)* or between lovers or married couples *(fūfu genka).* It used to be thought that families could settle such matters among themselves, but recently the police are increasingly becoming involved. There is still, however, a reluctance to interfere with a *fūfu genka,* a fact reflected in the saying *fūfu genka wa inu mo kuwanai* (even a dog wouldn't nip at a lovers' quarrel).

In such cases, one or both parties may be quick-tempered *(kenka-ppayai).* This term consists of *kenka* and a euphonic change of *hayai* (quick). *Katto naru, kakka suru,* and *kari-kari suru* all mean to become angry or fly into a rage; both *katto naru tachi* (temper) and *kari-kari kuru tachi* refer to a hot-tempered person.

The underground expression for *kenka* is *goro* and its verb form is *goro (o) maku. Sashi-goro* and *ya-goro* both refer to a knife fight. Another expression that is quite popular among younger hoodlums is *taiman.* This means a one-on-one fight, and it comes from *ittai icha* (one-to-one) and *man* (person). Its verb form is *taiman o haru.* The *ya* in *ya-goro* comes from *yaiba,* meaning blade.

Sashi, from *sashi-goro* comes from the verb *sasu* (to stab).

Deiri is a slang expression for a confrontation between the members of two *yakuza* gangs. It literally means coming in and going out, reflecting the behavior of gang members who frequently run in and out of the group's headquarters during such a fight.

Then, there are long, drawn-out gang wars. These are called *yakuza no kōsō* (struggles) or *yakuza-sensō* (wars) and often, in newspaper headlines, *jingi naki tatakai* (battles without justice). In such fights, *hajiki* or *chaka,* both meaning pistol or handgun, may be used. *Hajiki* is from the verb *hajiku,* which means to flip or snap, and *chaka* is an onomatopoeia for the sound of the trigger.

Yakuza like to fight even when they don't have a legitimate reason to do so. Consequently, they make up pretexts *(kōjitsu). Gan (o) tsuketa* (literally, you looked at me; figuratively, what are you staring at?), *ashi (o) funda* (you stepped on my foot), and *kata ni sawatta* (literally, you touched my shoulder; figuratively, you shoved me) are all typical "provocations" used by gangsters as excuses to fight. *Gan* (eyes) is a *yakuza* argot term, but now it's ordinary slang as in *gan-tsuke.*

Once the fight has begun, there are a variety of expressions one might hear. Besides the typical *nonoshiri* (swear words), *warukuchi* (bad-mouthing), and *akutai* (abusive language), *yakuza* have a number of set *kenka yōgo* (fighting terms), which are usually used in running, guttural combination.

Nan da temē and *nan da omae,* both used by men, and their feminine counterpart *nani yo anta* all mean who the hell do you think you are? *Kono yarō* and *kon'chikushō,* often pronounced *kon'chikishō* (literally, you beast), can be translated as you bastard.

Baka yarō (literally, fool) and the rougher *bakkayaro* are probably the most widely used quarrel words in Japan, and they can be translated you shit, you bastard, and so on. (Women usually simply say *baka* or *bāka*.) Even more offensive is *kusottare*, which literally works out to mean you shit-dripper. Such an exchange is described in Japanese as *uri-kotoba* (literally, words to sell) *ni kai kotoba* (literally, words to buy), rendered into English as those are fighting words. When the fight really gets going, these words are spoken explosively and gutturally, and the r's are rolled forcefully. These words are often used in combination with *urusē*, and *damare*.

Urusai and its tougher-sounding form *urusē* (obnoxious) mean shut up or get out of here. Again, its effect is immeasurably enhanced by rolling the r. *Damare* also means shut up.

Iikagen ni shiro (literally, that's enough to provoke me) means don't mess with me any more. *Yose (yo)* and *yamero* are stop it or more colloquially, knock it off.

Fuzakeru is an ordinary Japanese verb meaning to frolic or to play. It isn't so playful, though, in its informal negative form, *fuzakeru na,* which means, don't mess around with me. Cruder still, *fuzakenna* and *fuzzaken'ja nē yo* are equivalent to don't fuck with me. *Nameru na* and its slang variation *namen'ja nē yo* (literally, don't underrate me) again would be, don't screw with me. *Tobokeru na* and its slangy derivatives *tobokenna* and *toboken'ja nē yo* mean don't play dumb, while *ibaru na,* often *ibarun'ja nē yo,* means don't try to be such a hot shot. The verb *ibaru,* as we have already mentioned, means to be pompous or to swagger.

Jōdan ja nai, jōdan ja nē, and *jōdan iu na* can all be translated as don't kid with me. *Jōdan* is an ordinary and commonly heard term meaning joke. *Namaiki (da zo)* and *namaiki iu na* both mean don't be such a wise guy.

Jōtō da (literally, fine), implies you think you're so great, but just you wait—I'll kick your ass, while *atama ni kita* means you're really getting to me. *Omote ni dero* means get outside, and, by extension, let's fight! *Yatte yarō, yatte yarō ja nē ka,* and *yattarō ja nē ka* all mean

I'm going to beat you up. *Buttobasu zo* (I'll knock you on your ass) and *bukkorosu zo* (I'm going to kill you) are other idiomatic expressions.

The winner of a *kenka* will usually boast proudly of his victory. The verb *yattsukeru* and its past form *yatsuketa* are commonly used when one emerges as a winner in a fight or quarrel. The term derives from the basic word *yaru,* which simply means to do. *Yattsukeru* was originally used to mean to dare to do something. It later came to mean specifically to beat thoroughly or to let someone have it. Quite often, people add the mimetic adverb *koten-koten (ni)* or its slang form *koten-pan (ni)* to this verb. Thus, *koten-pan ni yattsukeru* means to beat the hell out of.

Buttobasu, buchinomesu, tatakitsubusu, and *tataki-nomesu* are other popular verbs used by the winning side in boasting of victory. They all mean to deal a crushing defeat. These are usually used in the past tense as in *buttobashita* or *buttobashichatta.*

As might be expected, there aren't as many expressions for defeat as there are for victory. The passive verb *yarareru,* often heard in the past tense, *yarareta,* is perhaps the most popular. *Maitta, maketa,* and *kōsan shita* all mean I've been beaten—you win. *Mairu* is to be beaten, *makeru* is to be defeated, and *kōsan suru* is to surrender. When someone is asked *dōshita?* (what happened?), the loser might reply *koten-pan ni yarareta* (I got my ass kicked). Other expressions for defeat are *hidoi me ni atta* or *sanzan-na me ni atta,* both of which mean I had a hard time, or I got the shit kicked out of me.

Instead of admitting that they were defeated, *yakuza* usually resort to some kind of euphemistic expression, such as *haji o kaita* (I was shamed) or *haji o kakasareta* (literally, I was humiliated), *otoko ga sutaru* (my manhood is thrown out).

When a person, not necessarily a gangster, feels humiliated or insulted after having been beaten in a quarrel or dispute, he might say *koke ni sareta* (he made an ass of me). This is slang for *baka* (fool or ass) *ni sareta*. *Koke* in *koke ni suru,* or its passive form *koke ni sareru,* is said to have come from the Buddhist term *koke,* meaning untrue, or a discrepancy between inside and outside. Subsequently, it came to mean thoughtless or foolish. *Koke ni suru,* then, means to make a fool of. *Koke no ichinen* (concentration) and *koke no isshin* (literally, single-minded), on the other hand, imply that even a fool can accomplish something if he devotes himself single-mindedly to it.

When a *yakuza* feels *koke ni sareta,* he will demand some kind of settlement from his enemy. This settlement is called *otoshimae*. *Otoshimae* and its verb form *otoshimae o tsukeru* are common slang terms referring to settlement of the issue or quarrel. The verb *tsukeru* can carry the implication of to fix something. The *otoshimae* is usually arranged by a *chūsai (-nin)* or *nakadachi (-nin)* (mediator). *Hanashi o tsukeru* and its slang variation *nashi o tsukeru* are popular verbs referring specifically to this kind of mediation. *Hanashi* is talk and *hanashi o tsukeru* means to work out a settlement. *Kuchi o kiku* means to speak to or put in a good word.

What is involved in *otoshimae?* First of all, the losing party must offer an apology (*wabi o ireru—wabi* means apology), if only to allow his opponent to save face. Often, the person apologizing will cut off his little finger *(yubitsume),* a practice we've already discussed. He might then give it to the mediator to take to the winner.

Once the formalities are decided upon and completed, the parties concerned hold a *teuchi(-shiki),* or reconciliation (ceremony). *Teuchi* (literally, clapping hands) is also used in ordinary conversation to mean strike a bargain or close a deal, is in *teuchi ni suru,* or the more popular *te o utsu.* There is no handshake, as the Japanese do not have a tradition of touching one another. At a *yakuza* reconciliation ceremony, the mediator would say *o-te o haishaku* (literally, lend me your hands; in other words, follow me) and lead the group in *sanbon-jime,* which is a special kind of clapping cadence that goes like this: clap, clap, clap; clap, clap, clap; clap, clap, clap; CLAP! After this is repeated three times, the parties concerned wind up the celebration by saying *gokurō-san* or *otsukare-san,* which are common expressions meaning sorry to have troubled you or sorry to have put you out. *Jime* here comes from the verb *shimeru* (to close, to put an end to).

Since we're on the subject, we'll digress a bit here to introduce some slang and underground terms used to refer to money-related subjects. *Gen-nama* or just *nama* both imply cash or ready money; *neka,* an inverted form of *kane* (gold or metal), simply means money. In ordinary conversations, people add the honorific prefix *o-* to get the word *o-kane.* Thus, such rough expressions as *oi, kane nē ka* (or *nai ka*)? (ain't you got any money?), and *kane (o) kure* (give me some money), would only be heard among very intimate friends or in the underworld. *O-satsu* is a bill or note, while *zeni,* with its underground inverted variation *nize,* and *bara-sen* all mean coin or small amount of money. The word *satsu-taba* literally means a wad of money or roll of bills, but it bears the same connotation of big money as wad and bundle in English. *Satsu-taba kōsei* (*kōsei* is campaign) means attempted bribery, while *kane-mōke* and *zeni-mōke* both mean making big money, the latter connoting by dirty or shady means.

O-ashi is another synonym for money. It is made up of the honorific prefix *o-* and *ashi* (foot). It comes from a euphemism for money used by women to mean base or foundation—the feet on which one stands. Now it is used by men as well, implying that money is a thing that constantly escapes as if it had feet of its own.

Maru (literally, circle) comes from the shape of a coin and is mainly used as telegram code, as in *maru okure* (send money). In Japan, when you make a circle with your thumb and forefinger, it means money. Like people around the world, some Japanese don't like to talk about money directly. So saying *kore* (this) *aru?* or *kore kashite* using the above-mentioned hand sign, means do you have any money? or, lend me some money, respectively.

What about those all-too-frequent occasions when one runs short of money? When you don't have any money at all, you might say *mon-nashi da* or *issen mo nai* (I'm broke or I'm penniless). *Mon* comes from an Edo era monetary unit, while *issen* comes from a sub-unit of the yen in pre-war days. *Okera* is another slang term for being penniless. It comes from *yakuza* language, but now it is quite popular among ordinary people as well. An *okera* is a kind of cricket that holds its forelegs in an apparently imploring position, as if it were saying look, I haven't got a thing.

Karaketsu and the more informal *karakketsu, sukanpin, gerupin,* and *kinketsu* are other popular synonyms for *okera* and *mon-nashi*. *Karaketsu* and *karakketsu* come from a slang term that was used in theatrical circles in the Edo era. *Kara* is empty, and *ketsu* is hole. Thus, *karaketsu* and *karakketsu* mean having nothing, penniless. *Sukanpin* means terribly poor, and it can be translated as being flat broke. *Gerupin,* mainly used among students, is coined from the German *gelt* (gold) and the English word pinch. Finally, *kinketsu* is comprised of *kin,* which is a different way of pronouncing the *kanji* for *kane* (money), and *ketsu* (lack or shortage). This expression is usually accompanied by *byō* (disease), so when you say *aitsu wa (itsumo) kinketsu-byō da,* it means he never has any money.

Sometimes when lower-ranking gangsters or *chinpira* don't have any money or want to throw their weight around, they resort to *roha* (free of charge) services. This term comes from the Chinese character for *tada* (the ordinary expression for free of charge); this character looks like a combination of the phonetic *katakana* symbol for *ro* on the top and *ha* on the bottom.

Juvenile delinquents and gangsters will often eat and drink for nothing (*tadagui* and *tadanomi,* respectively) at snack bars and saloons after threatening the staff. The next day, they boast about their adventures with sentences like *yube roha de tabetari nondari shichatta* (last night, I ate and drank for free). At other times, they ride the trains for nothing by menacing railway workers. *Satsuma no kami* is an archaic expression for riding for free. It came from Satsuma-no-kami Tadanori, which was a samurai's name. *Tadanori* literally means free ride, but people liked to use only the first part of the name as a euphemism. The official term for this is *fusei jōsha* (literally, illegal ride).

O-kura generally means warehouse or storehouse (*kura*), but in underground language, it's used to mean a pawnshop. *Shichi-ya* is the regular term for pawnshop. When you say simply *shichi,* it means both seven, and pawn or security, though the *kanji* for each *shichi* is different. Using these homonyms, people have created the slang term *ichi-roku ginkō,* which also means pawnshop. *Ichi* is one, *roku* is six, making seven, and *ginkō* is bank.

Tenjō, which means ceiling or sky, also refers to a ceiling in economic jargon. Thus, *tenjō shirazu,* meaning limitless price, refers to skyrocketing stock prices.

Ponkotsu, generally meaning junk or trash, can be used to mean extortion or blackmail in *yakuza* language. *Ponkotsu* or *ponkotsu guruma* (car or automobile) mean jalopy. *Ore wa ponkotsu da* could be translated as I'm completely burnt out or used up.

Kansai greengrocers have a tricky language that they use when discussing the prices of their commodities. In order to understand this jargon, we must first explain the different expressions for the 12 months of the year, which form its basis.

January is usually called *ichigatsu* (first month), but it is also known as *shōgatsu* (genuine month) or *mutsuki* (friendly month). February is *nigatsu* (second month) or *kisaragi* (heavy-clad month). March is *sangatsu* or *yayoi*. *Yayoi* is said to come from the idea that March is the month when plants start to grow *(iyaoi)*. April is *shigatsu* (fourth month) or *uzuki* (rabbit month), as the rabbit is the fourth animal of the 12 in the Asian zodiac. May is *gogatsu, samidarezuki* (early summer rain month), or *satsuki* (etymology unclear), and June is *rokugatsu, narukamizuki* (thunder month), or *minazuki* (water month). July is *shichigatsu, tanabatatsuki* (Vega month), or *fumitsuki* (writing month). August is *hachigatsu, hazuki* (month of leaves), or *tsukimizuki* (moon-viewing month), while September is *kugatsu, nagatsuki* (long month), or *kikuzuki* (chrysanthemum month). October is *jūgatsu* or *kannazuki* (no-god month). It is said that in October all the gods in Japan go away for an annual meeting. November is *jūichigatsu* or *shimotsuki* (frost month). Finally, December is *jūnigatsu, shiwasu* (even-the-monks-are-running-it's-so-busy month), or *gokugetsu* (ending month).

The Kansai greengrocers borrow from these terms to secretly express numbers. Thus, *shō* is one, *kisa* is two, *yā* is three, *ū* is four, *ame* (rain from *samidarezuki*) is five, *kami* is six, *hoshi* (star) is seven, *tsuki* is eight, and *kiku* is nine. So, for instance, *ame-man shō-sen,* would be 51,000.

To complicate matters still further, Tokyo greengrocers also have a secret language for numbers. *U* is one, *me* is two, *sa* is three, *ku* is four, *ra* is five, *ma* is six, *tsu* is seven, *ta* is eight, and *ke* is nine. These come from the names of trees: *ume* (plum), *sakura* (cherry), *matsu* (pine), and *take* (bamboo).

Similarly, *sushi* restaurants have their own words for the numbers one through nine. They are *pin, sokuban, geta, dari, mēji, ronju, sēnan, bando,* and *kiwa. Tekiya* equivalents are *yari, furi, chika, tame, shizuka, mizu, oki, atsuta,* and *kiwa. Chinpira* have the same words for the numbers one, two, four, six, and seven, but they change the others to *kochi* (three), *zuka* (five), *asuta* (eight), and *gake* (nine). Finally, musicians have their own number terms based mainly on the Japanized pronunciation of the letters of the scale. *Tsē* (C) is one, *dē* (D) is two, *ii* (E) is three, *efu* (F) is four, *gē* (G) is five, *ā* (A) is six, *sebunsu* (seventh) is seven, *okutābu* (octave) is eight, and *nainsu* (ninth) is nine.

3

Punk- and Juvenile
Delinquent-Related Language

(chinpira, hikō shōnen yōgo)

Furyō (no good) comes from *furyō shōnen* (bad boy) and *furyō shōjo* (bad girl) and has traditionally refered to juvenile delinquents. Now that juvenile delinquency has become a more serious problem in Japan, however, people have coined a new word to fit the current situation. For the past 10–15 years, *hikō* (misdeed) has replaced *furyō,* and *hikō mondai* (the problem of juvenile delinquency) is a much-debated topic.

Hikō gurūpu (literally, misconduct group) means gangs of juvenile delinquents; these delinquents have their own argot. Instead of the common expression *tabako* (tobacco) for cigarette, for example, they use *moku* or *enta*. *Moku* is the inverted form of *kumo* (cloud); it also has an association with the adverb *moku-moku,* a mimetic expression that is used to describe smoke rising voluminously. *Enta* comes from *en,* the Chinese character for smoke, which is then supplemented with the suffix *-ta,* either meaning lovely little thing, or added merely for euphonic purposes.

Shike-moku and *zuke-moku* both refer to a butt or half-smoked cigarette. *Shike* in this case is thought to come either from the verb *shikeru* (to become damp) or to be an inverted form of the noun *keshi* (the act of extinguishing). *Zuke-moku* is dirtier-sounding and more casual than *shike-moku*, and it implies a very wet butt. It comes from the verb *funzukerareta* (to be trampled).

Right after World War II, there were people called *moku hiroi* (butt collectors). At the time, money was very short, so these people either smoked the butts themselves, or sold them at cheap bars after re-rolling the tobacco. At that time, too, it was hard and expensive to get cigarettes from abroad. Such cigarettes were called *yō-moku* (literally, Western cigarettes); this expression is still used by young people who like to show off by smoking foreign cigarettes.

Yani means resin and is slang for tar, and for nicotine. *Yani ga kireta* is a kind of code phrase meaning I really want a cigarette. *Kireta* here means to have run out. At such a time, this person might ask *moku nai?* (do you have a cigarette?) or *yani aru?* (have you got a butt?).

Juvenile delinquents often play truant (*saboru* or *zuru-yasumi suru*) from school. The verb *saboru* comes from the English expression sabotage, while the *zuru* in *zuru-yasumi* comes from the adjective *zurui,* which is an ordinary expression for unfair, tricky, or sly. Young people who engage in such behavior are called *tsuppari.* It comes from the verb *tsupparu,* one of whose meanings is to take an antagonistic or aggressive attitude against society. *Gakuran* is the kind of uniform dress worn by these *tsuppari* rebels. Typical adolescents, they tend to think they're unique and different, but end up uniformly conforming to dress and other codes established by the group.

For male *tsuppari,* the *gakuran* is a specially ordered student uniform that has exaggeratedly long sleeves, jacket, pants, and a very high collar. The boys also adopt a unique hair style called *sori* (shaving), whereby they shave their upper temples. The rest of the hair is long in spite of the schools' ban on long hair.

For girls, the *gakuran* is a pleated school uniform skirt about four inches longer than those of the other students, worn with flat shoes. They often pull down their school neckties and leave their blouses open at the collar. Also, defying the school dress code, they wear their hair in long, frizzy permanent waves. In general, they look quite sloppy and are often called *zubekō,* slang for *hikō shōjo.* This expression comes from the adjective *zubera,* which means sloppy or untidy.

There is a great deal of hostility between teachers and these rebellious students. *Tsuppari* students often use the word *mukatsuku* (to feel sick) when they feel irritable, especially about their teacher. *Mukatsuku* originally meant to feel sick, but it has come now to mean to feel offended or to be angry, and the word is widely used by students in general. Students call teachers by the derogatory terms *senkō* and *senteki* instead of *sensei.* A result of the tension that exists between the teachers and these *tsuppari,* *kōnai bōryoku* (violence in schools) has become a serious social issue. There is even a special term *sotsu-rin,* which means attacking a teacher on the day of the graduation ceremony *(sotsugyō-shiki).*

Kōnai bōryoku is not confined to *tsuppari* students and their teachers. *Hikō* students constantly bully weaker students violently, and *ijime* (bullying) is currently one of the biggest social problems in Japan. In extreme cases, students are even murdered or driven to commit suicide. In 1993 three students in Yamagata Prefecture were arrested for a murder in which a student was stuffed into a gym mat where he suffocated. In high school and university athletic clubs, there are numerous cases of *ijime* against younger students in the form of *shigoki* (discipline using hard training), sometimes with fatal results.

Some students tell teachers and authorities about the bullying. The verb *chikuru* is the latest popular slang expression, meaning to snitch, or to tattle to the teacher. Other students just try not to get involved, and the word *shikato suru* is a popular expression for this. Originally, this word was coined by the *yakuza,* and it means to pretend not to be aware of something or to ignore something so that you won't become involved. A colloquial equivalent is *shiranpuri suru,* which comes from the ordinary expression *shiranu furi o suru* (to pretend not to know).

Shikatō originates from the Japanese card game *hana-fuda* (literally, flower cards). In this game, there are 48 cards in all, four for each month, with respective values of 0, 5, 10, and 20. The 10-point card for October shows the figure of a deer *(shika)* looking the other way *(soppo muku). Shikatō* (or *shikato*) is a play on words in relation to this scene.

A couple of synonyms for *tsuppari* are *o-kyaku-san* and *ochikobore. O-kyaku-san,* which literally means guest, implies that they're not really part of the school. While the rest of the students are learning, they just sit at their desks without paying any attention to what's going on. *Ochikobore* (literally, those left behind; figuratively, dropouts) is a more direct expression. It comes from the verb *koboreru,* which means to drop.

Daihen means answering to a teacher on behalf of an absent friend, or replying to attendance calls in class for someone else. *Sabori* (hookey) students use *daihen* often. The *dai* in *daihen* is the *kanji* for proxy. *Hen* comes from *henji,* meaning reply.

When they flunk their exams, truants are likely to be held back or to have to repeat a grade. *Daburu,* coming from the English word double, is a term for this, as is *kokeru* (to fall down). *Teikū hikō* (literally, low altitude flight) means barely being promoted to the next grade.

Hikō shōnen and *hikō shōjo* often hang out in coffee shops when they skip school. The expression for coffee shop is *saten,* which is an abbreviation of *kissaten,* the ordinary word. A synonym for this is *hiiko,* an inverted form of *kōhii* (coffee). *Saten* and *hiiko* are also commonly used by people in the entertainment industries.

Tamari-ba is the expression used by Japanese juvenile delinquents and truants to describe their favorite hangout, where they drink coffee and smoke. This word is derived from the intransitive verb *tamaru* (to collect, gather) and *ba*, which means place.

When they get tired of their *tamari-ba* activities, *hikō shōnen* often turn to drinking or drugs. *Kisu* is a term *yakuza* and juvenile delinquents use for alcoholic beverages. It is an inverted form of *suki* (favorite), as in *suki-na mono* (my favorite thing). *Kisu-gure* refers to a drunk or to being drunk.

Shinnā asobi (literally, thinner play) is recreational sniffing of paint thinner or chemical glue, which is much more popular than drinking among *hikō shonen*. *Fūsen* (balloon) is a synonym for *shinna asobi;* this term was adopted because thinner is often sniffed from inflated vinyl bags that look like balloons. *Hikōki* (airplane) means inhaling glue or thinner and getting high. *Anpan* (a sweet bean jam bun) refers to a sexual orgy after an episode of *hikōki*. Such sexual activity is also called *momoiro yūgi* (literally, pink play) or, in official police language, *fujun isei kōyū* (impure connection with the opposite sex).

In the past, *yakuza* and juvenile delinquents were roughly divided into two groups. One was called *kōha* (literally, hard group), who were the brawlers of their respective organizations. The other was the *nanpa* (soft group), which was comprised of the womanizers. *Nanpa* and its derivative verb *nanpa suru* are synonyms for the slang terms *onna-tarashi* (lady killer) and *onna o tarashi-komu* (to seduce a woman). But today's Japanese juvenile delinquents can't be divided into hard and soft groups, as they all tend to engage freely in sexual activities.

The verb *nanpa suru* is also used by ordinary young and middle-aged people, and it means to pick up members of the opposite sex. The target of *nanpa* for boys is *hakui suke* or *mabui suke*. The expressions *hakui* and *mabui* are used only by males when referring to females. *Hakui* is an underground word which means beautiful as in *hakui suke* (beautiful). It comes from *haku,* a pronunciation of the character for white, and it means to have a beautiful white face (in Japan white skin is particularly prized). Originally, *mabui* was used in the Edo era to mean to have a beautiful face. According to folk etymology, the word is derived from the adjective *mabushii* (dazzling, bright) and means dazzlingly beautiful. Later, it was adopted by the *tekiya* type of gangsters to mean the real thing, as well as beautiful. Finally, it came to mean a very beautiful girl, and it enjoyed its heyday as a popular word in the early 80s. It may be considered similar in tone and era to the American English word fox, as in she's a fox.

Sukekomashi (seducer) is roughly synonymous with *nanpa*. *Suke* means girl, and *komashi* comes from the Kansai dialect term *komasu*. This verb originally meant to give something or to do as one wills but later was adopted by the *yakuza* and *tekiya* to mean to seduce or to cheat on a woman. *Sukekomashi* is a type of gangster who hangs out around train stations trying to entrap young small-town girls who have run away from home. When he manages to attract a girl's attention, he sweet-talks her and later takes advantage of her. This is called *kui-mono ni suru* (to make something edible out of her). The verb *sukeru* (to play with a girl) is also used, particularly among *bōsō-zoku* or *kaminari-zoku,* both of which mean motorcycle gang.

Here, we would like to introduce some sexual expressions popular among young people, particularly among *chinpira.*

Keru, hegu, mame-doro, and *tsukkomi* all mean to rape. *Keru* literally means to kick and colloquially it means to reject. How it came to be used to mean rape is unclear. It may have come from the idea of kicking, beating, and raping a woman, or from that of neglecting or rejecting a woman's pleading. It can also simply mean to fuck.

Hegu and its verb form *hegu suru* probably comes

from the archaic *hegu,* meaning to strip off another's clothes or to steal someone's belongings. A modern synonym for the latter is *hagu. Mame-doro* is an abbreviation of *mame dorobō. Mame* (literally, bean) in this case is a slang expression meaning clit (clitoris), while *dorobō* is robber. And finally, *tsukkomi* comes from the ordinary verb *tsukkomu,* which means to thrust or poke into.

Gōkan means rape. *Rinkan* means gang rape. The *gō* in the former means forcing, and the *rin* in the latter is circle. The character for *kan* in both means rape. *Mawashi* and its inverted form *shiima* both mean gang rape. *Mawashi* comes from the verb *mawasu* (to turn or to pass on) because the victim in this case is passed around from one man to another.

Tsui-man is used for one-on-one-sex. It is said to have been coined from *tsui* (pair or twin) and *man* (cunt, or fuck). An orgy, on the other hand is called *o-matsuri* (literally, festival) or *sukiyaki (pātii). Sukiyaki* is a favorite Japanese dish cooked at the table.

Mii-man is coined from the English me and the Japanese *man,* and is mostly closely translated as my vagina. It is used by young women to refer to their own private parts. *Josei jishin* (literally, the female self) is the closest synonym for this.

A favorite linguistic device used by juvenile delinquents and *waru gaki* (bad boys)—following the example of the *yakuza* and *chinpira*—is inversion. *Bitere,* for example, is an inversion of *terebi* (television). *Oraji* is from *rajio* (radio), *waden* from *denwa* (telephone), and *shiitaku* from *takushii* (taxi). *Baso* is made from *soba* (Japanese buckwheat noodles), and *baso-ya* from *soba-ya* (*soba* shop). *Mengo* is an inverted form of *gomen* (sorry), and people often use it twice as in *yah, mengo, mengo.* It's often used without any real feeling of contrition.

Another favorite linguistic device used by juvenile delinquents is abbreviation, as in *dachi-kō, dachikko,* or simply *dachi,* all of which are shortened versions of *tomodachi* (friend). *Tomodachi* was originally a plural form of *tomo* (friend), but now it is also used as a singular form. *Dachikō* implies not only friend, but *nakama* (comrade) or *aibō* (partner, buddy). When a person wants to emphasize a friendship, he might use *mabu-dachi* (close or intimate friend).

Piikō and *piibō* are a couple of slang terms used by the younger generation for cop. They are derived from the first letter of the word policeman, and *-kō* and *-bō* are derogatory suffixes. These words express a sort of taunting attitude towards someone like a policeman who's supposed to embody a great deal of authority. *Pii-kā* (patrol car) also makes use of the first letter of policeman. This is a slang term, but the expression *pato-kā,* an abbreviation for police patrol car, is used in ordinary conversations and newspaper articles.

Geso (shoes, *geta, zōri*) is an abbreviation of *gesoku,* which means footwear that has been taken off and left in the entrance. It refers to footwear *(haki-mono). Sushi* fans may know that *geso* in sushi-shop language means the tentacle of the squid, and that *geso-wasa (geso* with *wasabi,* a kind of Japanese horseradish) is a popular delicacy in Japan.

Jan-sō is a shortened form of *mājan-sō* (more colloquially, *mājan-ya),* meaning mahjong parlor. Mahjong parlors are favorite places for *chinpira* to hang out. Mahjong is one of the most popular gambling games among salaried men and students in Japan. It's a four-person game that is exciting but tends to drag on for hours as the losers try to recoup. One round usually takes about an hour, and the match normally continues until the *shūden* (the last train—an abbreviation of *saishū densha*) is about to leave.

There is a number of slang expressions derived from mahjong terms. *Tsumoru,* for example, means to take a tile from the row, but it's often used by students to imply to make something one's own as in *kinō kanojo o tsumotchatta* (last night, I managed to seduce her). *Toimen* in mahjong jargon means a player on the opposite side, but it is now used in ordinary slang to mean anything on the opposite side. For example, *uchi no toimen wa gakkō* can be translated as there is a school in front of my house. In student slang *toimen* refers to a girlfriend, or someone of the opposite sex.

Paipan (literally, white plate, or the white tile used in mahjong), refers to a girl without pubic hair. *Paipan yarō,* means a guy of pale, blank complexion. *Chonbo* is another mahjong term for a fault. It is said that the expression originally comes from the Korean word for stealing. *Chonbo* and its verb form *chonbo suru* are now used in ordinary slang to mean *hema* (mistake or blunder); juvenile delinquents commonly use it for theft or shoplifting.

Manbiki (shoplifting) has become increasingly widespread among junior and senior high school students. Even elementary school children as young as kindergarten age are said to be involved. There are many euphemisms for *manbiki.* Among them are *itadaki* (a polite expresion for taking or receiving), *kaimono* (shopping), and *shikkei* (bad manners).

Manbiki committed on *deki gokoro* (sudden impulse) reached 56,000 incidents nationwide in 1992 alone, and more than half of them were committed by junior high or high school students. Exasperated by the increase, some supermarkets have begun to install *manbiki tanchiki* (shoplifting detectors), which cause an alarm to go off when items are passed through them without having been decoded at the cash register.

Japanese youngsters have almost limitless imaginations when it comes to creating new and fashionable words. Here are some more terms that are not only fashionable among juvenile delinquents in Japan, but can also be heard among adults.

Itchōmae, or *itchomai,* means being independent as a gangster or man. They are synonymous variations of *ichinin-mae,* which refers to a single helping of a meal, or one person in an adult group. When *itchōmae da ne* (you're doing pretty well) is said to a *furyō* or *waru-gaki,* it means that he is on the verge of being recognized as a full-fledged *kumi-in* (member) of a *yakuza* group.

Onomatopoetic expressions also play an important role in Japanese slang. For example, *gata-gata iu* means a loud complaint or objection. It comes from the onomatopoetic expression for making a rattling noise, as in *to ga gata-gata suru* (the door is making a clatter).

Kari-kari is a versatile expression with several meanings. Usually, it means hard or crispy, as in *kari-kari suru* (to be crisp). *Kari-kari suru*'s crispy meaning can also be carried over to describe a person with a brittle personality, someone who tends to get irritated easily. When the word is applied to eating, as in *kari-kari taberu,* it means to eat noisily. *Kari(-tto)* can be applied to the single action or noise of crunching, while *gari-gari* or *gari(tto)* is used for still noisier eating.

Gata(-tto) is used for the noise made when two hard objects come together with some force, and *gata-gata* is an expression for such noises being continued. *Kata(-tto)* and *kata-kata* are applied to smaller and lighter noises. Finally, *muka(-tto)* is an expression for the moment of becoming or feeling sick or angry. *Kare no kotoba ni mukatto shita* means I got angry at what he said.

The common words *awa* (bubble), *hako* (box), and *minato* (port) all have underground meanings.

Awa o kū is literally to eat bubbles, but also means to get flustered or to get shaken up. *Awa o fukaseru* is to cause a person to froth at the mouth, or to give them fits. *Mizu no awa* (literally, water bubbles) is used to refer to an effort that comes to nothing or something that goes down the drain. *Doryoku wa mizu no awa da,* or the same expression, using the same characters but pronounced differently, *doryoku wa suihō ni kishita,* means all our efforts went down the drain.

Abuku is a slang synonym for *awa,* but it can't be substituted for *awa* in formula expressions like *awa o kū.* The compound *abuku zeni* (money) means found money, the idea being that money, like bubbles, can easily disappear.

Let's take a look at *hako. Hako niwa* means miniature garden and *hako-iri musume* (literally, boxed-in daughter) means an overprotected daughter. In underground parlance, however, *hako* refers to a train or police box. *Hako-shi* or *hako-nori* are underground words meaning a pickpocket who works trains. *-Shi* means practitioner; *nori* means rider. *Hako-nori (shuzai)* is also used quite often in journalistic jargon to mean to have an interview with a VIP or criminal aboard a train or aircraft. *Hako-neta* is another journalistic word, meaning boxed news item, usually appearing on a political page, which does not deal with particularly serious matters.

Minato means port. *Fune* (boat) is used in the underground to mean the female genitals, again with some association with appearance. Since ships call on ports when they need maintenance, *minato* is an underground word mainly used among juvenile delinquents to mean *sanfujinka* (an obstetrics and gynecology hospital).

YOUNG PEOPLE'S AND VOGUE EXPRESSIONS

wakamonogo, ryūkōgo

1

Emergence of New Mankind

(shinjinrui tanjō)

In 1985, the *shinjinrui* (new mankind) emerged in Japan. Young people born after the 1964 Tokyo Olympics came of age at this time. These young people did not experience the hardships of postwar reconstruction, show little interest in politics, and grew up during a period of economic prosperity in which material gain was the ultimate ideal. They had totally new values and behavior patterns, and the adults who could not comprehend them labeled them *shinjinrui*.

The *shinjinrui* have their own language. According to a 1987 survey by Hakuhōdō, a large Japanese advertising agency, the ten most popular expressions among *shinjinrui* are:

1. *Maji* (short for *majime*, meaning honest, sincere)
   Maji is used to emphasize that something is really, honest-to-goodness true. *Maji* is also used as in *honto ni maji?* (is it true? really?), or *maji? maji?* (really? really?).

2. *Saitē* (worst)
   A short exchange using *saitē* might be:
   Q: *Ano otoko dō?* (What's he like?)
   A: *Mō, saitē!* (He's the lowest and stupidest!)

3. *Abunai* (dangerous)
   This word is near in meaning to *iyarashii* (indecent) and *kiwadoi* (risky feelings). It can be used to lightly

express the idea of something odd. Saying *abunai hito* rather than *iyarashii hito* is indirect and sounds softer.

4. *Ichiō* (sort of, to some extent, in a way)
A common trait of the *shinjinrui* is to be vague when they're not absolutely certain about something.

Q: Are you done with work?
A: *Ichiō*. (More or less.)

5. *Yabai* (no good or stupid)

6. *Chekku suru* or *chekku o ireru* (to check up, inspect, inquire)
Chekku suru is synonymous with *yoku miru* (to observe, to look carefully). It means to check out others' dress or privacy. *Chekku ga kibishii* means you're very (too?) severe in finding fault.

7. *Puttsun!* (Snap!)
This word is an onomatopoetic expression meaning to go crazy. It is often used to describe the thoughtless actions of *shinjinrui*. A *puttsun joyū* is an actress whose behavior is erratic, and *aitsu wa puttsun shite iru* means that guy's lost his mind.

8. *Kattarui* (to feel tired)
Kattarui originally comes from *kaina* (an old expression for arm) and *darui* (to feel tired, listlesss) to mean to be physically tired and feel lethargic. *Omae no hanashi wa kattarui* means I'm bored with your prattle. *Tsukareru* (to be tired) is used in similar situations, as in *omae no hanashi wa tsukareru n'da yo na* or simply *ah, tsukareru,* both of which mean your chatter is making me tired. It also means to feel burdened as when a *shinjinrui* finds something too hard to tackle.

9. *Betsu nii* (not particularly)
This term is similar to *ichiō*.

Q: *Eiga wa tanoshikatta?* (Did you have a good time at the movie?)
A: *Betsu nii.* (Not particularly.)

10. *O-sshare* (looking/acting smart)
This word is a derivative of *o-share,* meaning to dress up. This can also be used to mean tasteful or witty.

These words are still popular today. In the mid-80s, they were quite revolutionary in terms of fashionable language, and the phenomenon of *shinjinrui* language has been the subject of continuing media attention. In October 1993, the *Asahi* newspaper, carried a series called Tokyo Language Now. The first part was about ambiguous expressions that are now trendy, and the second part was about fuzzy conversations. According to the paper, the number of young people who do not clearly communicate is increasing.

The *shinjinrui* are also somewhat eccentric and bizarre in their choice of words. One newspaper story in the summer of 1994 reported that a young woman described her boyfriend as *bukimi* (weird). By weird, it turned out, she meant he wasn't very talkative. The proper word for this would be *mukuchi,* and the older generation would never dream of using *bukimi* instead.

In the 1970s, generation preceding the *shinjinrui* was criticized for *san-mu shugi.* Today's *shinjinrui* are criticized as suffering from *go-mu shugi. Mu-* is a Japanese prefix that can be translated as un-; *shugi* is a popular suffix meaning -ism. Thus, *san-mu shugi* and *go-mu shugi* literally mean three- and five-nothing-ism, respectively. The three nothings are *mu-kiryoku* (spiritlessness), *mu-kando* (apathy) and *mu-kanshin* (indifference). These three characteristics are referred to collectively as *shirake,* and young people of the 70s were dubbed the *shirake-zoku* (*zoku* is tribe or group).

With the *shinjinrui,* two more undesirable traits were added to create *go-mu shugi*: *mu-sekinin* (irresponsibility) and *bu-sahō* (bad manners). (*Bu* is an alternate pronunciation for the character *mu.*)

The *shinjinrui* can be divided into two types. One is *ne-aka* (naturally cheerful), and the other is *ne-kura* (naturally gloomy). These expressions were created in the early 80s, and they are still in wide use today. *Ne* means nature or root, *akarui* is bright, and *kurai* is gloomy. The *ne-aka* types are *hyōkin* (funny) and *chōshi ga ii* (sociable). Their *ne-kura* counterparts are *shiraketa* (apathetic) and *mukuchi* (reticent).

Shinderu (literally, being dead) is used by *shinjinrui* when they find somebody deadly dull. If you apply the expression to yourself, it means I'm totally exhausted, I'm sick, or I'm dead drunk. It can also be used as an antonym for *naui*. *Furukusai* (out-of-date or archaic) and *ryūkō-okure* (to be out of fashion or to be behind the times) are synonyms for *shinderu*.

Ochikomu (literally, to fall in or sink down) is used when someone feels very depressed. *Moro-ochi,* means being too depressed to get out of a terrible slump. It can also mean in a rut. The *moro* in this term is an abbreviation of *moro ni* (totally or utterly), and *ochi* is a shortened form of *ochikomu*. *Ochime* is adversity. *Zef'fuchō* is a newly coined word, an antonym of *zekkōchō* (in top condition), meaning in the worst condition. *Zetsu-* is a prefix indicating absolute, and *fuchō* means in bad shape or condition.

Auchi and *auto* come from the English word out and mean failed or no-go. *Ore wa auto da* can be translated as I'm hopeless or I'm helpless. *Gakkuri* resembles *auto*. It comes from the set expression *gakkuri kata o otosu* (to drop one's shoulders in a marked way). *Gakkuri* is an onomatopoetic expression for sudden action. *Gakkuri suru* and *gakkuri kuru* mean to be broken down or badly disappointed. It's a stronger expression than the ordinary word *gakkari* or *gakkari suru* (to be disappointed or dispirited).

Uttōshii, which is generally used for describing depressing or gloomy weather, is now used by young people to describe a person or thing that turns one off. Students use this expression when complaining about or after having been scolded by their teachers. *Ah, uttōshii nā* means it's troublesome, and *ano sensei wa uttōshii* means that teacher really bums me out. A slang variation of *uttōshii* is *utchawashii.*

The verb *aseru,* which is commonly used to mean to be impatient, has acquired the connotation of to be upset, confused, or uneasy. Thus, *asetchau nā* means I'm confused, and *yah, asechatta* is I was upset. *Aseru n'da yo nā* or *asetchau n'da yo nā* can be translated as I feel uneasy.

Bibiru, which comes from *biku-biku suru* (to become timid, to be frightened) is now applied to mean to feel small or to lose one's nerve. Similarly, *hiyoru* means to be wishy-washy or cowardly. This expression comes from *hiyorimi shugi,* which can be translated as opportunism. *Hiyorimi* means weather vane, implying that a person who makes his or her plans based on the weather is opportunistic. When you say *aitsu (wa) hiyotteru,* it means he's getting scared.

Zukkokeru is a popular slang expression meaning to mess up. It originally comes from *zuriochiru* (to slide down), and later came to mean to lose control. *Aitsu wa itsumo zukkoketeru* means he always screws things up.

Egui originally meant harsh or acrid. Over time, however, it and its derivative *egutsu nai* have come to be applied to people to cold-hearted or nasty. It was used in a broad sense to mean *iyarashii* (obscene), *dogitsui* (too much) and *kibishii* (hard, difficult). *Egui* is also a synonym for *kakko ii* (now, trendy, nifty). Students use this expression when somebody introduces openly bawdy words into an otherwise ordinary conversation. In such a case, they say *egui nā* (this is too much).

Makesō or *makkesō* (literally, I think I'm losing) were once popular exclamatory expressions among young people meaning all right, you win, or you're saying too much. *Mazui koto o shita* (I did something wrong), meaning damn, I messed up, can be abbreviated into a single verb, *mazuru*. This conjugates in the past tense to *mazutta* or *mazutchatta*. *Shikuru* is a shortened form of the verb *shikujiru* meaning to fail or to bungle. *Kimoi* and *kimotai* come from *kimochi ga warui* and mean disgusting or sickening.

Toroi and its inverted form *rotoi* both mean dull or sluggish. These terms come from the mimetic expression *toro-toro,* which refers to the state of a heavy, liquid running slowly, like molasses or glue. A similar English expression might be slow as molasses. *Toroi* is used by younger people more often than ordinary words such as *noroi* (slow) or *manuke* (slow of wit). Thus *aitsu wa toroi* means he's an awkward or sluggardly ass.

Mota-kō and *motai* are a couple of other fashionable expressions similar to *toroi.* The noun *mota-kō* (laggard) comes from the verb *mota-mota suru,* meaning to take a lot of time to do something. One can say *mota-mota suru na,* or else invert it into the still more casual *tamo-tamo suru na* to mean make it snappy, or hurry up will you.

Guzu or the more colloquial *guzura* are synonyms for *mota-mota.* *Guzu* comes from the verb *guzu-guzu suru* (to be slow, to hesitate, to be irresolute), which we introduced earlier. *Chintara* is an even rougher synonym. *Chintara* and a synonym, *tamo-tamo,* are particularly popular among gangsters. *Chintara yarō* is a lazy boy.

Shotteru (conceited) comes from the verb *seotte iru* meaning carrying on one's back. This came to be shortened to *seotteru* and then the more slangy *shotteru*.

Mosai is a newly invented word derived from *mosatto shitte iru* and *mossari shita*, both of which mean unrefined or stolid. These expressions originally come from the noun *mosa* which was used in the early part of the Edo era by the *kamigata*, the people of Kansai, especially Kyoto when they referred to Kanto people. People in the Kanto at that time often finished their sentences with *mosa*, Kanto which came from the verb *mōsu* (to say). Kansai folk regarded their compatriots as country bumpkins and used the term *mosa* to express that sentiment. Soon, *mosa* and *mosa-kō* came to mean an unrefined person or persons. The adjective *mosatto shite iru* (absent-minded) was created from these expressions.

Gattan-ko and *mondai-gai* are the latest expressions for an insignificant young boy. The former may come from the onomatopoetic expression *gatan* or *gattan* (with a bang) and *ko* (child or guy). *Gattan* is used when something falls down with a crash, like a see-saw hitting the ground with a bang. *Gattan-ko* also has the connotation of a guy fallen to the ground.

Mondai-gai can be literally translated as out of the question, but the *-gai* in this case is a play on words. It's used particularly to mean a "guy" that no one ever talks about because he's so insignificant. In ordinary conversation, you can use *mondai-gai* to mean it doesn't matter.

Choroi is a slangy adjective meaning easy. When someone says *aitsu wa choroi (aite da)*, it means he's an easy mark. Students often use this expression when a test is easy. *Shiken (wa) dō datta* (how was the test)? *Choroi, choroi* (it was a snap). A colloquial equivalent for this is *asa-meshi-mae*, which literally means before breakfast—in other words, very simple to do. The slang verb *choro suru* comes from *choromakasu*, and both mean to acquire something in a shady manner. The onomatopoetic *choro-choro* is used to describe a murmuring or trickling brook. *Ogawa ga choro-choro nagarete ita* means the brook flowed in a trickle. The verb *choro-choro suru,* describes something small that flits or sneaks about. This expression is often used by parents to warn their children not to flit about, as in *choro-choro suru na* or its feminine equivalent *choro-choro shinai de.*

2

Gyaru (Girl) and
Related Words

(gyaru kanren)

Young women *shinjinrui* are called *gyaru* (girl). The word *gyaru* has been used since the Japanese song "Oh! Girl" became a hit in 1979.

Burikko was one of the most fashionable expressions among young people in the 80s, and it can be called a predecessor of *gyaru*. It comes from the expression *kawai-ko-buru-ko* (a child who deliberately acts good or cute) and is used mainly for girls. *-Buru* is a verb suffix that comes from the expression *furi o suru* (to pretend or to behave like something). *Gakusha-buru,* for example, is to assume a scholarly air, *shijin-buru* is to pose as a poet, and *otona-buru* is to act grown up. *Aitsu wa butteru* (or *burikko shite iru*) can be heard in schools and means he is trying to become teacher's pet.

Burikko is still used, currently as a suffix, and it easily combines with certain words to form new expressions. For example, if you use *warui-ko* (bad child), you can make the new word *warui-ko-burikko,* which means a child who is intentionally naughty. *Shittaka-burikko* is a child who pretends to know everything or a know-it-all. This expression is coined from the idiomatic *shittaka-buri* (a person pretending to know; the verb form of this word is *shittakaburi o suru*) and *burikko*. *O-rikō-burikko* is a variation of *ii-ko-burikko* (a child who pretends to be good). *O-rikō* is made by adding the diminutive and honorific prefix *o-* to *rikō,* which means clever or clever child. *O-rikō-burikko,* then, implies a child who pretends to be good and clever in a hypocritical way.

Burikko is also used these days by middle-aged women. When a woman buys an accessory or article of clothing that is unbecoming or just too cute for her age, her friend might say *mā, burikko ne.* This implies *wakai-ko-burikko* (literally, a person who pretends to be young).

There are some other expressions, as well, that contain the *-ko* (child or girl) suffix. *Kido-ko* is a fashionable abbreviation of *kidotte iru-ko,* both of which mean a girl who puts on airs. The traditional term for this is *kidori-ya. Game-ko* comes from the Kansai dialect word *gametsui* (calculating, greedy), but it is used nationwide to mean a grasping or greedy girl. *Yume-ko,* an abbreviated form of *yumemiru-ko* (a girl who dreams) means a dreamy or romantic girl.

Jun-ko sounds like a woman's name, but it's used among young girls to mean a virgin. *Jun* is the Chinese character meaning pure. Her opposite is *sase-ko,* meaning an easy lay. It comes from the verb *saseru,* meaning to cause or make a person do something, and the suffix *-ko* for a young girl.

There are also a number of slang words using *-ko* or *-kko,* in which *-ko* means child. *Kagi-kko* (literally, key kid) was coined in the mid-60s when mothers began to work outside the home, and their children would come back and let themselves into an empty house or apartment. This term finds its direct translation in the expression latchkey child. *Hitori-kko* is an only child. *Ijime-kko* is a compound made from the verb *ijimeru* (to bully or tease) and the prefix *-ko,* and it means a bully.

Itazura-kko or *itazura-kozo* (mischievous child) comes from the noun *itazura,* meaning mischief. *Waru-gaki* (literally, bad kid) is a more current expression that implies both *ijime-kko* and *itazura-kko.*

Hahaoya-kko (literally, mother's child) is a child who is closer to his mother, a mama's boy. It's usually used with regard to a son. When a child looks like his or her mother, the expression is *hahaoya ni*. *Chichioya-kko* and *obān-chan-ko* mean papa's child and grandmother's child, respectively. *Oni-kko* (literally, devil's child) is the unflattering expression used for a child who resembles neither his mother nor father. *Tete-nashi-kko* or *tete-nashi-go* (literally, a child without a father) means an illegitimate child.

Jogakusei and *joshidaisei* are contractions of *joshi daigakusei*, female college student. The number of women attending college countinues to rise; their high profile and level of activity have received considerable attention in recent times. They drink along with the male students, engage enthusiastically in sports, and call male students *kimi* (you—a pronoun traditionally used only by men). *Burikko no joshidaisei* also appeared for a while on TV programs. They were called *hana no joshidaisei* (flowery female college students) or *run-run joshidaisei* (happy and cheerful coeds).

O-nyan-ko is an expression that emerged in the mid-80s, and it means girls who are cute like little kittens. It originated from the weekend TV program *Yūyake nyan-nyan*. *Nyan* is an onomatopoeia for the mewing of a kitten. The verb *nyan-nyan suru* was a slang expression used around 1980 for having sex. *O-nyan-ko* became extinct after about two years, superseded by *gyaru*.

In the 1980s, *shinjinrui gyaru* began to enter the workplace and to marry late, riding on the wave of the women's movement. They were not, however, hard workers like the men. So their male colleagues called them *san nai gyaru* (three-without girls): *hatarakanai* (do not work seriously), *kekkon shinai* (do not marry), and *kodomo o umanai* (do not have children). Instead of looking seriously for a lifetime mate, these girls began to keep stables of boyfriends who served them in various capacities. This phenomenon is called *bōifurendo no godan katsuyō* (five levels of boyfriends). The expression has been popular since around 1990. *Godan* means five steps, and *katsuyō* is practical use or practical application.

Here is a breakdown of *gyaru no bōifurendo godan katsuyō:*

1. *Benrii-kun:* A man who takes good care of his girlfriend and is very convenient *(benri)* to have around.

2. *Asshii-kun: Asshii* means *ashi* (feet or foot) and generally is a slang term for car. *Asshii-kun* is a man who has a car and is available to chauffeur a girl around.

3. *Mitsugu-kun* or *messhii-kun: Mitsugu* (literally, pay tribute) is a boyfriend who often gives gifts, a contributor. *Mitsugu* is a person with money, and *messhii* is a person who pays for *meshi* (meals).

4. *Kiipu-kun: Kiipu* is from the English keep. *Kiipu-kun,* then, is a boyfriend kept for the time being, until *honmei* (the favorite) appears. Therefore, this means the second favorite.

5. *Honmei-kun:* This is the most desirable, the favorite, and comes from *honmei* (the favorite) in horse racing.

In addition, there are other expressions such as *susshii-kun* (a man who pays for *sushi), nesshii-kun* (from the verb *neru,* to sleep, meaning sex friend), and *kōdo-kun,* the guy that sets up the *gyaru's* TV, VCR, and other gadgets for her. *Kōdo* means cord.

Unmarried women in their 30s have increased greatly in number in Japan. This is due to a more independent spirit among young women who set very high standards for their *honmei-kun.* Nowadays, they are called *hikonsha* (unmarried), a much kinder term than the formerly popular *ōrudo misu* (old maid) and *urenokori* (unsold).

The most desirable types for *honmei-kun* are *sankō* (literally, three highs). *Kō* is an alternate pronunciation of the character for *takai,* or high. The three highs are: *sei ga takai* (tall), *kyūryō ga takai* (high salary), and *gakureki ga takai* (good academic background). The *gyaru* also prefer second sons. Eldest sons in Japan traditionally assume the burden of caring for aging parents; by taking the next son, young women manage to avoid such responsibilities.

The counterparts to women who marry late or never are *ikazu sanjū otoko,* men who have reached the age of 30 and are still unmarried. Men around this age generally work long hours, leaving them little time to meet women or to date.

Out of the house and working, Japanese women have more spending money nowadays than did their mothers, and they are now actively involved in many kinds of leisure activities. *Tenisu* (tennis) *gyaru, sāfā* (surfer) *gyaru,* and *disuko* (disco) *gyaru* are the subject of occasional newspaper articles, and the following phrases have also become popular: *kyapi-kyapi gyaru,* girls who shriek merrily; *ike-ike gyaru,* girls who easily have sex or run around painting the town red; *bairin gyaru*, bilingual girls; and *āpā gyaru* (girls who are *pā*, or crazy; *āpā* is an inverted form of *pā*).

Related to *ike-ike gyaru* are *o-tachidai gyaru.* They dance provocatively on high platforms *(o-tachidai),* wearing practically nothing. They get an exhibitionistic thrill from doing this and seem to enjoy being drooled over by non-dancing customers in the audience.

In the 1990s, *gyaru* moved into fields that had once been the exclusive territory of middle-aged men like their fathers. These young women became known as *oyaji gyaru* or *ojin gyaru* (girl in man's territory). *Oyaji* (father) *gyaru* and *ojin* (middle-aged man) *gyaru* thought that if men enjoyed something, they should try it out, too. These girls began showing up at *aka chōchin* (taverns with red lanterns hanging in front of their front doors) in groups, and increasingly frequented *pachinko* parlors, *keiba* (horse races), and even *tachigui soba-ya* (stand-up noodle shops). They started taking *onsen ryokō* (trips to hot springs), where they dared to enjoy *rotenburo,* (open air baths in which the sexes often mixed), *gorufu* (golf), and *kabu tōshi* (stock investing). In contrast, there are also *obangyaru,* young women who act middle-aged, and *gyaru oyaji,* middle-aged men who behave as though they were young girls, eating sweets, chatting, and gossiping.

Gyaru-go is best described as evanescent, with words appearing and disappearing all the time. The following list, however, contains terms that have been around for a while and are likely to be with us a little longer.

Asashan (literally, morning shampooing): A *gyaru* expression for hair-washing in the morning. Japanese traditionally take a bath at night, but the morning shower has become increasingly popular, mainly among the young.

Baburukurasshu (literally, bubble crash): Uses the analogy of a bubble to describe the sudden and jarring end of the asset-inflated Japanese economy.

Bakusui suru: To fall asleep suddenly and deeply, as Japanese often do on trains.

Batsu-ichi: A divorced woman, or her status. Under the Japanese system of *koseki* (family registration), in divorce, the name of the person who joined the family (most often the woman) is stricken from the register with *batsu jirushi* (a slash mark). From this expression comes the expression *batsu-ichi,* one strike against (the woman). These days, however, *batsu-ichi* sounds bright and cheerful, suggesting a feeling of liberation.

Chibimaruko: The round-faced main character of a TV cartoon series that's been popular since the 1990s. It is used colloquially to mean a short and *maru-maru* (round) girl.

Chibiru (have a little, a leak): To leak a little urine when surprised or in a hurry. It comes from *chibitto* (a little bit).

Chin suru: To warm food using a microwave oven. This expression came into being with the spread of *reitō shokuhin* (frozen precooked food) meals that only a *denshi renji* (microwave oven) can cook. Single young people often don't want to spend a lot of their free time cooking, so they rely on *reitō shokuhin* and other prepared foods. *Chin* is an onomatopoeia for the oven bell signaling that the food is finished cooking.

Chū suru: To kiss. Comes from the Japanese onomatopoeia for kiss.

Daberu (chatter, jabber): A slang expression created by combining *muda banashi* (idle talk) and *shaberu* (to chat). *Nani dabetten no?* is what the hell are you talking about?

Derumo: An inversion of *moderu,* meaning model (flesh, not plastic).

Fajii (literally, fuzzy): As distinct from *faji,* a term derived from the revolutionary computer technology now used in household electric appliances, such as washing machines and video cameras. It refers to the quality of being able to smoothly take in, analyze, and output information.

Fakku suru (to fuck): To have sex or send a fax. The *su* has been dropped from *fakkusu suru,* and the word when used by young ladies at the office, now generally means to send a fax.

Furiita: An abbreviation for *furii arubaitā. Arubaito* is a common Japanese expression, taken from the German *arbeit* (labor), meaning a part-time job. Thus, *furii* (free) *arubaitā* refers to young people, many of them women, who have no permanent job.

Gochi ni naru: To be treated to dinner. *Gochi* is an abbreviation for *gochisō* (delicious food).

Hamaru: To get sucked in, become obsessed, or to be unable to get out of a part-time job. It is a slang meaning of the verb *hamaru,* meaning to fall or plunge into.

Kireru: To end a relationship, or to get angry suddenly.

Kiteru: To go crazy, to lose it.

Kuchaberu: To have a long or silly chat. It comes from *kucha-kucha,* an onomatopoetic expression for chatter, and *shaberu* (to talk).

Kurofuku, or *kokufuku:* Describes the male employees of discos who wear all-black clothing or dark uniform-like suits.

Memoru: To take or write a memo.

Namako: Literally, a sea slug. Figuratively, someone who is difficult to understand. Also, a man who seems warm and soft on the outside, but is cold and dark on the inside.

Ō-boke: Someone who is very flaky and unreliable. *Ō*

means big or great, and *boke* comes from the verb *bokeru*, which means to become senile.

O-mata: A casual abbreviation for *o-matase* or *o-matase shimashita* (sorry to keep you waiting). This expression is used by female students or *gyaru* who don't especially care if they're late.

Panion, pakon, or *konpani:* Young women who work as announcers at trade shows and exhibits. They are also called *konpanyā* and *pākon.*

Panpii from *ippan piipuru* (ordinary people): People who lack character and aspirations.

Sutchii/sutchan: A stewardess.

Suppin (unpainted face): A face without any make-up. This is now a commonly used word, but has yet to make it into the dictionary.

Takabii: A snob.

Tsūshotto suru (to two-shot): When a man and a woman break away from a group and engage in a one-on-one conversation. It originated from a television singles show by the comedy team The Tunnels.

Gyaru have a habit of adding the honorific prefix *o-* to all kinds of words. For example, *o-nyū* is coined from the prefix *o-* and new and means newly made or purchased clothes, shoes, and so on. *Supe,* from special-made, is another term for this. *O-hatsu* is an ordinary slang expression and is also used to mean new clothes. *Hatsu* in this case means the first time, as in *o-hatsu ni o-me ni kakarimasu* (literally, this is my first time seeing you;

figuratively, how do you do?), which is used by older people when meeting a person for the first time. Eating seasonal food for the first time is also called *o-hatsu*.

Antonyms for *o-nyū* and *o-hatsu* are *o-furu* (old ones), *chūburu* or *chūko* (both written with the same characters and meaning used), and *sekohan* (secondhand).

O-senchi means sentimental, and it is used as in *ara, o-senchi ne* (oh, you're too sentimental). The *o-namida chōdai* (literally, give us your tears; figuratively, tear-jerker) type of melodramatic movies was once fashionable. *O-netsu* (literally, fever) is an old slang term used by female students, meaning to become infatuated with someone. It's not used very much anymore. Instead, *fiibā suru* from the English fever is a popular expression meaning to get excited or aroused.

Ocha suru (literally, to do tea) is an expression that the *gyaru* started using in 1986, and it can be used for any non-alcoholic drink. To take a short break and chat is *ocha suru*. Terms using *suru* in this way, such as *ochake suru* (*ochake* is a baby word for *sake*), *biiru suru* (drink beer), and *gohan suru* and *meshi suru* (both to eat a meal) are often used instead of the standard verbs *nomu* (drink) and *taberu* (eat).

Finally, *o-gyā*, or just plain *gyā*, means mother. *Gyā-gyā* is an onomatopoetic expression for screaming or squalling. So nagging mothers are called *gyā-gyā* by their daughters. The ordinary expression for to nag is *gami-gami iu*. *O-gyā* is normally used for the crying of a newborn baby.

3

Young People's Language

(wakamono, gakuseigo)

In 1983, a magazine did a survey of words in vogue among elementary school children. In order of popularity, the most fashionable words were: *dasai, naui, yabai, sekoi, imo, chikuru, ojin, burikko (butte iru),* and *maji.*

Among these nine expressions, we have already introduced six. In this section, we will explain the remaining three: *dasai, imo,* and *sekoi.*

There are several theories as to the etymology of *dasai,* which means provincial and dull. The first is that it comes from the word *tasha.* The *kanji* for the word *inaka* (countryside, rural area) can also be pronounced *tasha. Tashai* is an adjective derived from this, and, with a slight change of pronunciation, becomes *dasai.*

The second theory is that *dasai* is a contraction of the phrase *datte Saitama da mon* (that's 'cause he's/it's from Saitama), to *da Saitama,* then *dasai.* Saitama Prefecture may be thought of as Tokyo's northern suburbs. It is known for its flat, dull bedroom towns where low- to middle-ranking salarymen make their homes.

The third school of thought suggests that it comes from *donkusai,* a word in the Kansai dialect. *Don* means dull, and *kusai* means to reek.

The word *dasai* came into use in the late 70s to early 80s and is still commonly used. It has several even more colloquial variations, including *dassē, dasē,* or *dashā.*

Dasai carries nuances of *yaboi* (vulgar), *mittomonai* (awkward or shabby), *akushumi* (tasteless or senseless), and *akanuke shinai* (unrefined). You may have seen or heard about the *takenoko-zoku* dancing in Yoyogi Park near Harajuku in Tokyo. These youngsters take pride in garbing themselves in the most *dasai* fashion—gaudy punk rock or 50s rockabilly style. It is said that the fashion was originally created by a boutique in Harajuku called Takenoko (literally, bamboo shoot). The *takenoko-zoku* (bamboo shoot group) admit that they are *dasai,* but at the same time, they feel that their very uncoolness is most *naui* (up-to-date).

Kakko warui and *ikasa nai* are antonyms for *kakko ii* (cool) and *ikasu* (hip), and both mean awkward or funny-looking. These are commonly used as synonyms for *dasai.*

A prefix that is sometimes appended to *dasai* is *chō.* *Chō* is an emphatic prefix meaning ultra-, and it has been in vogue among the young since 1988. *Chō kakko ii* (very handsome), *chō dasai* and its abbreviation *chō dasa* (very unfashionable), and *chō konde iru* (very crowded) are popular expressions.

Other prefixes current among the younger crowd include: *gero* (sickening), *meta, mecha,* and *mechanko* (all literally meaning absurdly), *moro* (all, every), *geki* (intensely, passionately), and *kuso* and the prefix *do* (both shit, damn), which are used instead of *sugoku* (the most common word for emphasizing).

Imo (potato) is a *dasai* person or *dasai* behavior, as in *aitsu wa imo da* (he's a bumpkin) or *imo-na hanashi da* (that story is dull). *Imo* is an amusing expression for anything that is senseless or tasteless. When used to describe a person, it can also imply *buki* (a clumsy, awkward person), *kappe* (a country bumpkin), *noroma* (a dunce), or *zunguri-mukkuri* (a short, fat person). *Imo* and *imo-na* can also describe a thing or event as in *imo-na kaisha* (deadend company), *imo-na nekutai* (tasteless necktie), *imo-na hanashi* (silly story), or *sore wa imo da* (that's nonsense). *Imo (-na) nē-chan* and *imo (-na) nii-chan* are now abbreviated to *imo-nei* and *imo-nii. Nē-*

chan is older sister or girl, while *nii-chan* is older brother or boy. These terms refer to an unattractive young boy or girl totally lacking in intellectual or other merits: a dweeb. After *imo* became fashionable slang, young people coined the adjective *imoi*. This adjective is used to describe someone who is *inakappoi* (hick) or *nibui* (dull). *Imo* can also be used in the sense of *dasai* or *bakamitai*. Synonyms for these words include *imo-ppoi* and *poteto-chikku*, both meaning potato-ish.

Tonderu (literally, flying), a close synonym for *naui*, became very fashionable after the publication of the novel *Fear of Flying* by the American feminist Erica Jong. It comes from the verb *tobu* (to fly) and has been used by youngsters to describe the feeling of being high on drugs or alcohol. Now it has taken on the broader meanings of surpassing and most up-to-date. A derivative, *tonderu onna*, refers to what we sometimes in English call a superwoman. A take-off on this is the phrase *tonderu onna, tondemonai onna,* which means a superwoman who is just too much. *Tondemonai* is a frequently heard word meaning no way or too much; it can also be used to mean you're welcome.

Susunderu and *koeteru* are the latest synonyms for *tonderu*. The former comes from the verb *susumu,* meaning to advance and has the connotation of being progressive. The latter comes from the verb *koeru,* which means to transcend or exceed and can be written with the same Chinese character as *chō*.

Sekoi is now used in various ways to mean unfair or stingy. *Sekoi* is said to have come from Edo era theatrical jargon meaning bad (actor), or from thieves' argot for painful or tough. Another opinion concerning its etymology is that it came from *seko-taketa* or the more colloquial *seken zure shita,* both of which mean too wise in the ways of the world. *Seko* and *seken* here are worldly affairs. Another possibility is that it is an inverted form of *kose-kose shita* (fussy or narrow-minded).

In any case, *sekoi* can now be used to mean all of the following: *zurui* and the more colloquial *zurukkashii* (sly, cheat); *mimitchii* or the rougher *ketchii* (mean, stingy); the above-mentioned *kose-kose shita, sesekomashii* (shabby); *kitanai* (dirty, unjust); and *yasuppoi* or *chachii* (cheap).

Another very fashionable expression nowadays is use of the word *kusai* to mean suspicious. *Kusai* usually means to smell bad or to stink, but in this case it's an abbreviated form of *usankusai* (suspicious looking). A synonym for *kusai,* is the expression *mayu-tsuba.* This comes from the idiom *mayu ni tsuba o tsukeru* (literally, to put saliva on one's eyebrows; figuratively, to be suspicious about something).

Japanese youngsters are also fond of coining slang that combines Japanese with English. We would like to introduce some of these words here, starting with the English gerund suffix -ing.

Bokkingu, from the formal term *bokki suru* meaning to become stiff or to become erect, is used to describe an erect penis. A mimetic synonym for *bokkingu* is *pin-pin.* When you say simply *pin,* it's an up-to date student slang expression for a throbbing penis. The opposite of *bokkingu* is *nō sutando* (no-stand), which means impotent.

The next -ing word is *saboringu,* a colloquial gerund form for *saboru,* to play truant from school. *Ningu* is an abbreviation of *kanningu* (cunning), and it refers to cheating on a test in school. *Gamaningu* adds the gerund suffix to the ordinary word *gaman,* which means patient or enduring.

Unchingu means having a bowel movement. *Unchi* is baby talk for number two. *Doko iku no?* (where are you going)? *Unchingu* (I'm going to take a crap). Connected with this is the expression *unchingu sutairu,* which means crouching style, as one sometimes sees in downhill ski racing.

The next group of words coined from English involve the suffix -tic. *Poruno-chikku,* for instance, comes from *poruno* (pornography), and the *-chikku* (-tic) adds the sense of pornographic. Similarly, *manga-chikku* comes from *manga* (cartoon or comic) and means cartoonish. *Okama-chikku,* which comes from *okama* (male homosexual), means to be swishy. *Otome-chikku,* which comes from *otome* (virgin), means behaving like a romantic, sentimental, young girl.

Japanese youngsters also combine Japanese words with the English suffix -less *(resu).* *Shūchi-resu,* for example, comes from *shūchi(-shin)* (a sense of shame), and it is used to mean a shameless person, someone who is cheeky. An antonym for this is *shūchi-furu* (shameful), meaning bashful.

Konjo-resu is made by combining *konjō* (guts or perseverance) with -less, and it means a spineless person *(ikujinashi).* *Tenbo-resu* comes from *tenbō* (prospect, foresight) and bears two connotations: someone who has no prospects and is totally hopeless, or someone who has no foresight.

Let's take a look now at a group of words that make use of the English word man. *Tatchi-man* (touch-man) is a molester. Likewise, *dasai-man* comes from *dasai* and means a boor. *Choko-man* means a cute little boy. This comes from the verb *choko-choko aruku* (to toddle around). *Eito-man* (literally, eight-man) is a playboy. *Eito* comes from the Japanese idiom *happō bijin* (literally, an eight-sided beauty; figuratively, an untrustworthy person who tries to be everyone's friend). *Sūpā-man* now can be given either the meaning of a conventional superman, or a father who goes shopping at the supermarket.

Here are some expressions that are particularly popular among female students. *O-shon* is derived from *shōben* (piss) and its slang form *shonben,* both used only by men. Adding the *o-* prefix and removing the inelegant-sounding *ben*, enables the expression to be used by women.

Rokuon (sound recording) and its verb form *rokuon suru* are word plays from *o-toire,* a polite expression for toilet made by adding the honorific prefix and *oto-ire* (*oto* means sound, and *ire* means putting in; they combine to form a synonym for *rokuon*). Thus, young girls use *rokuon* as a euphemistic expression sounding similar in tone to the English powder room. *Doko iku no?* (where're you going?) *Chotto rokuon shite kuru* (I'm just going to the powder room).

O-sashimi (sliced raw fish) is used to mean deep kissing or being kissed. *O-sakana* (fish) is a woman who has been seduced by a man. Instead of the hunting metaphor popularly used in the West, the Japanese refer to fishing when they're describing their efforts to catch a woman. Thus *onna o hikkakeru* (to catch a woman) is a popular slang expression with the connotation of catching on a hook. *O-sakana* (fish) is also used by young girl students to mean being caught by a man. There's an old Japanese saying that goes *tsutta sakana ni esa wa iranai* (no need to bait a caught fish). This expression might be thought of as equivalent to the English admonition about not needing to buy the cow when one can get the milk for free.

Mi no shita sōdan is a play on words of *mi no ue no sōdan. Mi no ue,* as we mentioned earlier, means one's personal affairs. Thus, *mi no ue sōdan* is a consultation about personal affairs. *Mi no shita sōdan,* then, puns on the *kanji* for *mi no ue* (literally, the upper part of the body) to mean consultation about the lower body: more simply, an exchange of sexual information and knowledge, an especially popular pastime among teenage girls. *M* or *emu* is used to mean menstruation, but can also be used to mean money.

Otaku (literally, home; figuratively, to stay home indulging in some specific hobby, then obsessive), and its synonym *otakkii* are now in wide use, replacing *hotondo byōki* (almost ill/crazy). These maniacs are collectively referred to as the *otaku-zoku*. Some examples of *otaku* are *pasokon otaku* (computer maniac) and *bideo otaku* (video movie maniac or addict).

A new version of *otakkii* loves *buru-sera*. *Buru* is an abbreviation for *burumā* (girls' underwear), and *sera* is an abbreviation for *sērā fuku* (sailor dress, like a female high school student's sailor-suit uniform). *Buru-sera* means exactly that: underwear (bras and panties) and school uniforms. Adult toy stores *(otona no omocha-ya)* discovered that middle-aged or unpopular men like used female *buru-sera* with stains or odors, and many high school girls now make money selling such items. Some female high school students who sell their *buru-sera* to retailers also engage in prostitution to make a little extra cash, and this has become a growing social issue since the fall of 1993.

Another very new *otakkii* offshoot is telephone sex. With the spread of AIDS, telephone sex witnessed a boom in the U.S., and Japan promptly followed suit. The number used is 0990, and the service is called *daiyaru kyūkyū* or *daiyaru kyūtsū,* which is sometimes written as Q^2. Many parents were shocked and outraged by the bills their sons racked up on these phone calls. It was also found that many young men used other people's phones to charge the calls. This service is closely linked to the widespread prostitution in Japan.

4

Other Fashionable Words

(sonota ryūkōgo)

The recession of the early 90s has brought a more sober mood to Japan. As a result the appearance of new, fashionable words has slowed down in recent times. This means that many of the trendy expressions used today were coined in the more prosperous 80s.

Still, the 90s have not been without their slang successes. For example, a popular television program concerned with the phenomenon of group dating has brought the masses the term *gō-kon,* a now fashionable word among young people. *Gō-kon* is an abbreviated combination of *gōdō* (joint) and *konpa* (company, or meeting).

Here, then, are some contemporary expressions for how a young person may feel at a *gō-kon*. *Notteru* can be very aptly and precisely translated as being turned on. The expression originated with Japanese jazz musicians, as did its counterpart in the U.S., and was used when a jam session really got into full swing. The verb *noru* means to join or to feel like doing (something). You can use it when people go all out for something, as in *yā, notteru ne* (you're really into it, eh), for example.

Gin-gin ni notteru and *saikō ni notteru* are more emphatic expressions. *Gin-gin,* which was originally used by rock musicians, describes someone who is sparkling, in a fabulous mood. When you add the verb *naru* (to become), to get the expression *gin-gin ni naru,* you get a phrase meaning to do something enthusiastically and in a showy manner. When you say *chōshi ga ii,* it means to be too smart or overly-sociable, or to be slick. There is also a fashionable word, *shii-chō,* which was originally created by musicians. *Shii-chō* comes from a Japanese musical term, *shii-chun* (C tone), which is regarded as a good tune. Later, however, it acquired a meaning similar to *chōshi ga ii,* of which it is also an inversion.

Atsuku naru (literally, to get hot) means to be crazy about or to be absorbed in something. The difference in connotation between *notteru* and *atsuku natteru* is that the former is used for a particular occasion, whereas the latter refers to a more habitual state. Taking it a bit further, the expression *atsu-atsu* (literally, hot-hot) mainly refers to being passionately in love with a person. Its verb form is *atsu-atsu ni naru* (to fall in love). Thus, *kare to kanojo wa atsu-atsu* means those two are having a hot and heavy love affair. *Atsu-atsu* can also be used to describe very hot (temperature, not flavor) food or drink, as in *atsu-atsu no nabe* (a piping hot stew) or *atsu-atsu-kan* (hot *sake* or wine). You can also use these expressions as in *keiba ni atsuku natteru* (he's totally absorbed in horse racing) or *kanojo ni irekonderu* (he's crazy about his girlfriend).

Let's now introduce some terms that appeared first as slang and have since come to be regarded as "respectable" words.

Hanakin literally means flowery Friday, or happy Friday, an abbreviation of *hana no kin-yōbi,* and has been used since the 1970s. On *hanakin,* young men and salarymen would drink and have fun until just before the last trains left for home, around midnight. Another night when bars and clubs do a booming business is *hana no kyūryōbi* (payday, once a month, on the 25th in Japan).

In the old days, *uwaki* (infidelity) was something men did outside the house. *Uwaki* comes from the expression *uwatsuita kimochi,* meaning restless feeling. But now with the increase of men and women who are staying single, a new word, *furin,* has been in use since the 1980s. *Furin* means immorality. *Furin* sounds lighter and has become a common word. Also, like *furin,* *tsumamigui* (literally, eat with the finger; figuratively, cheat on a partner), is often used. *Tsumamigui* is also used for social evils such as embezzlement of public funds. Another term for an unfaithful woman is *kintsuma* (Friday wife). This term originated from the 1985 TV drama *Kinyōbi no Tsumatachi* (Friday's Wives, or weekend lover), in which *furin* was the main theme.

An unfaithful wife may be dissatisfied with her husband, or even want to give up on her marriage. *Imaichi* (literally, a little more) means not satisfactory. Originally, this was student slang in the 80s, but now it's an everyday word. *Oriru* (literally, get off, disembark) was originally a slang term used by punks for give up, and it is now acceptable in general usage.

Osu or its prefix *o-* and its counterpart *mesu* or *me-* (female) are usually used when referring to animals, as in *osu-inu* (male dog) or *o-jika* (stag), and *mesu-neko* (female cat) or *me-gitsune* (vixen). By combining *osu* with melancholy, we get *orankorii*. This refers to a boy who's worried or unhappy because he's not popular among girls. A colloquial equivalent for this is *motenai otoko* (a man who is not popular with women).

The replacement of *me-* by *o-* can be found in another non-standard Japanese-English word, *onsu,* a play on the word *mensu* (menstruation or period). Some people say that women become irritable or even hysterical during their periods. So *onsu* refers to a time when a man is in a bad mood. It's used as in *kare wa kyō onsu da* (he's in a bad mood today).

Osu and *mesu* also appear in the expressions *odeito* and *medeito.* The former, made by combining the English date with the honorific prefix *o-,* was first used by young girls to mean date or to have a date. *Kyō wa dare to odeito?* (who are you going out with today?). *Ara, ya da wa. Itsumo no kare yo!* (stop teasing me—with the same one, as usual!). But now, *odeito* can also mean a date with a man and *medeito* a date with a woman. *Ne, kyō tsukiatte?* (say, can't you come along with me today?). *Un, de mo kyō deito na no* (I'd like to, but I have a date). *Odeito, medeito, dotchi?* (which, a date with a man or woman?).

The younger generation also uses another *o-me* pair of expressions, *odenwa* and *medenwa*. *O-denwa* is frequently used in the office when one receives a call for a senior employee. *Kachō, odenwa desu* (boss, there is a phone call for you). (*Kachō* means section chief.) Nowadays, however, young people also use *odenwa* to refer to a phone call from a man and the newly coined expression *medenwa* to mean a phone call from a woman. *Denwa da yo* (telephone for you). *Dare kara?* (from whom?). *Medenwa* (a woman).

Osutarugia and *mesutarugia* are another pair of expressions using *osu* and *mesu*. They're coined from nostalgia, and the former means a state of wanting to have a boyfriend while the latter refers to wanting a girlfriend. Elderly, nostalgic Tokyoites might remember the expression *ossu mesu (messu) gatchanpo* (male and female are easily hooked up), which was popular in their childhood. This was used when they wanted to tease a boy and girl who were discovered to be fond of each other.

Abauto comes from the English about, meaning half-hearted or perfunctory. *Abauto-na yatsu* is an irresponsible fellow. But *abauto de ikō* (*ikō* means let's go) has a more affirmative meaning to the extent of let's not worry over small details. *Fajii* (fuzzy) is now replacing this.

Gojikara otoko (literally, after-five man) refers to young men who don't work too seriously during the day, but become extremely active thereafter and enjoy their night life. This word came from a TV commercial. Of course, there are *gojikara onna* as well. These two phrases, to a great degree, sum up the *shinjinrui*. There are expressions like *hirugata ningen* (day-time person) and *yorugata ningen* (night-time person), but *gojikara otoko* is *yoru dake ningen* (night-only person). *Asa ga yowai* or *asa ga maru de dame* describes a person who is no good in the morning, either because he is *yorugata* or has *teiketsu-atsu* (low blood pressure).

Ageman (woman of happy fortune) is a word that spread from the title of a 1990 Japanese movie *Ageman no onna*. A synonym for this is *fukuman*. *Ageman* is a word from the Kansai region, and means a woman who brings success in life to her man. A woman who brings bad luck, on the other hand, is *sageman*. On the other hand, *ageru* means to push up or give, and *man* can be *o-mankō* (cunt), so that in slang among students, *ageman* is *yaraseru onna* (woman who is an easy lay), while *sageman* is *yarasenai onna* (a prude).

Recently, there are also groups of three words starting with the letter k, called *san-kei* (3K), that have become fashionable set expressions. A *3K shokuba* (*shokuba* is workplace) is *kitsui* (hard), *kitanai* (dirty), and *kiken* (dangerous). These are jobs such as construction work, trucking, and factory jobs. It's very hard to find workers to fill these positions unless high pay is offered. Instead of young men, *dekasegi nōmin* (farmers who work during the off-season) and *fuhō zanryū gaikokujin rōdōsha* (foreign workers who overstay their visas) fill the gap. There are many who wonder if these *san-kei yangu* (literally, *3K* youth) will be able to lead Japan in their later years or whether they will be part of the Japan whose "risen sun has set."

Another *3K* consists of *karōshi* (literally, death by overwork), *keiretsu* (big conglomerates, such as Mitsubishi and Matsushita), and *kenbei* (literally, hatred or dislike of USA).

Yet a third *3K* covers items that are often mentioned as important for cutting down on expenditures. First, there is *kōsaihi* (literally, social expenses; figuratively, expense accounts). To a certain extent, this money is not taxed, and thus, many salarymen in Japan enjoy *tadagui* (free meals) and *tadanomi* (free drinks) with this company money. Next comes *kōtsūhi* (transportation money). After wining and dining with *kōsaihi* until after the last train leaves, the ride home is by taxi. Taxi fares in Tokyo are the highest in the world, some four or five times higher than in New York City. Third is *kōkokuhi* (literally, advertisement expenditures). It was recently discovered that electric and gas companies were paying several million dollars annually as advertising fees to the newspaper of the conservative Liberal Democratic Party, and this has become a big issue.

Yokomeshi means dinner or lunch with foreigners. This word comes from *yokomoji* (literally, letters written horizontally; figuratively, foreign languages). This word has its roots in the fact that, in the past, Japanese was written vertically, as opposed to Western languages, which are written horizontally.

Masu-komi (mass media), *mini-komi* (small media), and *kuchi-komi,* which literally means communication by word of mouth, are three ways in which information is disseminated publicly.

5

Media- and Fashion-
Related Words

(gyōkai kanren)

Fashionable words often spread via TV and the movies. Here, let us introduce some words that were born in the world known as *gyōkai* and have come to be widely used. *Gyōkai* (literally, industry, or the trade) has been used for industries that are sensitive to trends and fashions, such as music, theater, movies, and TV, as well as the advertising and fashion industries. All of the people working in these industries are known as *gyōkaijin* and are much admired by young people of the opposite sex.

Okkake (groupies) refers to girls, mainly high school students, who gather at TV stations to catch a glimpse of famous TV stars who are filming. They are also known as *okkake gyaru*. *Nori* is harmony, fine feeling. Since the old days, the lines spoken along the *shamisen* chords in theater such as *kabuki* were said to be good or bad *nori* (harmony). This came to be used by the people in the music industry when a song successfully matched its accompaniment, as in *uta no nori ga ii* (*uta* is song, and *ii* is good). Later, in TV programs, when someone smoothly entered a conversation, this also came to be called *nori ga ii,* and good *nori* became an absolute necessity for TV performers. Furthermore, copying the tone or gestures of someone famous came to be called the *nori* of so and so. Now, it's a general word used by the young when a conversation goes smoothly. *Hanashi ni noru* means to join in the conversation well or to take part in the plan. *Sugu noru* is be eager and quick to join in a conversation or plan. These expressions are often heard in everyday conversation. A related expression is *noseru no ga umai,* and this refers to someone who is good at introducing another person into the conversation or atmosphere.

Ago (literally, jaw) means eating, or accommodation; *ashi* (literally, foot) is a mode of transportation. *Ago-ashi tsuki* (with *ago* and *ashi* attached) means accommodation and transportation allowance, especially for a business trip. This was originally industry jargon, but it is now in common use.

Karaoke was originally a jargon term used in the music and TV industry. It's a contraction of *kara ōkesutora,* meaning empty or no orchestra. Karaoke recording began as an emergency measure when the schedules of a band and vocalist conflicted. The accompaniment was recorded separately, and the singer listened to the tape and sang along. This was then mixed to complete the recording. Since 1977, there has been a *karaoke būmu,* in which the customer—usually in some kind of bar—sings along with a karaoke tape in the background. As technology advances, karaoke is now often accompanied by laser discs, which show the songs' lyrics along with pictures portraying the atmosphere of the songs. Now, there are even karaoke rooms or karaoke clubs where housewives and students go to sing in the daytime. Karaoke has become incredibly popular in Japan, and it has even gone overseas. It is currently an enormously popular form of entertainment in China, Taiwan, and Korea, and karaoke bars are also springing up in the United States and Europe.

In the TV industry, there's an axiom that, when going after high ratings, a *kui-mono bangumi* (food program) or *tabi-mono bangumi* (trip program) is the thing to do. Over 300 programs, such as specials on odd *rāmen* (Chinese-style soup noodles) restaurants or special feature programs on *rāmen,* curried food, or steaks are broadcast regularly. This is a result of the age of *ichioku sōgurume* (everyone is a gourmet). Recently, *pinku-mono* (literally, pink programs; figuratively, erotic programs) have become more risqué, and some network TV late night shows feature not only bare breasts, but girls in thong panties or even *tii-furonto* (thong-front) panties. *Jaritare* is industry jargon for teenage stars. *Jāmane* is a manager.

Warau is to put away the stage set and props. *Barasu* literally means to take apart, or to cancel a plan. This is used in general conversation too. In colloquial slang, *barasu* has two meanings. The first is to dismember or, by extension, kill. The second is to divulge a secret. The word *baremoto* (can't do any harm) is an abbreviation for *baretemo motomoto* from the verb *bareru,* meaning to be found out, and *moto-moto,* which means originally. The implication here is that even if something is found out, the situation will not change.

Karami (entwine) is industry jargon in pornography and adult video circles for sexual intercourse scenes. *Maebari* (literally, front patch) is used in the same circles for hiding the pubic hair, a very Japanese invention. Nowadays, though, instead of hiding the pubic hair, they often just circumvent the problem by *teimō,* or shaving (it).

Naki is industry jargon for the announcer speaking. The director says *hitonaki shite* (speak now) to signal when the announcer should start. *Ketsukatchin* is movie and TV industry jargon for the deadline by which the filming must end. This term is used in general conversations as well. *Oshi* and *makioshi* mean overtime, from *osu* (to push) and *maku* (to wind), as in *tokei no hari o maku* (wind a clock).

Next, here are some words from bars, *sushi* shops, and general restaurants.

Kuchiake (literally, open mouth) is the first customer

after the opening of the restaurant or bar. *O-temoto* (literally, at hand) is chopsticks. *O-tōshi* is the hors d'oeuvre of the day, and *tsukidashi* (literally, thrusting out) is the same. In traditional Japanese drinking houses, where the drinking is almost always done while eating, the owner automatically gives the customers a small portion of the hors d'oeuvre of the day with the first drink. In Western-style bars and nightclubs, this is called *chāmu* (charm).

Okami or *okami-san* is the female owner of a restaurant, *sushi* shop, or pub. In a bar, she is called *mama* or, more usually *mama-san,* and her assistant, if she is a woman, would be *chiimama* (little mama). *O-aiso* is the bill at restaurants. This word consists of *aiso* (good will) with the prefix *o-* added, meaning thank you very much. *Kanban* means sign, and then the closing time of a shop. At traditional Japanese restaurants, signs or *noren* (shop curtains) are put outside during business hours and brought inside at closing. *Kanban desu,* therefore, means we're closing.

O-agari or *agari* is a cup of tea. In the *mizu shōbai,* tea was a forbidden word since it was used in the expression *ocha o hiku,* originally to grind tea, or in other words, to have to kill time due to lack of customers. Instead, *agaribana* (literally, floating flowers), or simply *agari,* was used for tea. Its folk etymology claims that it is called *agari* because the customer drinks it when he is at *agari-doki* (the time of ending of the meal).

The next *agari* has a different Chinese character. This *agari* means total income from entrance fees. Like the *mizuage* (landing of fish) of the fisherman, *agari* is the gross receipt at a theater.

The word *hane* is used at theaters. This comes from *haneru* (to push aside), as in to push aside the mats *(mushiro)* at closing. The word comes from traditional Japanese theater, like *noh* or *kabuki,* where the audience sits on mats on the floor, but it's still popularly used in Western-style theaters or cinemas today.

Tsuke is a tab at a restaurant. If someone says, I'm going to put it on my tab tonight, the owner will reply *tsukete okimasu*. *Tsuke* comes from *tsukeru* (put down, write into the book). *Tsuke uma* is different from this *tsuke;* it is, rather, the restaurant employee who *tsuite iku* (accompanies) the customer to his home to collect the debt. *Tsuke bito* or *tsuki bito* is an attendant of a successful entertainer.

Nami no hana (literally, flower of the wave) is salt. *Murasaki* (literally, purple) means soy sauce; it's a common term derived from the purplish color of soy sauce. At *sushi* shops, *shari* is boiled rice, and *neta* is an inversion of *tane* (ingredients), or *sashimi,* that is put on top of it.

6

Oldies But Goodies

In this final section of our book, we'd like to introduce some expressions that we find particularly witty, interesting, or evocative, but are no longer used. We hope our readers will also enjoy these words and help reintroduce them into the Japanese language.

Tanmei ryūkōgo are short-lived fashion words, the fate of most slang. For example, the somewhat witty expressions using *hanashi ga* . . . (the story is . . .) that were popular among young people from the late 70s to the early 80s are no longer in use.

Hanashi (talk) *ga piiman* (green pepper), for example, meant the conversation or discussion is boring, of no substance, and the analogy here is quite clear: a pepper has nothing inside it but air and inedible seeds. Two ordinary synonyms for this expression are *hanashi ga tsumaranai* (boring) and *hanashi ni nakami ga nai* (there's nothing of substance in this conversation).

Other expressions built around *hanashi* include *hanashi ga kyūri* (cucumber) instead of *hanashi ga nagai* (long) for a long-winded person or conversation, and *hanashi ga kyabetsu* (cabbage), for a complicated conversation (instead of the more conventional *hanashi ga komitteru*). This derives from the fact that the insides of a cabbage stalk are complex and convoluted. *Hanashi ga renkon* (lotus root) refers to gossip coming straight to one's ears as if through a pipeline. This originated with the appearance of the inside of a lotus root, which has straight holes.

Then there is *hanashi ga satsuma* (from *satsuma imo,* or sweet potato) meaning that the conversation is somewhat fishy or smelly. This comes from the fact that, in Japan, it's thought that when a person eats sweet potatoes, he is likely to fart *(onara o suru).* A more commonly heard expression is *hanashi ga tsutsunuke,* meaning that a private matter comes directly to one's ears or leaks out completely. *Tsutsunuke* means direct or verbatim.

Hanashi ga unagi (eel) was used among students instead of the standard *torae dokoro no nai hanashi* (nobody can get to the point of the conversation), meaning there's no point in this discussion. This term obviously stems from the fact that eels are slippery and, therefore, hard to catch.

Hanashi ga pārman (a TV character who is invisible), used instead of *nani itteru no ka wakaranai* (I don't understand what you're saying) or *hanashi ga mienai* (the discussion is not visible), means I don't know what you're talking about. A creative person could invent many more such expressions, and we hope you do.

Wanpatān came from the Japanese-English expression one pattern and was very popular in the late 70s and early 80s, meaning stereotyped or in a rut. It was used by young people when talking of a person or the behavior of a person who always acts the same.

Shōyu gao (literally, soy sauce face) was a phrase that was very popular in the late 1980s for a person having a typical Japanese face with smooth features, a face with *hitoe mabuta* (smooth eyelid with no folds) and no bumps or depressions. The opposite is *sōsu gao* (literally, Worcester-sauce face) or *batākusai kao* (literally, stinking of butter; euphemistically meaning Western-style face). This latter expression doesn't mean that the Japanese dislike Westerners' looks; it is, rather, used contemptuously for Japanese who aspire to look Western, often with the help of plastic surgery. Other similar terms are:

miso gao (literally, bean paste-face; in other words, an extremely typical Japanese face); *mayonēzu gao* (literally, mayonnaise-face; figuratively, white, soft, pudgy, piggy face); *ketchappu gao* (literally, ketchup-face; figuratively, red and fat face); and *tabasuko gao* (literally, tabasco-face; figuratively, Mexican-like, macho face). These words are not used too often nowadays.

Other phrases that were popular in the early 1980s, such as *munekyun* (make one's heart flutter, burn with passion) and *run-run (kibun)* (an onomatopeia for a happy cheerful feeling) are now almost completely extinct. Extinct or not, it is in the spirit of *run-run* that we end this book. We hope you've learned from and enjoyed it.

OTHER TITLES IN THE YENBOOKS LIBRARY

Japan's Sex Trade
by Peter Constantine
Japan's Sex Trade offers a probing, step-by-step tour of the astonishing professional sex scene in Japan: love hotels, soaplands, S&M snack bars, and kinky salons. The highlight of each section is a listing of the language of these "floating worlds," with their service menus explained in detail. Scandalous and controversial, this book will fascinate the reader.

The Completely Non-Authoritative Guide to Japan
by Paul Nowak and Robert Urowsky
A zany, comically illustrated portrayal of Japan that is right on the mark! Page after page of hilarious cartoons lampoons the Japanese and Japan's foreign community. This lively guide takes the who, the what, and the *why* out of living in Japan. Though not the most erudite guide, it might be the funniest!

Making Out in Japanese
by Todd and Erika Geers
From the language used between friends to easy conversation in a bar, this best-selling book provides you with all the common words and phrases used in casual Japanese. Accompanied by a pronunciation guide and a key to male/female usage, this book will bring you to a new level of fluency and communication in Japanese. Similar books in this series are available for Chinese, Indonesian, Thai, and Korean.

Business Guide to Japan
by Boye L. DeMente
Everything you need to know to win at the business game in Japan is explained in this no-nonsense guide. Learn how to penetrate company bureaucracy, read subtle signs to come out ahead on the negotiating table, and master the art of after-hours business with this guide to doing business in Japan. All the practical tips and hints you'll need to be a success.

Yoshiwara: The Pleasure Quarters of Old Tokyo
by Stephen and Ethel Longstreet
Yoshiwara was for years the famed pleasure center of Tokyo. Authors Longstreet trace the rise and fall of this city within a city, a sanctioned preserve of teahouses and brothels that was not abolished until 1958. Discover the beautiful courtesans and geisha who inhabited Tokyo's former pleasure center.

Murder at the Tokyo American Club
by Robert J. Collins
Welcome to the Tokyo American Club, where club manager Pete Peterson's head has just been found bobbing in the swimming pool. A headless torso was found alongside it, but the body doesn't match the head. A swelling list of suspects is investigated as the police chief pieces together the puzzle, as well as the body parts. Comic intrigue unfolds as the private lives of club members are revealed.

Outrageous Japanese: Slang, Curses, and Epithets
by Jack Seward
Yes, Japanese people do swear—and so can you with this book! It covers threats, taunts, curses, sex, booze, money, and more. Fun and instructive, this book is perfect for students of all levels, as well as readers simply interested in Japan. Author Seward has been involved with the Japanese language as a student, teacher, and author for more than 25 years and will help you speak your mind—outrageously!

Tokyo Pink Guide
by Steven Langhorne Clemens
The first book to tell foreign men and women how to enter the doors of Japan's "anything goes" pleasure palaces. Learn what to expect at and beyond the front door and get tips on what to wear, dos and don'ts, and prices.